FIRST ACTS

FIRST ACTS
A Memoir

B. L. REID

The University of Georgia Press Athens and London

© 1988 by B. L. Reid
Published by the University of Georgia Press
Athens, Georgia 30602
All rights reserved

Set in Berkeley Old Style Book
The paper in this book meets the guidelines
for permanence and durability of the Committee on Production
Guidelines for Book Longevity of the Council on Library
Resources.

Printed in the United States of America

92 91 90 89 88   5 4 3 2 1

Library of Congress Cataloging in Publication Data

Reid, B. L. (Benjamin Lawrence), 1918–
First acts.

1. Reid, B. L. (Benjamin Lawrence), 1918–   —Childhood and
youth. 2. Louisville (Ky.)—Biography. 3. Louisville (Ky.)—Social
life and customs. I. Title.
F459.L853R45   1988   976.9′44   87-25577
ISBN 0-8203-1015-8 (alk. paper)

British Library Cataloging in Publication Data available

For Jane

Contents

Prefatory Note

When I decided, more than twenty years ago, to try my hand at biography, I did so in a mood of revulsion against what I felt as phoniness and floridity in the style of my critical writing. Enough flourishing of opinion, I told myself: try fact, and see if you can make your writing straighter, more modest and honest. I worked hard at biography, enjoyed the process, and in a half-dozen years, while teaching, produced big books on John Quinn and Roger Casement.

My own life has never been spectacular, and I had not thought of autobiography until I began to feel bored and deprived at the way my students and even my colleagues seemed to be perceiving and reporting their lives, as a set of accidents within privilege. My early life in the South had been tough and untidy, but it had always been *interesting,* at least to me. Would it interest other people, perhaps show them something strange yet representative, worth knowing and feeling? I resolved to try it and see. I would work in a historical and lightly monitory spirit, in a style deliberately flat—well, not *really* flat, but no toning up, little interpretation, little tracking of themes: let the course of small personal and familial events compose the whole narrative. It would be a straight chronicle of my parents' middle lives and the early lives of myself and my two brothers. I finally called it *First Acts*—350 pages that carried me to the age of twenty-eight when my wife and I began to teach. I have never wanted to write about my professional life.

Acknowledgments

It is both an obligation and a pleasure to list persons who have been importantly helpful in the production of this book, particularly to thank those who have helped me to find photographs, or to fill and straighten out tangled recollections: my wife, Jane Davidson Reid; my daughter, Laurie Reid McAnulty, and her husband, Michael; my brother, Isaac, and his wife, Eleanor; Jane's sister, Ruth Davidson Malcom, and her husband, Edward Vartan Malcom; Virginia Austin Southouse; Roy Finch; Kingman Grover and his sister, Vanessa; Ross Groshong. I owe a special debt to George Core, who printed most of chapter 7 in the *Sewanee Review* (Fall 1987), and to Sam Pickering, Jr., who noticed the manuscript kindly there and recommended it to the present publishers. At the University of Georgia Press I wish to thank especially Malcolm Call, Debra Winter, and Sandra Strother Hudson. I thank also all of those I don't know by name who have made a book out of a pile of typescript.

Traveler

1 was born in Louisville, Kentucky, in May 1918, but I was carried to Texas (I am told) at the age of six months. If I was trailing clouds of glory as Wordsworth says infant souls do, I was not aware of them: that vapor must have been smoke and steam from the train engine. My life has never been glorious, though it seems more and more interesting the more I think about it. The memories I retain from our three years in Texas are surprisingly numerous and clear, though not momentous. In fact my memory in general is not a very efficient one. Congreve remarked that you could tell a fool by his complaints about his poor memory. That hurts, but so be it. I have never put my fundamental brain power at a high figure, and I certainly do have a leaky mind: "All I know I keep forgettin'," runs one of the folk phrases that Sandburg quotes. (You can see what a literary fellow I grew into.)

My father was a Protestant minister, or as we always said, a preacher. The great family fact of my early life was the church. There had been so many preachers in my family line that I used to have a notion that the career was hereditary, like certain kinds of genetic disasters such as baldness in the male and ugly legs in the female. We once counted up thirteen preachers among our near forbears. Later in life I lost a chance at a teaching position in a denominational college, at a time when I badly needed a job, when I told the man who interviewed me that I had more religion in my background than in my foreground. (The tendency to make inappropriate jokes, to "act smart," is another habit in my family.) We belonged to a sect, quite numerous in the South, named the Disciples of Christ, seceders from "Scotch" Presbyterianism. But we always called ourselves, less in vainglory than in historical ignorance, the Christian Church: "You're a Baptist? I'm a Christian."

Our bloodlines were almost entirely British: Scottish or "Scotch-Irish"—

the commonest strain in the South and almost universal among poor whites, the class to which we belonged by economic reality though to the eye we passed for shabby-genteel. My father's father, Joseph Kendrick Reid, had been born in Missouri but had lived most of his life in Kentucky. He used to tell of seeing Civil War soldiers passing through when he was herding cows in the fields. He became a "Christian" minister, of course, and so, after the manner of our sect, he was generally known as "Brother" Reid, as was my father in his turn—not the classier "Reverend" or "Doctor." His friends and even his wife always called him by his initials: "J.K." A photograph in his early married years shows him in a Prince Albert coat, looking big and blocky, handsome and formidable, with a longish square-cut brown beard, next to his stately well-formed wife. By the time I begin to remember him he had given up preaching (I never knew why) and was always about the house, busy with one or another puttering task. He was tall and thin and grey, and his beard, which my mother, who disliked and resented him, said he wore to hide a receding chin, had grown white and scanty and ineffective. He was still formidable in a spiteful sort of way.

Most of his habits were irritating. He was always mumbling apples with his bad teeth and he would scatter cores and peelings about him wherever he sat. He was afflicted with a chronic catarrh and would hawk and spit into the fireplace or the coal bucket, or if neither was handy, on the floor, where he might or might not drag his shoe sole across the gob in the country way—as my mother stamped delicately away tossing her pretty dark head in disgust. Granddaddy was thought to be a diabetic, and he was ordered not to eat sweets; but if he was not watched he would slip out into the kitchen and bolt down a whole can of peaches or pears, juice and all. He could handle the whole maneuver inside two minutes.

My father's mother, Katherine or Kate Errett Reid, was also tall and good-looking, with glossy red-bronze hair, fair skin, and softly rounded features. Her figure was shapely and graceful, but she had a habit of turning out her feet when she walked—what was called slue-footed—which my father inherited. The Erretts were supposed to be Welsh, but I have never found anybody in Britain who had heard the name. Grandmother's uncle, Isaac Errett, dead by the time I came on the scene, was the nearest thing to a hero we could boast. My sister-in-law Eleanor, who is serious about such things, has traced him to County Wicklow in Ireland; so he must have been a southern Irish Protestant, a fairly rare animal. He had been the founding editor of a weekly religious journal that still survived with a modest national circulation. Grandmother talked often of Uncle Isaac and was impressed with the dignity of being his niece. She had had no college education but she had pretensions to culture; she read a good deal of a serious moral sort, and she played the piano and organ well enough to accompany a congregation's hymn singing. In later years she occasionally played the family upright with a vague indecisive touch. In fact I cannot remember her doing anything much, except quarrel with my mother, who resented our dependence on them and came as close to hating them as her principles would allow. Both my father's parents were ambitious but unimaginative people, turned first spiteful and later querulous by their disappointment with life.

My father was the steadiest as well as the most acute of their disappointments, though they took some comfort in blaming most of his chronic failures upon his wife. Their original hopefulness was attested by his name: Isaac Errett Reid. He was their only child, and in some ways he always seemed accidental in relation to them, a kind of sport of nature. It was hard to imagine, in the first place, how two such big people could have produced such a small son: only five feet four. In early life he had been slight and graceful, but later he was rotund most of the time, a rather womanish little figure with sloping shoulders, wide hips, no muscles, and his mother's slue-footed walk. His movements were brisk, energetic, nervous. His eyesight was bad and he wore glasses all the time; in my youth they were always rimless pince-nez, forever getting knocked off. I wish I had given him more love.

Dad attended Louisville Male High School, then a large public academy for boys, famous in the area for a good traditional or "classical" training. It must have been at this time that Granddaddy was preaching at Parkland Christian Church, his last pastorate of which I recall any mention. After Male High Dad was sent on to Transylvania College in Lexington, a decent, homely little denominational institution that went back to 1780 and called itself "the oldest college west of the Alleghenies." It is obvious that his parents were pointing him toward the ministry. I was never sure how much say he had in the matter, or how he really felt about it. Dad's life was always accidental in some sense. He was evidently a bright, gregarious undergraduate, singing in the glee club, acting in plays, joining all the clubs, making a lot of friends who all called him "Ike," to my mother's disgust. In the family he was always called by his middle name, Errett.

After college Dad worked for a year or so as a reporter on a small-town newspaper, an episode of which I remember hearing only his happy report on being corrected by his editor for referring to a man as having been "raised" in such and such a place. "Cabbages are raised," this genius said: "children are reared." Next Dad was sent to New York to study at Union Theological Seminary, where he took another degree. It was training of an uncommonly sophisticated kind for a minister of our sect, and it was always matter for debate in the family whether it did him more harm or good. Certainly something in his training, or in his genes or his stars, did us all a lot of harm.

Dad met my mother at Transylvania, and one of the treasures of my childhood was their college annuals from the first years of the new century. I leafed through them often, feeling excited and mysteriously comforted especially by my mother's portraits in the oval medallion style of that day, cut off at the bust. Mama was beautiful. Indeed she still seems to me one of the most beautiful women I have known. I remember her best from the later years of hardship and sickness, but even then, when her hair was long and grey, her face lined, her teeth gone bad, her eyes shadowed by suffering and bitterness, she was still so haggardly handsome that one wanted to go on looking at her. Her college photographs showed a pile of glossy dark hair, almost black, over a beautifully designed face: a rectangular forehead squared off by fine bones, strong brows over deep dark eyes, a perfectly shaped nose, a mobile mouth, ivory skin with a lot of light in it. The face showed, accurately, eagerness and intelligence and humor. Mama had a sharp tongue. Gay or bitter, it was always witty. When she felt contempt, and that was often, she could shrivel you with a phrase. Thank God I came on the scene soon enough to see some of her early beauty, and to feel her capacity for gaiety and affection.

Mama was quite small, only about five feet two, with a pretty body and dainty hands and feet. I still remember some of her supple kidskin shoes, low pumps or lace-up boots, with the elegant in-curved heels of the period. Occasionally I come upon something like them in an antique shop, and they give me a wrench. She loved clothes and she had excellent taste of a traditional sort, for herself and for the rest of us—better taste than we could afford. I suppose their short stature was one of the things that gave Mama and Dad the disastrous notion that they would make a tolerable match for each other. Being a native of Lexington in the Bluegrass, she was a local girl at Transylvania, and after her graduation she taught Latin and English in high schools in southeastern Kentucky hill towns for several years. That was what she was doing when Dad proposed to her from New York City by letter, and she accepted in the same way.

Mama's maiden name was Margaret Bright Lawrence. She was bright by any standard but she was not a true Lawrence. Her father had been born a Geers, of Scotch-Irish stock, but being orphaned as a boy had taken the name of Lawrence after being adopted by a family of that name. Hence none of us who have used the name (it is my own middle name, and my daughter's, and my niece's) has had any blood right to it. Grandfather Lawrence had died of tuberculosis before I was born, so I knew nothing about him except little things my mother told me. She thought of him, apparently, without strong feeling, with a forgiving humorous indulgence that was surprising in one with her deep and often acrid puritanical streak. He was a housepainter in Lexington, a good workman who made good money but was hopelessly gripped by the traditional addiction of his trade to strong drink. Mama remembered him as totally unreliable but gentle and charming. She could nearly always talk herself into forgiving anybody who was naturally funny and not actually vicious.

But her real love, like mine, went not to her father but to her mother. Grandmother Lawrence had been named Elizabeth Butler. She is almost as vague a picture to me as her husband: though I must have seen her fairly often as a small child, I actually remember only one occasion that I shall describe later. The only surviving picture of her shows another handsome woman, beautiful really: an erect figure, taller than Mama, a grave, intelligent face, with deep-set bright eyes and soft grey hair drawn straight back from her forehead. When I look at her I seem to see the fundamental source of all the good looks that keep cropping up in our family.

The Butler-Lawrence marriage had produced a son and another daughter in addition to Margaret, my mother. Mama's brother George was dead of T.B. by the time I heard of him. He too had been a "Christian" minister. Mama had loved him and she often got out his picture which showed yet another version of the Lawrence good looks: tall and big-boned but thin, with a long lean face and a handsome beaked nose, dark eyes and brows, and a wide, full-lipped gash of a mouth; what hair he had left was a glossy raven black, Indian hair, but he had already gone bald on top. George's son Lowell McGarvey Lawrence inherited his father's looks exactly, and he was one of the best looking young men I ever saw. George's daughter Lois, on the other hand, looked like my mother, small and dark and dainty, ravishingly pretty, with a lot of style in her ways, an unconscious sexy dash. What Lois had inherited was the family tendency to T.B., and she was already in a sanatorium in El Paso, Texas. I was to hear and see a good deal of these cousins in my early years.

Mama's older sister, Aunt Inez (pronounced I-ness, with the accent on the first syllable), was a delightful and yet a pitiful figure. She looked a good deal like my mother, with the same fine bright eyes and dark hair, but with a heavier, squarer face and body. In Aunt Inez's face my mother's alertness and wit showed shadowed by pain and disappointment; it was a face that had collected a lot of suffering, physical and emotional. One shoulder and one side of her back were badly twisted—a real hunchback, said to be owing to a fall from a porch in her childhood. In an angry moment one of her big sons had said to her: "You look like a tent walking down the street." She told us the story, bitterly, but with a humorousness that refused to relinquish the complex jokes involved. She was married to a Lexington man, Claude Allen, and her twisted body had been tough enough to give birth to nine sons, all of whom were young men by the time I came to know them.

Mama believed, not without reason, that a strain of corruption ran from Uncle Claude down through all his sons. Certainly they all "smoked" and "drank," and Mama thought they "took dope" of some kind. All of them I know of came to sad ends. Yet there was charm and talent in them too, except for Sandy, the youngest, who was blond and broken-nosed and sullen, a bit simple. All of the others were clever with their hands, good makers and menders, and they could all draw and paint with a quickness, accuracy, and flair for style that seemed to me—in fact still seems to me—miraculous, occurring in such mass. George Lawrence's sick daughter Lois also possessed this talent, but none of the rest of us has ever had a shred of it.

I grieve to say that as a child I was weak and cruel enough to try to avoid being seen with hunchbacked Aunt Inez in public. But I loved her, really, and she was wonderful company when she was not sorrowing over some sin of one of her ten scapegrace males. She had Mama's gift for happiness and comedy, and when the two of them were laughing together I felt an exquisite proprietary pleasure in seeing Mama as doubled, two of her in one room. The room was always poor enough, in the Allens' house or in ours, but the two of them seemed to shed a lot of light around them.

I am trying to get back to Texas, to the scene of my first memories, but it has seemed important to sketch in the backdrop of family that hung behind me in early years—generally at such a distance that I was only spasmodically aware of any part of it. The truth is that most of my life I have paid little attention to family life outside the immediate home circle, and in fact all of us Reids have lived that way, preoccupied with the private struggle and not visiting and corresponding with the passion of many families. It is only in the last few years, in middle life, that I have begun to feel what a mysterious and powerful thing a lineage is, and to feel a sort of homesick desire to uncover more of my own roots. Now I am sorry I did not have sense enough when I was younger to try to find out from my parents more about their lives and those of their parents and grandparents. My lack of curiosity now seems like stupidity, a dull and unworthy egotism.

I used to laugh at my high school friend Julian, who was always stopping off at the Louisville Free Public Library on the way home from school to look up some branch of his family in the big books of genealogy. Indeed he still strikes me as absurd, for his motives were mainly snobbish: he was convinced that if he looked long enough or cleverly enough he would come upon royalty; he was fairly sure he had already reached nobility. My motives are not snobbish; I know I would not find visible eminence in my family line. What I am moved by is bafflement, disorientation. I find the self, my self, any self, so strange and mysterious that I hunger for a family context that might make it come a little clearer in the mind.

It shames me to realize, for example, that there is a period of about ten years in my parents' lives, between their marriage and my birth in 1918, of which I know almost nothing. My father must have been preaching in country churches in Kentucky. He had had time to establish himself as an early failure, and my mother had had time to grow embittered over that and over the death of her first child. It startles me now to remember that I was actually the fourth born of my parents' children. I have no recollection at all of the first two. The first child was a girl, named Katherine Elizabeth and called Katie Beth, after her Reid and Lawrence grandmothers. That the second child, Joe, had been named Joseph Kendrick for his Grandfather Reid, probably implies that my mother's father was already dead. According to Mama, according to everybody, these had been beautiful children of infinite promise, and I do not doubt that they were so. By the time I became a conscious person they were both dead, carried off by one of those diseases such as diphtheria that attacked so many children and before which the doctors seem to have been fairly helpless. (I still have a scar on the side of my throat that is a mark of a minor operation during an attack of diphtheria, an event I do not remember at all.)

On vague grounds of neglect or impercipience, my mother blamed my father for the loss of her first two children, to her so fabulously promising. Dad of course denied it, flounderingly: it is hard to defend oneself against a charge so comprehensive and shapeless. I always took Mama's side in their disagreements, but in this, the commonest subject of their early quarrels (it went on for years), even I could see she was being bitterly wrong and unfair.

The first family photograph of which I was a part is before me now, a formal studio portrait in the usual sepia tones but less stiff in feeling than most things of the kind. We are mother, father, and three small male children. We are an attractive group, and we look much more elegant and peaceful than our situation can have warranted. In the center is a sort of Holy Family group. My mother sits in a high-back chair, and she is small and dark and lovely. She is wearing neat lace-up boots with a high polish and a dress I seem still to remember: a fine mocha silk with a wide white collar one wing of which is drawn down across her breast like a bandolier. The infant of less than a year on the right arm of her chair, who might be a boy or a girl, is actually myself. I am a pretty, delicate-looking baby, with a cap of short light hair over a perfect long oval face, my mouth slightly open, my eyes with a hurt, brooding, inward look, probably not far from tears. I have been called Benjamin Lawrence Reid, and recalling the origin of the name suddenly gives me a piece of those missing ten years before we went to Texas.

All our names had to be biblical, of course, but my Benjamin was also a tribute to Benjamin Rand, the founder of the Rand office machine business, later Remington-Rand. Mr. Rand had been my father's parishioner and friend in North Tonawanda, New York, and my name was a testimony to my parents' respect and liking for him and no doubt for his wealth. My mother kept up a correspondence with him for some time and I think he used to send an occasional friendly small check. I can recall one troubled interval a number of years later when Mama, bitterly ashamed of her necessity, wrote Mr. Rand and begged for what she probably called a loan. When he sent a hundred dollars we all reacted with a mixture of shame, relief, and disappointment: a hundred dollars was something we did not often see, but I suspect Mama had hoped for more. It would have made her embarrassment over an act she felt she could never repeat more nearly worth the cost.

In the photograph we are posed against a stylized sylvan studio backdrop, probably wallpaper, *faux* Barbizon in style. But there is a real Oriental on the floor that I should like to get my hands on today—Herez, I think. My mother supports me on the arm of her chair, her right arm around me, her left hand under my long white dress, undoubtedly holding one of my ankles. She looks at me, her youngest, with what appears to be interest, affection, and some amusement. Something white has fallen onto the floor behind her chair: it cannot be my diaper, it must be her handkerchief. The only person who looks to be on top of the occasion, my older brother Isaac Errett Reid, Junior, my noble Buddy who was to be my good friend all my life, sits quite independently on my mother's chair, his right arm around her shoulder, his feet in sturdy white shoes resting on her skirt which is spread out on the seat of the chair. As he is a year and nine months older than I am, having been born in North Tonawanda, he must be nearly three at this time. Whereas he too wears a white dress, his looks short on him and he possesses quite discernible sturdy legs. Under his crown of short dark hair he rather glares at the camera, looking puzzled and unappeased, a bit truculent.

Next to him my mysterious lost brother Joe stands on the rug. He looks to be about four. He is dressed all in white, in a suit of starched cotton with a long buttoned coat like a tunic with a lacy Buster Brown collar and tight cuffs, long wrinkled white stockings, white leather slippers. His glossy hair is cut Dutch fashion, high across the brow. Like Buddy, he has my father's eyebrows, sloping downward at the outer corners. He looks gentle and sensitive and amenable. It can only be my own hindsight that makes his tentative posture, his rather baffled little half smile, seem attitudes of one who quietly suspects he is not long for this world. He must have died within the year, for I do not remember him, and my memories begin very soon now. I am sorry he could not have stayed: he looks a grave, intelligent, generous boy.

My father stands behind, only half visible beyond the central cluster, looking down at us all with dispersed benignity. I am surprised to see he has a full head of brown hair, parted on the left. Otherwise he looks familiar, though slenderer than I remember him. The pince-nez is there, and he is a dapper small figure, wearing a white shirt and a neat dark tie under a suit of what looks like khaki serge. From the modest epaulets and flapped breast pockets one can tell it is a uniform he is wearing. Judging by my own age in the picture, the time must be somewhere around the end of the war in November 1918. His situation as a clergyman and a father, as well as his small size and bad eyes, had kept Dad out of the draft, so he had joined up as a Salvation Army chaplain. Very likely the opportunity had been a godsend: he was never able to hold on long to his job in any church.

So there we are, a neat little group, the nuclear family of Reid. We look like what we were: nice enough folks, clean, quiet, well-mannered, intelligent people, but unconcentrated, rather tentatively related to the real world—pretty fragile, pretty vulnerable.

We lived in Texas for three years as I say, but as I was less than four when we went back to Kentucky, I recollect the period with no effect of continuity or sequence, in fact with no sense of time at all. What I have retained is a random set of single scenes, snapshots or still lifes chopped off on both sides, flashes that are clear but suspended, unattached in space and time. A few photographs have survived, and there was one now lost that showed Buddy and me playing about a toy wagon in our dusty backyard with our best friend, a little chocolate boy named Gustus, the son of our black cook. His name must have been Augustus, but nobody ever called him that. Mama always felt herself, as a lady, entitled to at least one servant, and felt mistreated when she had none, which was most of the time. In the South one's servant was always black, or as Mama would say, carefully, Negro—never, never Nigger. Mama always liked her Negro helpers, and they tended to become friends, companions, carrying on a soft, comfortable dialogue as they worked together about the house that was pleasant to be around.

The surviving photographs show me as a pretty little boy with a Dutch look. My face had got rounder, and I had deep blue eyes and the fair, full-blooded skin that blushes easily and has a terrible time with sunburn, a thick cap of blond hair cut in rounded bangs—a real white or platinum blond, the kind of hair that gets a child called "Cotton" in the South. As a matter of fact, I am afraid I was called Bennie Laurie. The name did not bother me in the family but it made me cringe when others used it. The second syllable of Bennie soon got elided, however, then the Laurie dropped away, and it was a great relief a few years later when everybody began calling me simply Ben. I had passed out of infancy, I felt, and at the same time become officially male. In one of these pictures I am sitting in a trapped and nervous fashion on a spotted pony provided by one of the itinerant photographers who used to tour the South, seducing fond parents. In another I am standing on the porch of our white frame house in Forney, dressed in a white sailor blouse buttoned to blue velvet knee breeches, and holding a white wooly lamb with a bell on a ribbon round his neck and mounted on a little wheeled platform. I remember him perfectly well.

But there is one charming studio portrait of Buddy and me, seated, full-face, in our Dutch-boy cuts, I very blond, he very brunet. He looks, as he was, handsome and good-humored and tougher than I, a good deal more equal to the world. He is wearing a standard "sailor suit," with a wide-collared navy blue middy-blouse. The costume I am wearing is one I recall clearly after more than sixty years: heavy Irish linen of pale green, with a wide oval white collar and white cuffs on short sleeves, and huge round black buttons. It was beautiful, and so stiffly starched that it was torture to wear. Mama had powerful and snobbish ideas about clothes, and her taste was far too good for her pocketbook. She believed that the minister's family should set an example of neatness and even elegance to the community, whether they could afford it or not. But she really loved beautiful things, fabrics or design, for themselves. She was especially fond of Irish linen and of starch, and washing and ironing were mighty events in our house.

It seems to me we were always talking about clothes, and it is probably owing to her influence that we all grew up with an extravagant affection for clothing. In fact I still have it, and I can take a sensual satisfaction in a handsome coat or shirt or pair of shoes. Yet, though I love to buy clothes, for myself or to give to other people, I care little about wearing them and I go about most of the time in nondescript cottons, and I am happier barefoot than shod. Mine seems an odd aesthetic passion in which clothes become an artifact, lovely to possess and to look at, not really to be otherwise used.

It strikes me now that my Texas recollections, perhaps too trivial to be worth the carriage for anyone but myself, can only be given order in terms of several effects of light. I remember scenes in three main kinds of light: full, bright, hot sun; a soft, shadowy suppertime twilight; black dark cut through with lurid flashes. For example, I have a very clear, wholly detached recollection of standing with my father on a wide wooden dock in Galveston, staring at the Gulf of Mexico. The sunlight was absolute, and everything but the planks of the dock was a pure cobalt blue: the endless plain of the sea, the huge inverted bowl of sky. What were we doing there? My father must have taken us "to see an ocean." If so it is the only time I can recall our going anywhere for the pure sake of travel. The Texas darkness I associate with gypsies and the Ku Klux Klan. The Texas twilight gave me the only image I possess of my mother's mother, Grandmother Lawrence.

That was a beautiful scene to me, though I suppose to anyone else it may seem featureless and rather dull. My grandmother must have come from Kentucky for a visit. I had gone upstairs in the late afternoon while it was still broad daylight, had fallen asleep, and had been allowed to sleep through supper. When I got up and straggled downstairs, still half asleep, darkness was falling, and everyone had left the big plain kitchen except my mother and her mother, who were washing dishes in two big white enamel pans at the sink. I was given something to eat and sat alone at the table, watching them silently and drowsily as they worked by the light of an oil lamp. They talked softly together. Fat junebugs pinged dully against the screen door, and outside fireflies flashed on and off and katydids buzzed. Against the screen of the open window above the sink big white moths flapped softly. Everything was soft: the air inside and out, the pool of light about the two beautiful small women, so far apart in age yet so much alike, the murmur of their voices, the way their hands moved. That is all there was to it, but the scene has stayed with me ever since as a sum of beatitude. Things never again seemed so trustworthy. Grandmother Lawrence must have died within the next couple of years, for I never saw her again.

My nighttime memories are mostly lurid, as I say, and not numerous. We seem to have had three general family phobias. One was "mad dogs," malignant rabid animals, victims of "hydrophobia," who were rumored to be numerous and constantly on the prowl. I never saw one or knew any-one who had, but local children were always being warned against them, with colorful descriptions of their symptoms such as "foaming at the mouth" and the ghastly consequences of their bite. In any case mad dogs were mainly a daytime anxiety. We worried about "gypsies" all the time, but they seemed to show up mainly after dark, probably because they liked to camp outside our town, Forney. I don't know whether they were real gypsies or just itinerant Mexicans or poor whites: probably some of each. They carried a reputation as great thieves and kidnappers, stealing anything that was loose and especially children. They would appear on the dusty road, moving slowly and stubbornly, one or two or three ramshackle canvas-topped wagons hung about with clattering utensils, accompanied by their surly dogs and often leading a goat or two or a mule or a cow. The people looked dangerous enough, dark and dirty and sullen, but they stared straight ahead and paid no attention to anybody they passed. When somebody called out "Gypsies!" we would run into the house and lock the doors and windows and pull down the blinds: an atavistic instinct, I sup-pose, a retreat to the cave.

There was a bit of delight in our trepidation over the gypsies: we only half believed they were dangerous. But there was nothing equivocal about our terror at the Ku Klux Klan. They were particularly awful because they came with no warning. We children had never heard of the Klan, and I imagine that even to our parents they had been no more than an improba-ble rumor. Suddenly they were there one black summer night, a line of flaring lights coming down the road. Buddy and I ran into the house.

Mama turned off all the lights and pulled down the blinds. Kneeling on the floor at the front windows, we raised the blinds a crack and watched the procession in pure horror. "What is it, Dad?" we asked. "It's the Klan." We were no wiser. It was like something erupted out of one's worst nightmares, or out of another world one had never heard of. They marched past, a line of perhaps a hundred men (were they men? we wondered), each one covered from head to foot in a long white robe topped with a conical mask with eyeholes, each carrying a long torch flaring against the black sky, and some with mysterious tools—rods or whips or rifles.

My father stamped about the house, nearly hysterical with outrage and fear, and Mama clutched at him. He knew that "as a minister of the Gospel" he should "do something." But what could he do, except go out and harangue them, and he lacked the nerve for that. So we watched them from our window slits, dumbfounded and insulted. After a while they collected about a big bonfire across a field, and we could see dim white forms moving ceremonially against the flames. They looked absurd and terribly powerful, reduced to their common deadly purpose, and invulnerable in their anonymity. They should have been funny, but they were far from it and we all knew it. I do not know whether they "did" anything that night, aside from parading, but next day the talk was that "niggers" had been lynched or perhaps only beaten.

I remember those whips very well, in Texas and later in Kentucky, "muleskinners'" whips, "blacksnake" whips: often six or eight feet long, braided of finest leather, with a stock of wood or bone or weighted leather and a thong to go about the wrist, flexible and tapering like a snake or a fabulous penis down to a thin tip rayed out in several thongs that cracked with a spiteful snap like a pistol shot at the end of the long curling stroke. It was a beautiful and brutal instrument, the tool of a bully and a dandy and a sensualist. The whip was so clearly an aggressive instrument, made to wound, and turned a man's arm into something stylish and deadly.

Lord knows what had taken us to Texas in the first place. I imagine Dad had "lost his church" in North Tonawanda, then come back upon his parents' hands in Louisville, in what was to become a fixed rhythm, before finding a new post in Forney. In our Protestant denomination a minister had to find his own church, in competition with men like himself, and he had to please his congregation to hold it. The congregation fixed his miserable salary, and paid it, and in Dad's kind of country churches one lived on uneasy sufferance and close to poverty. The fact that Mama's pretty niece Lois was in a T.B. sanatorium in El Paso, on the Rio Grande at the Mexican border, can have had little to do with our going to Texas, for Forney was hundreds of miles to the east, and we never saw Lois in El Paso, though she sent us enchanting little watercolor sketches she had made of the semidesert country, with cattle and horses and riders in big hats. No doubt her little paintings had a lot to do with my notion, an obsession till my early teens, that I was going west to be a cowboy when I grew up.

I don't remember Forney as a town at all, or even remember my father's church. It was cotton country, and one of the sunlight images I do retain is that of the Negro pickers, men, women, and children, crawling down the long rows, plucking the marshmallow tufts and stuffing them into the long sacks tied round their necks and trailing behind them on the ground. Those sacks must have seemed bottomless. I also remember the big rawboned cotton gin at a crossroads, and the big burlapped bales of ginned cotton going by on flatbed wagons to be piled high on freight platforms for shipment by train. Years later I would see tobacco, in bales and hogsheads, hauled in the same way out the Dixie Highway in Louisville, except that the wagons had turned into trucks and trailers. In Forney, Buddy and Gustus and I used to play in bins of cottonseed in the barn—fluffy, dry, mealy stuff—in the way most children play in sandpiles.

We lived a mile or two outside the town on what must have passed for a main road, for there was a good deal of dusty traffic going by. We had no car and my father went back and forth by bicycle, with his trousers drawn down in a peg-top effect from his pudgy hips to his cuffs bound in by black spring metal clips. Mama bickered about that of course, thinking his appearance shamefully inelegant for a minister. I remember the country as flat, hot, bright, and dry. There was a good deal of grass about, but also a lot of bare brown earth, sometimes dusty, sometimes curling into thin flakes the size and shape of pie plates. I recall vividly what must have been a year of long drought, in which our big muddy pond went slowly dry, and finally what seemed hundreds of silvery fish flopped handsomely and helplessly in the shrinking shallow pool that remained inside the shelving banks of cracked mud.

One of my father's stubbornest delusions was that nature had meant him to be a gentleman farmer. Our ten acres and the ragged white frame house in which we lived must have been the remnant of a worked-out farm. The house had screened porches, a cyclone cellar that was a mere cave or pit with a bulkhead and a ladder, and there was a small barn and a privy, a two-holer. I can't remember that we grew anything, though Dad probably had a vegetable garden. He was actually quite a good gardener, though stronger on theory than on order or persistence. He could also make a neat job of simple carpentry if you gave him plenty of time. His specialty was tool boxes, with a remarkable inner tray and a hinged top, the whole thing grown too heavy to lift, finally.

We had chickens and a milk cow, and Buddy and I were always setting up a wail for a pony, which got us nowhere. Mama loved cows and the things to be made from the milk: butter and cottage cheese, cakes and fudge, gallons of ice cream. She always wanted her cow to be a Jersey: aside from the rich milk, she was drawn aesthetically and snobbishly by their lustrous brown eyes and fine-boned, delicately lifted heads. The milking was Dad's job, and he seemed to have a good deal of trouble with it, especially from his pince-nez, which were always getting brushed off by the cow's flank or her swinging tail. While he was groping about in the straw the cow would be stepping on his glasses or into the milk bucket.

We always had dogs and cats, of course, and one of the grisliest memories of my early childhood is that of coming upon a scene behind the barn where a man hired for the occasion had just finished butchering, with an ax, a litter of unwanted puppies. Dad would have lacked the nerve to do it himself. The usual country method of disposing of superfluous puppies or kittens was to drown them in a pond in a sack. Dad did try, once, to drown a litter of kittens, but he lost his courage half way and pulled the sack out of the water. The kittens were very much alive, and they stalked off in a rage, snarling and spitting and shaking out their paws.

We played outdoors through the long bright days in what seemed an infinity of space and time. We loved to fly kites, but sooner or later they usually broke loose, and I can remember trudging for what felt like miles across country on the trail of a big box kite that we finally found crumpled in the top of a tree. Buddy and I often walked across the back fields to a tiny roadside Negro store where you could buy a huge cake of homemade peanut brittle for a few cents. The proprietor was not very selective about his nuts, but after a few shocks we learned to eat carefully around the black ones. Local nuts were plentiful and cheap and we usually had a big burlap sack of paper-shell pecans in the kitchen, delicious in cake or ice cream.

Evidently I had a passionate infantile curiosity about what women had under their skirts, for I recall Mama cutting me across the legs with a limber switch (the only time, I think, she ever punished me severely) after I crawled on the floor to look up under the skirt of our colored hired girl as she stood at the ironing board. Another time when she and a friend stopped off at our privy on their way home from work, Gustus and I ran to try to peek up at their bottoms from the opening near the ground at the back of the little shed. But the place smelled so bad and the data were so confusing that we quickly gave the whole thing up. Love has pitched his mansion in the place of excrement, as Yeats says.

Forney was situated about midway between Fort Worth and Dallas, and Dad or Mama went fairly often to one city or the other, traveling back and forth by "jitney," big dusty open touring cars with folding jump-seats in the space behind the front seat, which carried country passengers for a trifling fee. (A nickel was sometimes called a "jitney.") "Bring me back a present," Buddy and I always demanded. I usually asked for a popgun, a toy shaped like a real carbine that broke in the middle for cocking and flung out a cork with a satisfactory "plop." It was as close as I could come at the moment to the cowboy life. I thought of life in general as a routine affair illuminated by presents. Birthday parties were the saturnalia of presents, which along with the ritual cake and ice cream justified the strain of shoes and starched clothing. There was a good deal of rather nasty invidiousness about this whole business of giving and receiving presents. I can remember standing by the front door at my third birthday party, poised to seize the present as each boy or girl arrived. When Buddy or I was allowed to go along on the trip to Dallas or Fort Worth, it was a glamorous event for us. I think we never went anywhere except to Woolworth's or Kresge's and the big department stores, but to persons of our possessiveness and greed those seemed heavenly places.

As usual, I cannot be sure why we left Forney and moved to Houston. Either Dad had "lost his church" again or he had taken up with something that seemed a better opportunity. He kept his optimism, poor man, as long as he lived. I have a vague impression that he had taken some sort of minor "executive" job with the Salvation Army or the Red Cross. At any rate the venture was a failure and we never felt anything but tentative and temporary in Houston. We spent our last six months of Texas there, but though I was a bit older there, my memories of the city are confused and almost featureless. I cannot recall taking any pleasure in the new experience of living in a city: there were a lot of people but they were not friends. We occupied a two-story white frame house on a side street, and we had a cat who was locally famous for her habit of jumping off the roof of the porch, at the level of the second story. Buddy was going to school for the first time, in the kindergarten of a public school, and I was tried out for a day or two at a nursery school operated by a spinster in the neighborhood, mainly on her glassed-in porch. But after I had demolished some electric wires that ran around the porch in a niche of the wainscoting, I was invited not to return.

We had always been hard up, always living beyond our small means. My parents seemed to have a fixed idea that they were people entitled to a good living. Whereas they never had a good living or anything like it, they operated as if they could create money by spending it, or by promising to spend it. So we were always in debt, always "overdrawn" on our absurd bank accounts. Years later I came across some old letters that seemed to suggest that Dad had got involved in a small, quiet scandal over money in Houston. He had apparently held back and spent on family obligations a sum of money, not large, that he should have turned over to his employers. It was a piece of countrified, small-time peculation in which he would have acted in weakness and unrealism, our family's kind of schizophrenia, never doubting that the money would appear when he "needed" to account for it.

I am sure that Grandfather Reid bailed us out of Houston, as he had done before and would do again. He must have come through in fairly handsome style, for the next thing I knew we were rattling endlessly cross-country by train, heading back to Kentucky, and each of us had a "berth" to sleep in. I can remember Mama waking us up at a night stop, raising the green blinds with the pinch-latches at the bottom, and telling us to take a look at Little Rock, "where Daddy was born." I looked groggily about, through the flaring lights, trying to see the mysterious rock. The scene reminded me unpleasantly of the marching torchlit Klan, and after a bit I went back to sleep.

TWO

Country Boy

Happily I can also remember little of the new interval in Louisville that followed, though it lasted more than a year. I can imagine the tedious and uncomfortable kind of thing it must have been for my parents, back on Granddad's hands with no income and no work to do, but I seem to have passed through it in a vague dream. Granddad was preaching then in a hideous white frame church (we "Christians" had a positive genius for ugliness in our buildings) at the corner of Eighteenth and Gaulbert, and he owned "property" that was equally undistinguished, though necessary in our neediness: a two-story frame house on a narrow lot next door to the church, a tiny frame "bungalow" a couple of blocks away on Hill Street, and "the building" at Thirty-fourth and Market Street in the West End, a rawboned red-brick box smeared with peeling pebbly stucco, which he had bought cheap after it was abandoned as a brewery and was converting in his slapdash way into little stores and apartments. The four of us moved into the bungalow on Hill Street, a vulgar toy of a house, some speculator's crack-brained crackerbox, with only three or four tiny chambers running straight back in shotgun fashion on a lot barely wide enough to hold it. Mama despised the place, of course, and despised us for being there and Granddad for offering it. We were all miserable and we survived by assuming, with our usual weird optimism, that our condition was only temporary.

Of this period I remember clearly only my wicked little friend David Dutez (accent on the first syllable), who was believed to lead me into infamous courses. I recall nothing more heinous than long restless walks about the streets with David, climbing a few forbidden fences, and hopping onto the back step of Dutch Kessler's ice wagon to steal chips of ice, delicious on a hot summer day, while sparrows fluffed and chattered about the horse dung at the curb. The Thirty-fourth Street building was far enough away across town so that we almost never went there, but we saw a great deal of the house on Eighteenth Street, which Granddad had painted a nauseating purplish chocolate brown, not because he liked the color, but because he had got hold of some cheap paint that turned more and more toward vomited raspberry as it faded over the years. Granddad and Grandmother lived on the second floor and rented out the first to "Dutch and Inez"—the giggly muscular little red-haired ice man and his pretty round-faced brunette wife, both of whom went far toward making the neighborhood tolerable.

We come now to what I still think of as "my town," and the place where I "grew up," though indeed we lived there less than five years and I was only ten when we left to retreat to Louisville once more. Those years in Crestwood have left me thinking of myself all my life as a country boy. Both of my parents are buried in the beautiful little graveyard south of the town, one of the two or three places on earth where I would not mind resting myself when the time comes. At an academic party recently, in a long, emotional, and slightly bibulous conversation with a colleague, a civilized woman who likes to make rubbings of old gravestones, I was surprised to realize that this question of a last place is one that I care about.

Dad of course had been looking for a new church ever since we left Texas with our tails between our legs, and one day I heard that we were to be moving to a place called Crestwood about twenty miles east of Louisville. We got hold of a car somehow and drove out to have a look at the area. Though I can't recollect how I learned to read, it is clear that I was reading then, for I remember lying on the back seat of the car and spelling out a big sign, white letters on a blue ground. that said "Oldham," which I naturally pronounced Old ham. That must have been LaGrange, the country seat of Oldham County, a larger town a few miles east of Crestwood. Over the years we grew dismally familiar with the road between Louisville and Crestwood. Coming out of the city you drove first through the busy suburb of St. Matthews, with a stop, if cash allowed, at a wonderful German bakery, Plehn's, then ambled out through the countryside on narrow black roads, through Lyndon, past the ominous grounds of Lakeland, the state insane asylum on a hill off to the left, through the pretty, old-fashioned town of Anchorage, with a real sea anchor hung up in a big hoop of steel by the post office, on past other hamlets, till you came to Peewee Valley, a mysterious little toy town that seemed to have no center to it. Peewee was notable as "The Home of the Little Colonel"—the home, that is, of Annie Fellows Johnston, the author of the much-loved "Little Colonel" books for children; and also as the site of the "Confederate Home," a handsome big yellow frame house, the strange-smelling last refuge of a score or so amazing old relics of the Confederate army. Beyond Peewee Valley a mile or so, most of it up and down a single long hill, you came to Crestwood, set in pretty green farming country, pleasantly mixed of woods and fields, with enough roll in it to make it graceful and interesting.

I think we all loved the town; I know I did. It was just a hamlet, really, supposed to contain about four hundred souls, and many of those must have been counted from the surrounding farms. The town was bisected by the highway and the railroad, a main line of the "L&N," the Louisville and Nashville. A freight siding ran close in behind Mr. Stoess's warehouse where there was usually a big open gondola or two filled with sand or gravel or coal, waiting to be unloaded or waiting empty to be shunted back onto the main track and hauled away. We used to climb all over those cars, using the ladders and the big steel couplings, and I'm surprised, thinking back, that nobody broke a leg or a head. There was also a hopeful little passenger station, now hopeless. I don't think the big passenger trains can ever have stopped in Crestwood, and the "Interurban," running single long yellow cars between Louisville and LaGrange, gave up the ghost about the time we moved to town, perhaps embarrassed at the inaccuracy of its title. Passenger trains, particularly the great "Pan-American" every night at six, coming back from exotic places in the East, rocketed through the town at top speed with no sign other than a sarcastic hoot from the whistle. There was joy and awe in those trains, in their sleekness and power and purpose.

The so-called highway, "the LaGrange road," was only a dirt track when we came to Crestwood, and I remember scuffling barefoot in its dust in summer and skidding in its icy ruts in winter. The widening and paving of the road was a remarkable event of our interval there, attended by a good deal of excitement. There were awkward motorized graders and rollers, but much of the work was still being done—this was about 1925—by horse-drawn steel skids shaped like a huge sugar scoop with a flat bottom, pulled by a single horse and guided by a heavy-muscled man who had to control not only the animal but the two short handles at the back of the big tool, and throwing the weight of his body this way and that to make the scoop dig in or tip as the case required. My friends and I watched all this with fascination, dividing our admiration between men and horses.

The "business" part of town was small and simple and closely clustered: a little grey stone bank, a little Chevrolet agency that was also the only filling station and the only auto repair shop, a ramshackle blacksmith shop that was usually busier and certainly more interesting than the garage, two general stores, Waugh's on one side of the tracks and Stackhouse's on the other. We traded at Stackhouse's because it was larger and nearer, but we sometimes turned to Waugh when our credit ran low with Stackhouse. We gave them, as we did the bank, a great deal of trouble. These were the typical untidy, wonderful stores of the day, where you could buy anything for daily country living, from a pound of coffee to a pair of overalls. Shelves of canned and bottled goods lined the walls from floor to ceiling. A long wide counter on either side of the store would be partly filled with glass cases holding cheap candies, tobacco in all its forms, medicines and toiletries. Bins and barrels held sugar, flour, meal, nuts, pickles, dried beans and fruits, hardware. Tables and pillars would be stacked or draped with clothing, hats, boots, rope, wire, horse harness of all kinds, even saddles. These were places of complex and powerful odor, the dominant smells being probably those of tobacco, leather, and dill pickles.

Mr. Stoess (pronounced as if it had no "o") was said to be the richest man in town and no doubt was so, though that was not saying very much. Everybody was more or less poor. We were poorer than most, though we passed for genteel. The Stoess enclave occupied an irregular U that enclosed the master's big white house, where I especially admired the inside bathroom and a smaller house where lived a brother-in-law employee and two children, mad little Dutch Engelhardt and his dolly blonde sister Mary Louise. One horn of the Stoess U was occupied by a little funeral parlor (the hearse doubling as an ambulance) and the other horn tipped by a little ice cream parlor and "sweet shop." Behind the sweet shop was a big bare room in one corner of which sat the roll top desk where my parents' friend Frank Measle kept the books of Mr. Stoess's complicated little empire. In this room the Boy Scouts held meetings, and occasionally a traveling judge of some kind sat to hear local cases, chairs being brought in from the ice cream parlor for spectators. Sheds and lofts in the body of the U held Mr. Stoess's stocks in trade: hardware, sand, gravel, lumber, sacks of plaster, cement, chicken and cattle feed, roofing, fencing, and so on, and ice and coal according to the season.

Buddy and I poked around these places a good deal, partly because Clayton Stoess was a friend of ours. In one of those shed lofts Kenneth Maddox, a dark, soft, effeminate older boy, dazzled me one day by demonstrating how he could "shoot off" (semen) from the top step clear to the bottom. There were two other young Stoesses, Milton Carl and Muriel, but they were generally outside our ken, being teenagers and in high school. I preserve a grateful memory of Muriel (pronounced "Murl" by everybody), for she was the first person to give me a glimpse, quick, veiled, and exhilarating, of the female genitalia. Sousing in the brown water off the dock at the Scout camp, I looked up and there she was, sitting cross-legged in a tight white wool bathing suit. I could see the long cleft with the cloth drawn into it, surrounded by astonishing wiry spikes of curly brown hair sticking straight through the porous cloth. The whole ensemble seemed to me mysterious and beautiful.

Aside from the main road running straight through town there were no streets, nothing but rambling dirt or graveled tracks that must originally have linked the outlying farms to the railroad and the highway, gradually taking on a bit of consequence as they got settled, still sparsely, by small holders along the way. Aside from the problematical Kenneth Maddox across the road from us, the Stoesses and Engelhardts near the center, and the two Griner boys at the greenhouse beyond the church, all of our friends lived in this little loose web of roads near town or farther out on actual farms. The Scout camp was far enough out to be in another township, and we went there rarely. But Camp Kavanagh was only a mile or so out of town in the opposite direction, and we saw a lot of that in summers: a handsome hardwood grove, a ragged cluster of cabins with an open assembly and dining pavilion, swarming with flies and yellow jackets, a couple of weed-grown clay tennis courts. The camp was a "Christian" amenity, used for regional gatherings of our sect—mostly the young, the place being too uncomfortable for civilized adults—but I think we also lent or rented the place to brave groups from other denominations.

Our church stood, or squatted, by the main road at the east end of town, with the parsonage next door, the two together occupying a couple of acres of flat ground with grass and trees but no other cultivation. A hundred yards beyond us was a large handsome white house with pillars and a porte-cochere reached by a circular drive. I can't remember who lived there, and it seemed to be empty most of the time. Beyond this house was nothing but countryside: the town had ended.

Our house was separated from the church by a couple of hundred feet of underfed grass. We thought the place reasonably comfortable and roomy, though it seemed to have shrunk by about half when I saw it again twenty years later. It was like millions of other turn of the century houses standing in country towns and city neighborhoods, a plain two-story house of white clapboards under an angular tarred tin roof, set in a rectangle of lawn with shade trees and a straight gravel driveway to a small detached garage. An open porch with round white pillars crossed the front and turned the corner of the living room to the front door. Inside was a sizeable hallway with a stairway rising with one right-angle turn to the second floor. Sliding doors off the hall opened into the living room, behind which was the dining room, and behind that the kitchen, all three rooms being roughly square and about the same size. Off the kitchen was a good-sized pantry lined with shelves, with a window in the end and a bare light bulb hanging from the ceiling. A door off the corner of the kitchen led to a small screened porch, outside which was a concrete cistern and a bulkhead into a small dirt-floored cellar, dark and dank and useless except for storing coal. Upstairs was a duplicate of the lower hall, with a couch under a sunny front window where I did much of my reading, and three more or less identical bedrooms running in series from front to back of the house. For some reason Mama and Dad took the middle room, Buddy and I had the brighter front room, and the back bedroom was soon occupied by our glamorous and problematical cousin Lowell.

What furniture had survived our family's moving about was shabby and disunified. Mama was ashamed of it but we could not afford better things. I remember mainly a big ugly oak china cabinet with glass doors, the kind of thing that for some strange reason people are now pursuing again at absurd prices, filled with cut glass pieces and gold-bordered Haviland china, probably surviving wedding presents. We used this stuff all the time, operating on the kind of economy that mistreats expensive and beautiful things because it lacks the cash to buy cheap utilitarian alternatives. We could hardly ever afford "help" now, and I'm afraid our house looked dingy most of the time. Mama hated dirt but she also felt, as a lady, socially superior to it, and so her housekeeping was spiteful and spasmodic. Buddy and I were soon drawn into what cleaning was done, and indeed we worked at it until we grew up: washed dishes and made beds, washed and ironed clothes and linen, dusted and mopped, and swept out the rooms with old-fashioned corn brooms after sprinkling the carpets with water to "keep down the dust."

Cutting the grass in summer and carrying in kindling and coal and tending the fires in winter were our other principal chores. We grumbled and dawdled and felt abused, but we did not have to work nearly so hard as the farm children did, for example. It seems to me now that we had endless free time, summer and winter. Furnaces being almost unheard of in a small Kentucky town in the twenties, our house was heated by stoves and grates burning the handsome "soft" coal that we broke into lumps of the right size with a hammer or hatchet. Laying a coal fire with the right ordering of crumpled newspaper, kindling, and small lumps, getting it started and keeping it going with the right intensity can be an artful and absorbing affair, and a good open coal fire is a lovely thing.

In the kitchen stood a big flat-topped cast iron stove that served for heating as well as cooking, keeping the room pleasantly warm in winter and stifling in summer. As we had no bathroom we took our baths in the same galvanized tub we used for laundry, in water heated on top of the stove. One bathed in the kitchen near the stove, or if one wanted privacy one dragged the tub into the pantry and closed the door. In the dining room stood a cylindrical black "parlor" stove, about which we spent most of our time on cold evenings, reading or playing innocent card games such as "Rook," about which we got very passionate. Mama considered "real" playing cards instruments of the devil, but Rook was all right. The living room and the front and middle bedrooms upstairs had small handsome open coal grates, but the back bedroom had no heat of any kind. Dad partly solved the problem, after Lowell moved in there, by making what he called a "register," simply a square hole cut through the dining room ceiling and the bedroom floor, framed off and covered with hardware cloth, through which warm air from the stove could pass upward.

One could sit peacefully for hours, doing practically nothing, in front of a coal fire, which is even better than wood for dreaming into, deeper and more mysterious. I especially loved the little private grate that Buddy and I shared in the front bedroom. The most luxurious single sensation I can remember from my childhood is that of being tucked into my bed by my mother, then lying there with my hands behind my head, looking drowsily at the fire or watching it flickering on the ceiling overhead.

Our outbuildings were few, small, and simple: the garage, usually empty; a little woodshed where we kept tools, coal, and scrap wood for kindling (handy also when Dad wanted to give one of us a disciplinary whacking); the privy, a two-holer, with a sack of lime and a piece of shingle or an old kitchen spoon with which one dipped out a portion and dropped it on one's deposit to keep down odors, and an old Sears Roebuck catalog whose leaves served as a Spartan toilet paper. Except in cold weather, when one was not inclined to dawdle, I used to linger on my seat to study the pages given over to models showing women's underwear—my country pornographia, the best I could find. Two or three old fruit trees produced hard green inedible peaches and yellow-green apples that weren't bad at all. Nearby was a small stable affair partitioned down the middle. On one side we usually kept a few chickens; on the other side were a stall and feedbins which, as I was constantly pointing out, would have accommodated a pony nicely, but which held a cow instead, when we had one. This area was the scene of two of my disasters, one small and one large but both disturbing.

Buddy and I and most of our friends more or less constantly carried slingshots, or "gumbos" as we called them, stuck into a back pocket when not in use. We gave a lot of time and thought to the making of a gumbo, looking for just the right Y-forked stick, cutting it off at the right points and peeling the bark, calculating length and width for the two strips of old rubber inner tube that supplied the power, carefully shaping the piece of old shoe tongue that formed the pouch for the missile. Every boy got into the habit of picking up and saving every likely small stone he came across. We were forever popping away at something, including each other, usually with little consequence. Most boys shot at birds, but Buddy and I disapproved of that, and we usually aimed at something inanimate such as a barn, which we could be fairly sure of hitting and which gave back a satisfactory thud. Sitting on an old stump in our backyard one afternoon, I idly took aim at a young leghorn that was strolling by about ten yards away. To my amazement and horror his head on its long stalk folded straight over toward me like a snapping stick. I had caught him square on the neck and he was stone dead. We were an inefficient bunch in our family, but we never wilfully wasted anything. When I carried the little corpse to Mama she was very angry, but I could see she was also amused by my astonishment and touched by my chagrin. She decided to stew the chicken and give him to me that night in a broth—mingling, I suppose, discipline and forgiveness. To kill the creature and then to eat my victim seemed to me close to cannibalism; but a couple of sips cheered me up: he tasted just fine.

There was nothing funny about the other episode. After a period without a milk cow, we had somehow managed to get hold of a beautiful new Jersey, and Mama especially was pleased and proud. Dad warned Buddy and me repeatedly that we must never leave the door of the feedbin open: the cow would overeat and infallibly "founder" and die. We took note and went on about our business. But one hot afternoon a bit later I noticed that the wheeling buzzards that were a common sight high in the sky were circling lower and lower over our yard with a distinct air of purpose. Rounding the corner of the shed I saw our beautiful new cow laid out on the ground, her sleek sides swollen into a balloon at the point of bursting, her four legs protruded stiff as sticks, her eyes popping, her tongue lolling and drooling: a foundered cow if there ever was one. She died under our eyes as we stood, baffled and recriminatory, awaiting the wagon of the renderer who would pay us a pittance for "hide and tallow," borne down by the thought of so much beauty and usefulness reduced by pure carelessness to a little pile of offal.

The carelessness, everyone agreed, could only have been mine: only I had been mousing about in the stable, only I could have left the feedbin open for the silly cow to eat herself to death. It was no help that I could not remember even touching the feedbin; that only made me feel more guilty, not only criminal but stupid. I was young but I was old enough to know a disaster when I saw one, and to feel the bitterness not only of costing us the cow but of taking away her life. After a couple of hours of hysterical anger, Dad typically appeared to put the whole thing out of his mind. But we had had the cow long enough for Mama to fall in love with her, and though she forgave me swiftly, she mourned the cow for many days, almost as if she had lost a child.

In fact Mama gained a child at about this time, her fifth child and third to survive, my little brother Paul. Buddy and I were mysteriously left in Louisville for a couple of days with our grandparents, and when we got back to Crestwood the baby was simply there. I was surprised and pleased, but I can't remember feeling especially puzzled or curious about his provenance. Mama must have been looking pregnant but I certainly had not noticed. Whereas I thought more or less constantly about what passed with me for sex, I did not associate it with the creation of children, and I don't think it ever crossed my mind that Dad and Mama must have copulated occasionally; I would have thought the idea comical and improbable and pretty repugnant. Paul looked a good deal like me, blond and blue-eyed. Soon he was a happy, active child, and Buddy and I found him interesting and fairly trouble-free.

A mile or so out the road to LaGrange there always seemed to be hordes of children in the little settlement of yellow board-and-batten shacks maintained by the L&N for track repairmen and their families; but these were an itinerant crowd and the children were always moving on about the time you began to know them. You could always recognize them by their bad teeth, a consequence of sucking all day on cheap hard candy. A familiar sight on the railroad line was the little open flatbed car of the repair crew, usually propelled by two men bobbing up and down at the handles of a pumping mechanism. Later, when the cars were given little putting gasoline engines, they were faster but less picturesque. When a real train approached, the crew would jump off and simply lift their whole car off the track. Their work was handsome to watch: the big square-cut creosoted ties aligned precisely across the roadbed, the clean broken stone carefully raked and tamped to bed them in, the shining new rail louvered into exact alignment, finally the steel tie-plates nailed to the sleepers with heavy square-cut spikes driven in by two men swinging long limber sledgehammers in perfect rhythmical sequence. I have always found it easy to understand Thoreau's seemingly confused feelings about the railroad, a spectacular new thing in his day: on the one hand the admirable power and purpose and steadiness and efficiency of the enterprise; on the other the mechanization, the noise, the invasion of the landscape, the awful cost in hard mindless labor that gave him his terrible image of railroad ties, or "sleepers," as endless rows of the bodies of sacrified men—"sound sleepers I assure you."

Hanging about the tracks was dangerous, and I don't know why we children were not forbidden to do it, but we spent a lot of time there, in random play in the box cars and gondolas on the siding, or walking the line from one point to another. The roadbed sometimes produced odd and interesting items dropped or thrown or flushed from passing trains, and of course it was an endless source of stones for gumbo-shooting or mere throwing at a mark. It was fun to see how long one could walk a rail, one foot whipped rapidly in front of another, arms teetering out to the sides for balance. Walking the ties looked attractive but proved frustrating. For a comfortable step adjoining ties were too close, alternate ties too far apart, and one found oneself panting along in a spastic stagger of mincing and leaping. We were warned never to touch the rails in cold weather, and one of our friends was famous for tearing the skin off his tongue when a crazy impulse directed him to apply it to a frozen rail.

Most of our friends from school and church lived along the roads rambling out from the center of town. Years later, when I came across the character Aminadab in Hawthorne's story of "The Birthmark," I thought at once of Lemuel Slaughter, though Aminadab was smarter. Lemuel was a stepson in a family named Wellman who lived on a farm to the east, a big, stupid, charming, totally good-humored lad several years older than Buddy. He apparently did most of the work on the farm, and I'm sure it never occurred to him to complain. He used to come to our house in the evening and stand about chuckling and scratching his head with his big cracked red hand. We all loved him but it was impossible to resist making a butt of him. Lemuel was almost immune to language, but being very verbal in our family we passed a lot of time in kitchen spelling contests and word games, one of which involved testing each other to recognize words spelled out in distorted syllables. We tried Lemuel Slaughter on his own name, and shrieked when he made it Lemon-mule Salu-tator. Buddy and I owned a much-prized Benjamin air rifle, which fired lead BB's with a velocity governed by the number of times one had pumped a plunger in a chamber under the barrel. Buddy used to let people shoot him "in the tail," at a distance carefully proportioned to the number of pumps. One night Lemuel managed, by pulling the trigger with his big toe, to fire a BB into the ball of his thumb. He stared at his thumb with a pained slow smile, scratching his head with his other hand.

In the hills to the south lived the Clore boys, almost albino blond, with pink-rimmed piggy eyes. Farther out to the east lived our good friends the Stampers, Everett and Verlin and their black-haired, violet-eyed tomboy sister Gladys, who was considered to be a little sweet on Buddy. She once broke both arms in a fall from a cherry tree and went about for weeks with the two casts in a sling like a muff across her belly. The Stampers would sometimes invite Buddy and me, town boys, overnight for a real farm outing. We would ride the gentler horses, grab the tails of the big hogs for a full-length skidding ride across the corn stalks in the feed lot, catch catfish with our hands in the shallow pond, and smoke "long green" (half-cured tobacco leaves rolled into a loose cigar) behind the barn. All this was glorious, but the big hungry mosquitoes in the unscreened bedrooms at night were another matter. Even then one could look ahead to hot biscuits with country butter and thick blackberry jam for breakfast. (Mama made delicious biscuits, too—of white flour, very short, with a lot of yellow cheese in them, or "Graham" biscuits of fine-ground whole wheat flour.)

Among our closest friends were Bobby and Geneva Love Measle (so help me), who lived near town on the north. Their father, Frank Measle, was a tall thin man with a long dark tensely humorous face. He spoke with an excruciating stammer that he survived with resigned exasperation. Mr. Measle played the trumpet, the only person in town who had mastered any instrument other than the piano, and it struck me as odd that he could produce a long melody without a stammer. Mrs. Measle was a pale pretty woman with light red hair and exquisite manners—what we called a real lady. Bobby was rosy and gay. Later he grew to be very tall, and he became a very good lawyer. But Geneva Love was the pearl of the family: tall, slender, blonde, gentle, altogether lovely. She and Buddy were particular chums, and I think the four parents already dreamed of making a match some day. I would not have admitted that I loved her too. Twenty years later Buddy and I saw her again, when our mother was buried in Crestwood, and she was still gentle and lovely, though a little tired and faded, married to a sound young local man and with a little girl of her own.

In a rundown cottage beyond the Measles lived a strange pitiful family of four named Meadows: father, mother, and two daughters. The older girl, Emma, was a sallow, strapping high school girl who was said to be "bad." I took this to mean that she smoked cigarettes; and I could see that she wore her stockings rolled down around her ankles in a bad-girl style. Nina (pronounced with a long "i") was a furtive giggly little dark girl whom I bullied in an unrewarding confusedly sexual way. Everybody in town knew and imitated Mrs. Meadows's manner of calling her girls, who needed a lot of calling: "Ni-nooo . . . Em-mooo. . . ." She was a tall awkward woman with a long soft Dickensian face who did odd lots of laundry and housecleaning around town to keep a bit of food in the house. Mr. Meadows, a big, baffled, wordless man, was a former laborer struck down and bedridden with what was whispered to be cancer, a mystifying ailment I had never heard of before. I remember that once he lifted his dark fetid bedclothes to show us a big inflamed knob low on his belly that looked like a red lantern in the gloom. The Meadows family were not so much friends of ours as dependencies of Dad and his congregation, which meant that they received occasional gifts of food or clothing or coal or cash. What they needed was a miracle.

Off the main road toward Peewee Valley, in a big rambling white house with a tennis court, a croquet ground, and even a paddock, lived a rich city banker named Ott. We did not see much of the Otts, nobody did, but we certainly aspired to their acquaintance. The Otts had several cars, including a black electric coupe, which crept about in eerie silence with Mrs. Ott's spinster sister at the steering lever, and they even had a pony cart with a smart little round-bellied black and white pony. I find I can't call the Ott boy, Buddy's age, to mind at all, not even his name. But I certainly remember his younger sister, Mary Louise, very well: a little princess with shiny straight blonde hair who always seemed to be wearing navy blue velvet with a lacy round white collar, which probably means that we saw them almost entirely on Sundays. Mary Louise is a figure in one of the few complete scenarios I retain from those days: she played the bride in a "Tom

Thumb Wedding" in which I was the embarrassed groom. This was one of the absurd standard charades of the day, probably got up to raise money for a church purpose, and probably a scheme of Dad's. It sounds like one of his.

One of our best friends, Lewis Deible Miller, always called "Dibes," we saw less and less often because he lived farther away on the road to Louisville and because he moved so frequently. Mr. Miller was a small contractor who built one or two houses at a time "on speculation." When he sold a house he built another; when one was slow to sell he simply moved his family into it until he found a buyer. The Millers' line of movement held steadily westward, until finally they landed in the Louisville suburb of St. Matthews. On our bicycles Buddy and I followed their moves for visits until they reached Anchorage, but our one trip there we found so exhausting that we gave up the cause thereafter.

I regret to say that I remember our visits to the Millers mainly with chagrin because of the damage we did. On one trip we were playing a game of some sort with Dibes on the still unsealed hardwood floor of his bedroom in one of his father's new houses. Buddy and I were wearing new high-top leather boots of which we were very proud, laced almost to the knee and with hard black rubber soles. We played hard and heedlessly, down on our knees on the floor. When Mrs. Miller came in she was near tears when she saw what the toes of our boots had done: dozens of long black crescent-shaped scrapes that would need sandpaper to remove. On another occasion I terrified Mrs. Miller when in pure stupidity and carelessness I fired Dibes's new .22 rifle straight through the kitchen ceiling. One does not forget one's acute embarrassments.

Of course there were also friends of an older generation, really our parents' friends, most of them members of the church, most of them with children of their own who had grown up and moved away or set up on their own nearby. Little Mr. West and huge Mrs. West, whose weight tilted the whole body of their black Model T sedan, lived back in the country; years later they showed up again, transplanted to Louisville like ourselves. There were the Lowerys and the Lowery Lewises. There were Mrs. Pryor and her maiden sister, Miss Annie, both very sweet and genteel, and Mrs. Pryor's son, Dr. Will. Will Pryor was a local hero, and not only of his family, for he had "done better" than anyone else ever produced by Crestwood: he had not only gone away to college but continued on to medical school and had become not merely a doctor but a "specialist," of the awkward eye-ear-nose-throat category; furthermore he was in practice in the city, in Louisville, with an office in one of the classiest buildings, and he was being called the best man of his kind in the metropolis. That he remained a modest man and a kind man seemed most remarkable of all.

One of the places we went oftenest was not the house of friends but the Confederate Home in Peewee Valley, a rambling, sunny, yellow-painted frame house set in pleasant grounds like a small park. Dad took it as a pastoral obligation to visit the old men regularly, and the whole family often went along on Sunday afternoons, doing our best to think of it as an outing. It was a strange little backwater community of perhaps a score of spectacular ancients cut off by time, by their families, and by the world in general. They looked like a crew of retired pirates, with a lot of white hair and big white moustaches, and several showing old scars or a peg leg or an empty sleeve. They did nothing but sit or amble in the bright wide halls and porches and talk and spit tobacco juice into shiny brass cuspidors. They were waiting with a general air of peacefulness to die, and as there were no more recruits to come the little band could only grow smaller. If they were bona fide veterans of the Civil War, as I suppose they were, most of them must have been pushing ninety or better.

I recall the place mainly in terms of odors and effects of light: the sickish smell of a flowering bush by the front verandah; the old men's faded skin and hair and clothing, their air of heroism faded beyond identification; the long light hallways, beautifully clean, where the housekeeper's soap fought a losing battle with the steeping of urine and of more solid matter. All of the men were more or less addled and more or less incontinent, and as you sat talking, or more often listening, to one of them he usually gave off a faintly ammoniac air. Each of them had a well rehearsed life story, and these were interesting, the first time through. The whole place left a strong but confused impression upon a small boy: so sad and so funny, the romance of big deeds grown distant and improbable.

The middle and late twenties, when we lived in Crestwood, were a very interesting period in the development of American transportation. The automobile was still a new enough thing to be a phenomenon in itself; cars fascinated us all, and we talked about them constantly. The various makes had more character and were more sharply differentiated than they have since become. We watched very closely the changes in the few established lines and looked eagerly at the new makes that kept hopefully appearing, often for only a year or two of life. But the automobile was by no means universal in a small Kentucky town at this time, and it was only beginning to be clear that the horse had seen his day as a creature of general service. On the farms around us horses and mules were far more common than tractors. The blacksmith still had as much work as he could do, and his work with his fires and his bellows and his hammers was handsome and vivid to the eye and ear and even to the nose. One still saw, moving along the roads or outside business places or public gatherings, under saddle or drawing buggies or wagons, fully as many horses as automobiles. It was obvious from the shape of the car bodies that the designers were still making horseless carriages, and the same was true of the early rural gasoline stations that one now passes abandoned: little frame shacks with a canopy extending out to cover a gravel driveway and a pump or two, clearly remembering the porte-cochere.

By horse and buggy was a most ingratiating way to travel, at least in good weather: quiet enough for talk, fast enough for any reasonable purpose, slow enough for looking about or for reverie, open to country airs and light and the complex rich smells of the horse and harness. One of the pleasantest sensations I know is that of driving through a long covered bridge in a buggy, the hard rubber tires going suddenly silent on the board floors as the sound of the hoofs goes louder and sharper, the sudden dimming of the outer lightness, with the sun striking through the cracks in the siding boards, the square of brightness at the far end of the corridor looking mysterious and lovely, an occasional glimpse through a gap in the floor of clear water sliding past underneath. Another mysteriously beautiful experience was that of sledding by moonlight behind a horse and buggy. Occasionally, when conditions were just right—cold enough, bright enough, the right kind of snow or ice—the owner of a rig would invite children who owned sleds to form a party. As many as ten or a dozen sleds, each carrying two or three children, would be tied in tandem behind the back axle of the buggy like a little train of cars, and we would glide over the winding narrow back roads until bedtime and beyond. At first we were gay and raucous, but after a while we would fall into a kind of trance, dazed by something magical in the scene and the feeling, the marvelous smoothness and silentness.

Fords and Chevrolets were the standard cars in Crestwood, though one occasionally saw something fancier, a Dodge or a Reo or an Essex, usually only passing through. That Mr. Stoess drove a Buick sedan was one of the signs of his affluence. He also owned a Packard hearse for the mortuary part of his business, a great black ark of a thing with faded magenta curtains. By doubling as an ambulance it covered most of the range of standard country disasters. We were in the great last days of the Model T Ford, and in fact the Model A arrived, amid universal excitement, before we left Crestwood. The Fords and in a slightly more bulbous way the Chevrolets were stark, simple, indomitable vehicles that seemed to take on a primitive or organic relationship with their owners, as in the sharp list to the right of the Wests's Model T under Mrs. West's weight. The sporty little roadster came on the scene about this time, with the trunk that opened out to offer a roofless rumble seat for two, into which one stepped more or less dashingly by climbing upon a cleat set in a back fender. But most cars were sedans, many with only isinglass side curtains, and all with wide running boards, attractive and dangerous for overflow passengers. Roads were miserable and tires were worse. One anticipated at least one puncture on any journey but the shortest, and usually got it. Every car carried a jack, tire tools, a pump, and a repair kit, and there was a complete folklore dealing with techniques for fixing a leak. All of this meant, aside from trials of the temper, an endless supply of abandoned inner tubes to be adapted for gumbos, swings, and other boyhood artifacts.

Like everyone else Dad was crazy about cars, and felt entitled to own one, and Mama too agreed that the dignity of "the minister's family" required an automobile. But the simple truth was that we could not afford to buy a car or to run one, and most of the time we did without. Fortunately Louisville was almost the only place we went that was beyond walking distance, and we could usually cadge a ride with someone into the city if one or more of us really had to go. But one day Dad showed up with a car, second or third hand of course, which he exhibited to us with a pride that we were glad to share. It was a Graham-Paige, which Dad reckoned among the world's finest and most exotic brands. It was an enormous black open touring car, very much like the arrogant machines that later got associated with the German General Staff, and though it was grander, it reminded us at once of the big jitneys that we used to ride into Dallas or Forth Worth. The Graham-Paige had huge protruding round headlights, a windshield that could be tilted by hand, leather upholstery throughout, jump seats behind the front bench, and long wide running boards on each of which was mounted a spare wheel and tire and a steel chest for tools and such. As a "tourer" it dispensed with side windows but offered a complex system of demountable isinglass curtains that turned out to be almost impossible to manage. Dad took Buddy and Paul and me out for a demonstration, and we were thrilled to see, on the long hill coming down from Peewee Valley, that the speedometer registered twenty miles per hour. "Don't tell Mommie!" Dad cautioned us delightedly; he was as excited as we were.

Now that we had a car it was determined that we must pay a visit to Aunt Inez and her big family in Lexington. Perhaps the wish to make the trip had been the motive for buying the car in the first place: our economy was addicted to that kind of logic. We were in the middle of a long hard cold spell in the dead of winter, and we prepared for that journey of sixty miles as if we were heading for the North Pole. Dad made a trip to an army store in Louisville and came back with charcoal heaters, heavy woolen blankets, scarves, gloves, and socks, and for each of us an aviator's helmet, a bit of the surplus equipment that supplied poorer people for a generation after Armistice Day in 1918—made of smooth leather lined with itchy olive drab wool, with a stubby visor and side panels that enclosed the face and buckled under the chin with a strap. I think even Mama wore one, and Dad's moon face and pince-nez buckled into one of those helmets made one of the funniest sights of my life to date. Given the polar draftiness of that big touring car, our elaborate preparations were not so absurd as they sound. The Graham-Paige did carry us to Lexington and back again, but it disappeared soon after: another of our habitual bad guesses.

In Lexington we children got our first sight of the fantastic Allen clan, Aunt Inez, Uncle Claude, and their nine "boys," grown young men really, stuffed into a modest frame house on a side street. The house was "on the car line," and riding the little yellow trolley downtown was another delightful new experience. (A standard bit of childish mischief was to telephone a house so situated: "Is your house on the car line?" "Yes." "Then you'd better move it; there's a car coming." Hang up with many giggles.) Mama had warned us of the wicked ways of the Allen males. It was easy to see that they "smoked," which was enough to seal the case for her, but she also believed they "drank" and that at least some of them "took dope," unspecified. Buddy and I slept upstairs in the attic that had been turned into a dormitory for the nine sons. The air was stifling from the fumes of the cigarettes they rolled from Bull Durham tobacco out of little cloth sacks with a drawstring top that sold for a nickel.

The episode I remember best from the Lexington visit was a silly crisis I created myself. I had come down with a feverish cold and a doctor was called to the house. For some weird histrionic reason I turned hysterical, refused to see the doctor or to take any medicine, ran into the bathroom and locked myself in and stayed there for hours, resisting the pleas and threats of the other fifteen people in the house. Finally one of the Allen boys climbed in through the bathroom window, turned the key, and pushed me out in disgrace that even I could see was deserved. For several years I had been building a reputation as a mysteriously sickly child. I had occasional headaches, but my real specialty was stomachaches. I think they were real enough; I can't remember ever faking them or taking any pleasure in them. The pain would simply hit and double me up. Doctors could find nothing wrong with my "system"; they spoke vaguely of indigestion and prescribed medicines, probably mostly alcohol and codeine, that did give me some relief. A couple of years later the pains left me for good of their own accord, just as they had come. I suppose I had been going through nerve-storms of some sort. We were a pretty tense bunch of people in our family, within the hectic simplicity of our lives.

The main consequence of our visit to the Allens was that Mama and Aunt Inez had got together and decided that our side of the family would take over responsibility for Lowell Lawrence, the teenage son of their dead brother George. In Crestwood we had recently been through the distressful pleasure of our only visit from Lowell's doomed sister Lois, on a sort of furlough from her T.B. sanatorium in El Paso. We children had never seen her before, though for years we had been fascinated by her vivid letters that usually enclosed bright little watercolors and drawings. Now it was like having a beautiful small ghost in the house for a few days. Soon she was gone back to El Paso, and the next news we had from there was of her death. In earlier years Lois and Mama had been very close when Mama had been her girlish aunt in Lexington, and Mama now mourned her heart-brokenly. I think she saw much of herself in Lois—so small and dark and lovely, so gay and quick-minded, so much ability and promise helpless under the doom that seemed to hang over the Lawrence family. Lowell arrived in Crestwood and moved into our back bedroom. He was to be an interesting and problematical part of our lives for about ten years.

Lowell was probably sixteen years old; I was nine, Buddy eleven, Paul four: a good distribution for resentment or hero-worship. Lowell couldn't help looking romantic whether he was so or not; he always looked more significant than he actually was. The Lawrence good looks took a striking form in him. He never grew much over middle height, but he was so well made, slender and fine muscled, that he always seemed tall. He wore his gleaming black Indian hair rather long, parted in the middle and combed back, and there was a good deal of curly black hair all over him. His face was a system of perfect curves: thick black crescent brows, deep-set hazel-grey eyes, a long thin aquiline nose, a wide, red, full-lipped, mobile mouth. He looked aristocratic but wasn't; his instincts were basically vulgar and worked in a narrow range. He also looked more intelligent than he was; his mind was no more than shrewd and pragmatical. He looked energetic, and he could be so when it suited his purpose, but he had a deep streak of laziness or luxuriance, defensive and self-serving. He was not incapable of good humor or kindness or generosity, but his good will never stretched very far beyond his own interests. Perhaps his limited and egotistical personality was a consequence of his early orphaning, the need to attend to his own survival. At any rate Lowell fitted into the real world with a smoothness and efficiency that none of the rest of us ever managed.

He brought into our house certain whiffs, romantic or a bit fetid but always exciting, of a different side of our village world. Of course his friends were older than ours. He went out of nights and came back late, sometimes smelling peculiar. Even a backwater like Crestwood, in its countrified and impecunious way, was not immune to the thin hectic energies of the Jazz Age. Young people swarmed over the few available cars and drove about the narrow roads, whooping and hollering and Lord knows what else (probably less than we supposed). Mama suspected Lowell of drinking and carrying on with girls, and we knew he smoked, even in the house, over Mama's vehement protests. We could smell tobacco, and sometimes see a blue haze when we looked up through the improvised register Dad had cut through Lowell's bedroom floor. In a small town high school a boy like Lowell was bound to cut a romantic figure, and he was a social lion and an athletic hero. The only school sports were basketball in winter and baseball in spring, and Lowell was a star at both, but particularly in basketball.

Basketball in the twenties was very different from today's game, and in fact the modern game was only beginning to be defined at the end of my own playing days in the early forties, after the center jump following each basket had been ruled out. Today's players, accustomed to their pell-mell pistonlike movement up and down the floor, their repertory of leaping shots, and scores of 75 to 100 or more for each team, would find the older game quaint and comical. There were really only three accepted kinds of shot: the two-handed set shot, often from far out and often delivered underhand; the "crip" shot (layup), driving for the backboard from left or right, the only kind of shot in which it was thought permissible to shoot with only one hand or without both feet planted in balance; and the foul shot, always delivered underhand (in Rick Barry's style) and with deep bending of the knees. Because the ball was brought back to the middle of the court for a toss-up after every basket, it was important to have a tall center who could "control the tap"; but young giants were fewer forty or fifty years ago, and there were plenty of country high school teams on which no player measured as much as six feet. Commonly whole teams scored fewer points than a single player hopes to make nowadays, and game scores such as 18 to 15 or 14 to 12 were perfectly normal.

Modern basketball is often compared to a ballet, of a fairly brutal sort, but the older game was really closer to a ballet, or perhaps a minuet, with far less body contact than is now permitted. One tended to think the matter over carefully before taking a shot, and the kind of player who is now called a "gunner" soon felt the weight of general disapproval. Precise and stylish passing was admired at least as much as shot-making. The players and the ball moved in intricate patterns, and people seemed to do a good deal of standing about in *poses plastiques*. Minutes might pass without anyone letting fly at the basket. Still, it was a complex, modest, and handsome game; when a game was dull it was dull in a less hectic and pretentious way than is now the case.

I go into the matter at length partly because I still love the game, having put so much sweat and passion into it (though I have passed sixty I still have an occasional basketball-playing dream), and partly because I am trying to give a clear image of the kind of ritual in which my cousin Lowell appeared at his poetical best. When Lowell soared for the basket, scored, and attracted a foul, then posed tragically at the foul line, his chest heaving, his cabled muscles shining with sweat, his black hair falling in twin scimitars around his face as he sank nearly to his knee to shoot, we understood perfectly well why the maidens palpitated about us in the bleachers. It was lovely to have a hero in the family at last.

It was easy for Buddy and me to get to school, for the building was only a couple of hundred yards due south of our house. We crossed the road, then an acre or so of thin woods, then the railroad, and there it was, a raw red brick structure of two stories from the turn of the century, set in an untidy playground. The small auditorium served also as gymnasium. No meals were served and everyone brought his own lunch, with heavy emphasis on peanut butter and bologna. All the grades from first to twelfth used the same building. Crestwood's was called a "consolidated" school, which meant that it served all the families from farms and hamlets in a radius of six or seven miles. Buses were unheard of and pupils got to school as best they could: on foot, on bicycles, a few on horseback, many delivered from farms by car or horse and buggy. The farm children's attendance was desultory, especially during planting time in the spring and harvest time in the fall, when they were most needed at home. They often smelled of tobacco, a staple crop of the region, or of horses, too often of skunks. In the grade school the girls wore cotton dresses and the boys wore work shirts of cheap blue chambray and either corduroy knickers or bib-top blue denim overalls, which got paler and more comfortable the more they were washed. We boys went barefoot or wore tennis shoes or laced high-top boots, and sweaters or sheepskin-lined coats, depending on the season and the state of the family purse. My family continued to be dressy beyond its means, but I really preferred the easy plain country clothes, and I understand very well why the young have once more made a cult costume of them.

I remember very little about academic work in Crestwood Consolidated School, aside from the extraordinary amount of time we spent in spelling drills. The old country tradition of spelling contests or "bees" was still very much alive, and I'm sure that pedagogically it was not so silly as it sounds. Spelling was a parlor sport too, and we were always trying each other out on new or difficult words at home or in the houses of friends. If Granddad happened to be on the scene he was sure to drag out "antidisestablish-mentarianism," a proud relic of his clerical past. It seems to me we had a spelling contest in our classroom every day, and once a year it got for-malized in a schoolwide contest in which the champions of the first eight grades tried to spell each other down. This was a considerable occasion, for the winner was sent to LaGrange to compete against winners from all the other schools in the county. All the county winners then competed for a state championship, and finally the state winners for a national champi-onship, an eminence comparable to being elected president or flying solo across the Atlantic.

My day of glory came when I won the championship of the third grade, then of the whole school, and so became Crestwood's representative in the county contest. Mama naturally saw this as an occasion calling for new clothes, and I was refitted from head to foot. I remember that suit very well, a double-breasted jacket and knickerbocker trousers in a handsome hairy pale grey tweed. I felt my responsibility gloriously but confidently; I expected to win the county and the state and then to become the youngest winner ever of the national championship. At LaGrange I stumbled quickly and stupidly, forgetting to capitalize the word "Yankee." That was the end, for the rules allowed no second chance. I tried to feel mistreated, but I could see I had no real case.

Aside from our constant anxiety over money, thickening periodically into crises, I lived a very happy life at Crestwood. The ordinary routine of things was pleasant in itself, easy and varied enough to satisfy a boy of nine or ten or eleven with no real responsibilities. Moreover, one's year rose and fell with a heartening rhythm about a few great days: Christmas, Easter, the Fourth of July, Halloween, Thanksgiving, birthdays. Thanksgiving did not come to a great deal, only the mild pleasures of a heavy feast and a couple of days off from school. Halloween produced little real mischief accomplished, but there was intense excitement in concocting impossibly elaborate schemes, the mere failure of which was a satisfying tribute to the brilliance of the conception. The tensions of the day usually got placidly dissipated in an evening party with costumes and spooky games and bobbing for apples in a washtub full of water. But the Fourth of July was unmistakably a great day, centering on systematic noise and the excitement of risks successfully run. There was never any public ceremony or display at Crestwood; it all came down to the cash, nerve, and ingenuity of the single boy and his friends. Fireworks could be freely bought, but a boy was fairly strictly limited by the money in his pocket and his parents' detailed prohibitions.

In buying firecrackers, the staple of the day, one finally had to choose between size and numerousness. If one had fifty cents or a dollar to spend, was it smarter to spend a nickel for a couple of three-inch crackers (the largest we were allowed) each of which would go off with a single loud roar, or for a string of about twenty-five tiny "Chinese" crackers, which yielded as many small single cracks or a machine-gun effect if you lit the whole string at once? One thought such an issue through carefully, and then faced the same dilemma in choosing between rockets, which sent a single fiery projectile into a gloriously high arc, and Roman candles, which shot off a half-dozen sizzling fireballs seriatim. Other options were not many but they were cheaper: cherry bombs, jawbreaker size, great to throw as well as hear; spittin' devils, red paper-wrapped wafers which you placed under your foot then crushed with a stylish spin of your body, sending sputtering particles in all directions; "sparklers" on a wire which you swung in arcs at the end of your arm—pretty but tame, rather effeminate we thought. In practice one made one's purchases according to a logic that would string out the day's sensations as long as possible and still allow for a few crescendoes, great moments. It was an awful moment when a boy had not only fired off his last but could not find a single friend with anything left to explode, and one had to listen to the return of silence or merely daily noises.

Christmas and Easter were two times in the year when our underdeveloped religious ideas did come together with warmth and coherence, but I'm afraid we boys thought of them, as of birthdays, primarily as occasions for receiving presents. To the extent that we could afford, Easter was new clothes day, and also a day for dyed hard-boiled eggs and enormous eggs and rabbits of rich chocolate and marshmallow, luscious and sickening. But Christmas was the year's great day by all odds, delightful not only in the event but in prospect and retrospect. For months before the day Buddy and I, and by now Paul as well, intensified our usual study of the big "Fall and Winter" catalogs from Sears Roebuck and Montgomery Ward, accumulating long lists of our requirements, complete with catalog numbers, prices, and shipping weight, most of which we incurably expected to receive. Then began the systematic waiting, counting off the days, deliciously tantalizing. If the family happened to have any cash or unexhausted credit, we could count on a day's orgiastic shopping in Louisville. Then came the last day of school before the long holiday, with a party in each classroom with small presents exchanged according to names drawn by lot. Then Christmas Sunday at church, with the best of all hymns to sing, and a present of candies for each child in a square box with a string handle like an animal cracker box. By this time the big mail order package would have arrived, and we would have pinched and poked and even smelled it, trying to make out what it held for each of us. I have never smelled anything more delicious than the aroma of new leather the year we opened a box containing a new pair of high-top boots for each of us, each with a new "Boy Scout" knife in a holster sewed onto the right calf. We had more than one Christmas when money was impossibly tight and we spent the day in spectral suffering silence. But most years Mama was able to mobilize our small cash or credit to provide us with a fair portion of the things for which we had entertained a serious hope.

Our day was like anybody else's country Christmas. One woke already tense after a brief dream-crossed sleep and raced downstairs through the icy house. It might be an hour or two before anybody would have sense enough to light a fire. Delaying the central issue as long as possible, one first attacked one's bulging Christmas stocking, stuffed with big oranges and apples, pecans, walnuts, almonds, and Brazil nuts, chocolates and candy canes, gimcrack toys. Then the real presents, opened in feverish sequence amid a hectic clutter of boxes and paper. After a bit one began to slow one's movements in order to string out the pleasure, foreseeing the awful moment when there would not be a single present left to open, even by somebody else. Christmas was not a feast day at our house; Thanksgiving took care of that, and we were all too busy and too full of nuts and candy to think of sitting down to a long slow meal. When we had opened everything, and gloated and chattered and tried out a few things, somebody would suddenly say, "Let's go see what Bobby Measle got." Carrying or wearing or riding one or two special treasures to exhibit, we would start a round of our friends' houses that would take all afternoon. Looking at our friends' trophies was almost as much fun as opening our own, and we felt little invidiousness in the process; we all knew that most people's presents would come in for shared use in the weeks ahead.

Life in a southern village felt so pleasant and right that all the other ways I have lived since boyhood have seemed to me more or less unnatural, and preferably temporary. One luxuriated in amplitudes of space and time, and in a pace modulated under one's own control—no crowding, no hurry. There were enough people about for any reasonable purpose, yet so few that there was nobody one did not know, though there were a few one did not particularly like. If you saw a stranger, he was just passing through, or visiting one of your friends, or, rarely, just moved to town. As most people were fairly hard up, there was comparatively little class distinction or snobbery, rivalries were not bitter ones. Such at least was a small boy's sense of the town.

Rural Kentucky was a place of four distinct seasons, all of them pleasant in some way. In New England I resent not the severity of the winter but the fact that it goes on so long, and the way it seems to leap right over spring and collide head-on with summer. In Kentucky months behaved the way they were supposed to do. (Years later, when daylight saving time came in, I felt a sneaking sympathy for the silly people who wrote letters to the newspapers denouncing the scheme as a tampering with "God's time.") March was transitional, with gusty winds and broken sun and clouds. April was spring itself: soft showers, long or short, light winds, a mild young sun, air clean and odorous with earth and greenery and blossom. There came a day when Mama said we could take off our long underwear, grown shabby with wearing and washing, then a day when she said we could take off our shoes and go barefoot, one of the glorious sensations of the year, like being let out of prison. May was a perfect month, warm and clear, blue and green, illuminated early by my birthday and late by the closing of school for the summer.

Summer was long and hot and free, an idyl that ran past the reopening of school in September. Unlike the farm boys who sweated in the corn and tobacco fields, Buddy and I had little work to do and could dispose the long days much as we pleased. I had a habit of rising early and roaming about alone until I could collect a companion or two. Baseball was our great game and we often spent whole days at it. In such a small town it was hard to get nine boys together for a team, and impossible to collect eighteen for a real game, but we played pickup forms perfectly happily, taking turns at bat and practicing fielding flies and grounders. Two or three boys could spend an hour or two without boredom simply throwing a ball back and forth. Baseball equipment always appeared on our peremptory Christmas lists, but our supply could not possibly keep up with our needs and our tools remained few and shabby. Nearly everyone possessed a glove, lovingly oiled and molded to form a pocket, but bats were scarce and usually kept going by glue and small nails with an overlay of wrapped tape. A new baseball was a sensually beautiful object, the perfect hard sphere of fine white leather, the raised seams handsewn with heavy waxed thread, lovely to feel and smell. But balls were expensive and easily lost, and if a ball did not get lost it soon popped a seam and then developed a hanging flap of leather, after which one could only wrap the whole sphere in a cocoon of black friction tape. I have never got over the shock of the prodigality with which balls are used in a professional game: think of boxes containing a *dozen* new baseballs. As we could not afford cleated baseball shoes we played barefoot or in sneakers. I have never lost the thrill of finding, abandoned in a closet in an empty house in Peewee Valley that we were inspecting, a pair of real baseball shoes, the old-fashioned type that came up to the ankle bone. Dad said he could see no reason not to take them, and I agreed entirely. I took them home and immediately started racing up and down the yard; the shoes were so much too large that the front cleats fell under my toes instead of under the ball of my foot, but I still felt as if I had grown wings. If our equipment was primitive our spirits were high, and the separate crafts involved, in throwing, catching, hitting, running, were all intricate and engrossing, each with its own mystique of style. Life offers few pleasures so pure as that of taking a clean level swing at a hard-thrown ball and sending it with a sharp crack on a line into the outfield.

In our last two summers in Crestwood Buddy and I took up tennis as well as baseball. Aside from the Otts' private court there was only one court in town, oddly placed in the middle of things, tucked in between the railroad embankment and a side wall of the town bank. The court was treated as public, but I think it may have been an amenity of the Stoesses, whose white shed formed a visually confusing backstop at one end. The surface of the court was of hard dry brown clay, but it always carried a thin skim of the small cinders thrown off by passing trains, making gritty and rather slippery footing. Catgut strings would bend a frame into a ghastly bow if you left a racquet out in the rain, but otherwise tennis equipment was simpler and easier to keep track of than baseball stuff, and there was the advantage that only two or four players could play a real game. We often played through a long hot afternoon until the Pan-American raged past overhead and we knew we had to go home to supper. Dad loved sports of all kinds (to Mama's disgust), but he particularly approved of tennis because, as he said, it was his game. Buddy and I laughed at that, until he challenged us one day and we were amazed to see the speed and accuracy and even grace with which he flung his short round body about the court. He had more style than either of us.

Autumn too was a pleasant season, with an exhilarating monitory nip in the air morning and evening, and high blue skies: "Dian skies" Keats called them in a beautiful letter. Our colors were less brilliant than New England's, but our maples and oaks and hickories gave off a rich quiet glow. Even with school squatting across much of the day, afternoons were still long and largely free, and there were always weekends. Even raking leaves was fun, given the fact that we were allowed to burn them at the end. Fall was a great time for rambles out into the country with a gumbo and a burlap sack, looking for unguarded apple or pear or persimmon trees and the nuts of hickory, hazel, and black walnut. In their thick hard rinds of apple green, walnuts were plentiful and we brought them home in hundreds. The trick there was to throw them in a heap on the floor of a shed and leave them till the rind started to rot and turn brown; then you simply pounded them with a wooden mallet until the wrinkled black shell of the nut came free. The spattering juice from the husks left a very characteristic rich brown butternut stain that was almost indelible, and for weeks in the fall boys wore that stain on their hands and overalls like a local uniform.

Winter cold in Kentucky is likely to be damp and penetrating, but it really grips hard only in January and February. There were no skatable surfaces near us, but we welcomed snow for sledding and snowballing. The year reached its peak at Christmas, which we tended to extend into a season in itself. But certainly the characteristic element of winter was the long evenings about the coal fire, rich and satisfying when they were not broken by a parental quarrel. School homework would have been easily disposed of before supper. We often popped corn or cracked some of the fall nuts, and we played records on the wind-up phonograph or listened to the radio, a new phenomenon in general life, for an hour or so. We had begun with scratchy little crystal sets but moved on to a glorious awkward secondhand battery-powered machine called a Fried-Eismann, which showed a kind of family resemblance to the big old Graham-Paige touring car. The radio gave us Lindbergh's flight and the great Dempsey-Tunney fights, but most of the offering was primitive stuff, quite acceptable to our uncritical ignorance. Much of the fare was a kind of song-and-joke patter that derived from the old music halls by the same kind of genetic logic that brought the automobile out of the horse-drawn carriage, but Dad especially had a bottomless appetite for such chaff. His favorite was a popular turn called Jones and Hare, puffing Interwoven hosiery, who came on with a bouncy jingle:

> Socks! Socks!
> We're the Interwoven pair.
> Now we're coming *on* the air;
> We're Billy Jones and Ernie Hare,

and took leave with a classy counterturn:

> Socks! Socks!
> Now we're going *off* the air. . . .

But the long winter afternoons and evenings were above all a time for reading. Buddy and I would begin with the daily paper from Louisville, with emphasis on the sports page and the "funnies," where I followed with special passion a cowboy hero named Dick Dare. Then we might leaf through a magazine or take a turn at the mail order catalog before settling down for a solid two hours with the book of current choice. If not necessarily occupied in some other way, I tended to read all the time the year round, and people used to worry about my eyes; but I was blessed with a good pair. It was lovely to read till one was sleepy on a winter night, then climb up to the bedroom where Mama would have lit a fire in the grate to take off the chill, and drift off to sleep with the flames flickering across the ceiling. One could feel them through closed eyelids.

I read hundreds of books in these early years, and God knows how many short stories. Most of what I read was trash, but I did not care; I was totally, ignorantly uncritical. I required of a story only that it be interesting, and I had an endless hunger for romance, sentiment, melodrama. I suppose it did me no real harm, though it kept my head drifting in an assortment of unreal worlds. There was probably some protection in the fact that the worlds were so many and so contradictory that they tended to cancel each other out and dissolve into a standard vague and glorious dream of heroic effort and high courage.

In our extravagant way we subscribed to a half-dozen popular magazines at a time: things like *Collier's,* the *Saturday Evening Post, McCall's, Redbook, Cosmopolitan,* the *Ladies' Home Journal,* the *Woman's Home Companion.* If I had nothing more engrossing on hand I read such pap quite happily. Buddy and I also received *Boys' Life* and *American Boy,* and those we read from cover to cover, loving especially the tales of sports and adventure, and soaking up the basically Puritan "sportsman's code" of strenuous effort, skill, stoical endurance of exhaustion and pain, modesty, magnanimity. We also got another children's magazine, *John Martin's Book,* that moved on a higher plane aesthetically and intellectually, and I enjoyed that one thoroughly too, though guiltily, for I thought it sissy. At the other end of the scale were the pulp magazines our cousin Lowell brought home, things like *Argosy* and *Wild West.* Mama despised such things, and I had to devour them in secret, excited and rather frightened by their sadistic bloodiness, one benign effect of which was to give me second thoughts about my aptitude for a cowboy life.

Works of higher quality that fell into my hopper did so by pure chance; I had no standards. I did read a good deal of Scott and Stevenson and bits of Dickens and Irving and Cooper, all of whom we owned in "sets." Natty Bumppo (the Deerslayer, La Longue Carabine) was one of my top heroes. I also read, again and again, various retellings of tales of Robin Hood and of the knights of the Round Table, for they gripped me in a magical way. I always put off reading as long as I could of the death of Robin or Arthur or Lancelot, for I knew they would make me cry and I didn't like to admit to myself that I was susceptible to tears, so alien to the sportsman's code. One of the standard parlor pictures of the day, G. F. Watts's *Galahad,* the knight in black armor, posed in outline with his helmet in his hand, his head bowed, and one knee bent stylishly, hung over our mantelpiece and I used to spend a good deal of time in familiar communing with it, privately.

Still, most of my reading for nearly ten years was cheap pap. I lapped up anything to do with sports and anything that went on in a wild frontiersy setting: the Kentucky hills, the wild West, the north woods, the Arctic, the jungle, and so on; and I had an endless tolerance for "boys' books," preferably the kind that ran in inexhaustible sequence: the Rover boys, the Hardy boys, Tom Swift and his this-and-that. The Frank Merriwell books offered heroic views of both sports and college, and *Stover at Yale* implanted a romantic vision of my own academic destiny that I never really got out of my head. The Kentucky stories of James Lane Allen and John Fox, Jr., shook me with special intensity because they seemed, though they were not, so nearby, so "real." Gene Stratton Porter's books about the suffering young, such as *Freckles* and *Girl of the Limberlost,* seemed the next nearest to me in space and time. Beyond that my mind floated madly and luxuriously. My method was to find a writer whose settings I liked and then read everything of his I could lay hands on: Jack London and James Oliver Curwood on the north, all of the Tarzan books of Edgar Rice Burroughs, and Zane Grey, Ernest Haycox, and Clarence E. Mulford on the wild West—still my first love. I must have read at least twenty-five Zane Grey books, some of them several times. Perhaps some unconscious critical sense is suggested by the fact that the supreme favorite book of my boyhood was Ernest Thompson Seton's *Two Little Savages,* a restrained and realistic tale of two lads involved in a series of modest woodland adventures in the course of which they pick up a good deal of real knowledge of the natural world. I must have read it at least a half-dozen times.

In those years one could buy a sound new small car, a Ford or a Chevrolet or an Essex, for five or six hundred dollars, and Dad had somehow got together enough money to buy, or to make a down payment on, the only new car we ever owned, a neat square little black sedan called a Star. We were perfect set-ups for advertising, ideal victims who believed that people habitually told the truth. The Star was a new brand, and it lasted only a year or two, but its early advertising had convinced Dad that it represented the wave of the future. He was proud and excited about our new car and talked about it all the time. Having the car meant that the whole family could make the twenty-mile trip to Louisville quite easily, and we began going to the city nearly every Saturday, that being the day when we were free of both school and church. We would arrive at our grandparents' house on Eighteenth Street in time for lunch, or dinner as we called it, always featuring weiners ("weenies"), which one ate in sections buttered with a dab of margarine, which Grand-daddy for some reason out of his country past called Omohundro. Mama was hard put to conceal her contempt for such a meal. She scorned to serve weiners at home, though we boys loved them, and she detested "substitutes" such as margarine or canned milk and identified them with the penny-pinching habits of her husband's parents. After dinner we took a street car downtown to the movie that was the real point of the day for us boys. My taste in films was governed by the same dubious principles that directed my reading.

The twenties and thirties were of course the great days of the films—the movies that soon became the talkies. We always spoke of a film as a picture show, or more commonly and shortly as "the show." Films were a universal entertainment, aside from radio almost the only one, and we accepted them thankfully and uncritically as a gift of God. Every city was full of movie houses and almost everybody went to "the show" at least once a week. The standard price of admission was twenty-five cents; it was a terrible shock when it went up to thirty-five a few years later. Children got in for fifteen or twenty cents. Downtown Louisville had a half-dozen first-run theaters within a couple of blocks on Fourth Street, as well as the Kentucky, which did reruns at a reduced rate, and fifteen or twenty neighborhood theaters scattered about the city. If you missed a film in the first run you could usually count on catching up with it at the Kentucky or in one of the neighborhoods, and sometimes we saw a favorite film in all three settings.

Our favorite house was the Alamo, which specialized in westerns, or in our idiom, "cowboy shows." I was mad about the cowboy star Tom Mix and his pinto "wonder horse" Tony and loved them as personal friends. Tom Mix seemed to me a miraculous incarnation, a transformation into reality, of my comic-strip hero Dick Dare and the brave men of the Zane Grey stories. Next to him we loved Rin-Tin-Tin, the noble, brave, phenomenally intelligent "police dog" or German shepherd. If both of these failed us we would settle for Jackie Coogan, who played richly pathetic big-eyed waifs in all kinds of trouble. A week without one of the three I considered a spiritual desert. Occasionally Mama would sit through the bill with us, but more often she would give us a nickel apiece for popcorn, follow us in to see where we sat, warn us several times to stay together and talk to nobody, and go off on shopping or errands of her own.

This was before the advent of double features, a stratagem of Depression times, and the two-hour program always contained the same elements in about the same order: Pre-Vues of Coming Attractions; a newsreel accompanied by portentous band music, usually Fox Movietone, beginning and ending with a shot of a camera with a turning crank, shown first in profile then swinging round to stare you in the face as the words "The Eyes and Ears of the World" appeared across the lens; a half-length "comedy," rich farce usually involving Charlie Chaplin, Buster Keaton, Harold Lloyd, Laurel and Hardy, or Our Gang; finally the feature, all the more delicious for the delay, and one went awash in the weekly dream. Then Mama would come groping and peering down the dark aisle and we would straggle up to the back of the theater and stand whispering together while we checked to see who had dropped a hat or a glove this time. Nearly always we begged to be allowed to "see it again," and occasionally, if Mama felt especially indulgent or had errands still to do, she would let us straggle back to sit through all or part of the program again.

Like the books I was reading, the movies of these years have all gone to mush in my mind. I remember them not as single events but as a state of nerves in an atmosphere, a dream place for which one longed like a drug and from which one reentered the street world feeling stunned and dislocated. Then came the long ride back to Crestwood, with everyone tired and quarrelsome, a sleepy slapdash late supper, then straight off to bed, feeling less sure that the day had been delightful.

THREE

Church People

Of the three churches in the small
town we Christians stood in the middle, socially and perhaps doctrinally.
We thought of the Methodists as a bit remote and probably a grade above
us: cold, theoretical, rather elegant types; and we had no doubt that the
Baptists ranked beneath us: noisy, ranting, vulgar, a bare cut above the
Holy Rollers, whom we really knew only by lurid reputation. Our church
building was the usual graceless square white pile, seating perhaps a hundred and fifty but rarely full. I can't recall that it had a single handsome or
interesting feature. Dad's great struggle during the first couple of years was
to collect funds to remodel the church building, and he did bring that off,
though the remodeling seemed to consist only of a skim of grey stucco over
the clapboards, and a new basement, dug out by the same kind of horse-
drawn scoops that graded the highway. A feature of the basement, however, was a new baptistry: a concrete pit entered by means of trap doors in
front of the pulpit. One rolled back the carpet, laid the doors back and
onto the floor, and descended by a little flight of concrete steps into
warmed water. It all seemed sensible and mildly dramatic; but though the
baptistry was kept empty most of the time it tended to stink faintly and
constantly.

We Christians practiced total immersion, an enthusiastic mode that
troubled us sometimes as tending in the direction of Baptist vulgarity. Baptisms were held whenever there was an accumulation of perhaps four or
five people who had "joined the church," and it was the ceremony that
sealed their commitment. Baptisms were held separately from regular services because they made such a mess. My own motives in watching them
were mainly voyeuristic, as I remember the case: one sometimes got an
instructive impression of the bodies of the girls after their comprehensive
wetting down. Mama and Dad always argued about the proper costume for

him to wear in carrying out the ritual. She favored a plain dark suit, but he held out for a formal baptismal robe, a long black gown weighted with lead in the bottom hem to keep the skirt from ballooning up around him on top of the water. The girls had the same problem, to my joy, and they didn't have weights.

Dad would wade in a stately fashion into the water, then reach up to guide the convert down the steps. They stood together in the water while Dad went through a form of words, then he would place a folded white handkerchief over the subject's mouth and nose, spread his other hand behind his or her back, and lower the whole body quickly into the water and lift it out again. Usually there was a considerable floundering of arms and legs and a gasp or two, then the person would climb out of the pool and splash off to the side, presumably beatified and certainly bedraggled, to be led off behind the scenes by a relative for a change of clothes.

Church naturally took up a great deal of our time, though I am shocked to think how little real religion, in fact or thought, occupied our family's spiritual space. Services began with Sunday School in mid-morning, a general gathering with a prayer and a hymn and announcements, conducted by a superintendent, following which we broke up into classes by age groups, each with a teacher who led a short period of Bible study and discussion of practical ethics, after which a good many people, especially children, slipped out and went home for the day, ideally with a slightly guilty conscience. Those who "stayed for church" or who had chosen to miss Sunday school now shared the main service of the week. We usually began with a rousing hymn sung by everybody but led by a small and inexpert volunteer choir, unrobed of course, and accompanied by an upright piano or a breathy little foot-pumped organ when that was working. Then came a prayer, impromptu and fairly long, delivered by Dad or by some dependable citizen he called upon, followed by another hymn. Then Dad would read a passage from the Bible in which his text for the day was somewhere contained and would launch into his sermon. I always tried to listen but soon grew baffled or bored, or embarrassed by his attempts at drama or humor, and passed into a dreaming daze broken by short prayers of my own that it would soon be over.

After a final prayer came communion, a ritual that I liked because it was simple and felt authentically reverent. The communion table had been sitting in front of the platform all morning with the "emblems" under a snowy linen cloth. Two elders and four deacons came forward and stood quietly about the table as one of the elders spoke briefly about the significance of the ceremony. The elders drew off the cloth, folded it, and handed the communion vessels to the deacons, then sat down in big chairs at either end of the table facing the congregation. The deacons served the minister, the choir, the congregation, then came forward and served the elders and were served in turn. Then the same men passed the collection plates and brought them forward after their rounds. After a final energetic hymn Dad would pronounce the benediction, then bustle down the aisle to shake the hand of everyone as he left—a gay, chatty process that he greatly enjoyed.

The morning service ended about noon, then everyone went home to Sunday dinner, the rich meal of the week, centering on great days on turkey or country ham (or both), but ordinarily featuring roast chicken or a cheap cut of beef baked to softness, with mashed potatoes and gravy, peas or beans, perhaps celery or olives, hot biscuits and preserves, cake or pie or homemade ice cream, which was delicious and gave one a bit of welcome exercise in turning the crank to rotate the freezer within its cocoon of broken ice and rock salt inside the big wooden bucket. While one of us went to Stoess's for a block of ice in a burlap sack, Mama would be mixing the batter, lots of real cream and sugar, flavored with plain vanilla or chocolate, or vanilla mixed with fresh strawberries or raspberries or peaches when one of those was in season, or best of all with ripe bananas or stewed dried apricots. We ground away by turns at the crank until the dasher would no longer move, then the dasher was drawn out and scraped and licked, and the gallon can covered and packed in ice under the folded burlap.

After dinner one was stuffed with food and stiff with clothing, divided between a need for exercise and a wish for sleep. Buddy and I envied the scapegrace families in which boys could slip into something comfortable and throw a ball about or stroll out into the country with the old gumbo. The minister's family was obliged to attend evening services as well as morning ones, so there was not much percentage in changing clothes in the afternoon, and as we were supposed to set an example in keeping the Sabbath our only attractive option was reading.

The Sunday evening service drew a much smaller crowd and was much simpler: perhaps a hymn, a prayer, a very short informal sermon, another hymn, a benediction. It was usually preceded, however, by meetings of the Christian Endeavor Society, an invention of our sect to keep the young out of mischief and interest them in a mixture of social service projects, foreign missions, and orderly good times. Buddy and I attended Christian Endeavor until we were young men. Our church also held prayer meetings on Wednesday evenings, solemn affairs of a hymn or two and numerous prayers or sober propositions of moral sorts from seniors attending. Buddy and I were forgiven the prayer meetings, but even so I went occasionally if I felt especially reverential or gloomy and craved a chance to steep the mood.

Really the hymns were the only aspect of our worship that gave me pure pleasure. They were the standard numbers that had been accumulating within the evangelical tradition for two hundred years: sad or happy, frightening or reassuring, stark or sentimental, but all simple and rhythmical and in one way or another invigorating. We sang hymns all the time, in church and out, and sang our favorites so often that we knew dozens by heart, all four or five verses. In fact my head is still full of them and I find myself singing them in the shower or whistling them as I work. It is symptomatic of our life that one of my early favorites was a song that seemed to blend religion and economics in an absolutely ideal way. It began, "My father is rich in houses and lands, He holdeth the wealth of the world in His hands," and went on to an opulent catalog: "Of rubies and diamonds, of silver and gold, His coffers are full, He has riches untold." That sounded good to me; I made the transposition between the heavenly father and the earthly one very easily. I even looked up "coffers" in the dictionary, and decided that we had plenty of them, if we could only get the stuff to put into them.

Mama had no faith at all in Dad's vocation or his talent as a minister, and I am sure she was right about it, though I often wished she would phrase her disappointment less contemptuously. She was disgusted but she was also grieved, for she did not doubt the greatness of the calling. In various branches of the family a great deal of baffled speculation went on as to why Dad not only failed to rise in his profession but even failed to "hold" the little churches they all considered unworthy of his powers and his training.

The usual consensus was that he was fatally over-educated for his parishes, that he "talked over their heads." I think now that it was more a matter of personality: he simply had no knack for making and holding contact with people at any level that mattered to them, intellectual, or moral, or emotional, or practical. His relationship to people was always turning nervous and somehow trivial—abstract, inconsequential, unconsecutive, with no firm root in either thought or feeling.

Mama denounced Dad as lazy, but that was off the mark. In his way he was energetic and active, but his busyness never seemed to point toward anything remunerative or even moderately useful. His habits—if courses so veering and broken can be called habits—remind me of the political candidate who assured an audience that he was "thinking about something or other all the time": Dad was always busy about something or other that made no particular difference to anybody, not even to himself when his whim had passed. He seemed incapable of concentrated purpose or consecutive action. (Our reaction against the disastrous consequences of his habits has turned his three sons into dogged, over-achieving types.) Mama chided Dad for paying too little attention to his professional work, especially in the pulpit itself—for preparing his sermons carelessly, for using old sermons over again, and so on. In that she was probably right. Dad put as much work into his sermons as interested him, and no more. He believed in a simple, practical, traditional morality, and I think he enjoyed the small prominence of talking about it in public. But I believe he was bored by theology as a body of knowledge or speculation, and untroubled by or even unaware of the emotional crises that intersect complex moral issues. I was too young at the time to judge, but I cannot conceive that his sermons ever cut very deeply into doctrine or belief.

Mama also denounced Dad's "lack of dignity," by which she meant mainly his tendency to chumminess and apparent frivolousness, an agitated gaiety of manner. But Dad was helplessly friendly and gregarious; he genuinely liked people and liked to be around them. And he was chronically good-humored, an optimist in his bones (like that superannuated schoolmate of Dr. Johnson's who told him that he had tried all his life "to be a philosopher" but failed because "cheerfulness was always breaking in"). Dad was the kind of person who in riding a street car would post himself directly behind the motorman and drive the man half crazy with an unbroken line of chatter until he reached his stop, if he didn't ride past it. He was not really frivolous, he was scatterbrained, incurably trivial-minded. And the truth is that Dad "lacked dignity" in a sense that was even less controllable and more damaging: he *looked* inconsequential. When he sat in his chair in the pulpit with his neat ankle crossed on his knee, his chin in his hand and a vertical index finger indenting his cheek, trying to embody dignity, it was very hard to believe that a creature so short, so plump, and so bland was about to get up and speak moral profundities.

Dad never did anything but fail, but I thank God that he never doubted that he was about to succeed. He was one of the world's losers. He really had no talent for anything but chat and putter. He was a gay companion, and tolerable enough if you were willing to rattle endlessly about nothing much. He had little vanity, and he really coveted nothing for himself. Partly because he was pure in heart, partly because he had so little clear identity, he was probably the most unselfish man I have ever known. His only ambitions were for others, particularly for us, his sons, who roused in him the only pride I ever saw him show. He was deeply, naturally kind, and almost suicidally generous. When he possessed something he could hardly wait to give it away. He was an absurd man in this world, and it is still a toss-up whether he did more harm or good. To respect him one had to keep wrenching away from ordinary standards. I cringe to remember how little real affection I gave him, God rest his bones.

At home we talked about the church all the time, but it was always in terms of personalities and problems, how to keep things running or how to hold onto our place. Of theology we can hardly be said ever to have thought seriously. Prayers and hymns and sacraments and even sermons could put us into warm or distressful moods, but neither the process nor the emotion was in any way intellectual. Of religion as a philosophical phenomenon or even a historical one I cannot recall that we were even invited to think. I found the Old Testament stories stark and dramatic, the psalms lyrical and picturesque, the gospels tender and morally luminous. I thought of heaven and hell as real and reasonable places, and thought the charts for getting to either place also quite plain and reasonable. It was almost thirty years later, long after I had severed any formal commitment to the church, that I began to be moved by religion as anything more than a set of stories, diagrams, simple feelings. It happened when I began seriously to study and to try to teach Milton and American writers, who are so haunted by *Paradise Lost* and the King James Bible.

Yet it would be quite wrong to say that religion did not affect our lives fundamentally. As ethical principle and discipline it established our whole moral program, literally directed how we lived. From church teaching and our parents' reinforcement we boys absorbed the whole ethical program of Protestant Christianity; with the Ten Commandments and the gospels as absolute texts we learned what it was to be good men. We tried hard to be kind, charitable, loving, temperate, humble, and I think that to a remarkable degree we succeeded. None of us would have dreamed of cheating or stealing or doing a willful injury, and if one of us told a lie it was a rare and terrible event, to himself and to the whole family. Christian doctrine made us honorable, hard working, and I think generally pleasant people, with nothing noisy or self-righteous about the carriage of our morality.

Where we fell down, and only moderately after all, was in forms of lust or covetousness. Partly because we were always so hard up, partly because we all had an aesthetic hankering for handsome things (it had little to do with enviousness or mere modishness), we could never cure ourselves of longing to possess things—ordinary, unexotic things. The lust of the flesh was still more powerful though I suppose less contemptible (I speak now, necessarily, mainly of myself). That we did not fornicate is hardly praiseworthy, for we were too young for efficiency and anyway we didn't get a chance: the girls we knew did not offer it, and we did not dare to ask. But I lusted for them, constantly, helplessly, phantasmagorically. Our only recourse was masturbation, and all the boys of my age practiced it, most of them secretly and privately but occasionally in pairs or larger groups, and confused by the guilt and fear that followed from the dire warnings and prohibitions we all heard from our parents. I have described Kenneth Maddox's performance on the steps of Mr. Stoess's loft. I recollect nothing that can be called homosexual behavior among my acquaintances, and in fact I never even heard of the idea until years later when I was in high school.

I do remember, with a lingering creeping of flesh, a dark summer evening when Kenneth Maddox, then perhaps thirteen or fourteen, collected a group of us younger boys and invited us to go along to see a show he would arrange with an older boy, Roger, with whom he evidently had an understanding of some sort. Roger was an oxlike youth of about eighteen who helped out in the blacksmith shop, where he looked as much like a client as an employee, with stiff brown hair falling over a low forehead and an immensely powerful square body with the brawny smith's arms that seemed heroic to us slender-limbed lads. Kenneth called him away from the forge into the weedy shadows behind the shop, where we sat in a puzzled circle. Then Roger pulled out a huge stiff organ, bigger and harder than my forearm, and Kenneth invited each of us to feel it and give it a pump or two. There was no doubt that the thing was phenomenal, and even admirable in its own way; one could see it was a marvelous instrument. But I was glad when the event was over, and it left me confused and shamed. The organ itself seemed outside the order of nature in its hairy enormousness, but that was less disturbing than the general furtiveness of the scene, or Roger's pleasure in showing himself, or the satisfaction Kenneth took in showing him, like a captive freak or a sacred bull. The little I knew about sex and the much more that I imagined had always been cleaner, more private and poetical, than that night's work, and I wanted to keep it that way.

What I have been describing in general is the happier side of our life in Crestwood, and I think there is no doubt that that side dominated, at least for us three boys in our irresponsibility. Our parents were happy there too, in as much of their lives as they could hold above the wash of anxiety and dishevelment. Certainly we were all happier than we would ever be again. But the truth was that things were falling apart for us in Crestwood. Sooner or later things always fell apart for our family. Our lives were a process of unraveling, more acute at some times than at others; we rose and fell within a low range, near the bottom of the general scale of fortune.

Our problems were simple, basic, closely related: Dad was failing at his job; we didn't have enough money. I don't know what Dad was earning, but I know it was little and that it was not enough; and he was losing his grip on even this inadequacy. Both of my parents were naturally extravagant, though the word seems too grand for the actual sums involved. Our style of life was modest, God knows, but not modest enough. Both Mama and Dad hungered to possess things, and both of them actively enjoyed spending money, whether they had it or not. Dad's hunger was mainly for gadgets of all sizes, from cars on down. Mama lusted for the accoutrements of genteel living, especially "good" food and "nice" clothes—for all of us, of course. Both of them felt entitled to such things, and they couldn't face the fact that we could not afford them: it didn't make sense for such nice people to be so poor. So they tried to beat back the reality, to spend it away. The problem was clear: not enough money came in to meet the tide of appetite.

Dad's habit was to write checks, for cash, or to pay bills, or to cover a purchase, assuming with his uninstructable optimism that the money would be in the bank in time to cover his check. Of course charge accounts were our downfall; at Mr. Stackhouse's general store or in the Louisville department stores we were always saying "charge it" with greater or less composure depending upon the current state of affairs. I remember trudging down to Stackhouse's with a list of provisions and being turned away curtly: "No more credit." Our anxieties were chronic, but they collected into periodic crises that were terrible in the approach, in the event, and in the shame and recrimination of the aftermath. More than once, when all checks had bounced and all credit had been cut off, and debts had accumulated to four or five hundred dollars (a formidable sum for us, representing probably a third of my father's annual salary), Granddaddy Reid came out from Louisville and paid everybody off and went back home after scattering rage and scorn upon us all, but particularly upon Mama, whom he blamed for all our troubles. He, after all, was getting along, and even laying by, on a small income. But he had the knack of parsimony.

In such times Mama would be in a terrible state, shamed and bitter, lashing about at Dad for his failures, at Granddaddy for the mean spirit of his benefaction, at herself for being forced to submit to it all. Our parents quarreled all the time, or so it seemed to us; probably memory overdramatizes a tension generally tacit. I imagine they could have lived together peaceably enough if Dad had ever had any professional success. The habit, the atmosphere of failure, was unbearable to my mother, almost incomprehensible. Their quarrels nearly always turned on a question of money, but the deep issue, which usually emerged before the thing was over, was my mother's disappointment, amounting to contempt, over my father's failure as an intellectual and a professional man. He did not amount to enough, and she could not forgive him. She had ambition, though it was not extravagant and could have been satisfied with a moderate accomplishment, and she had a great deal of built-in, perfectly organic pride and dignity. It would be wrong to call it vanity: she did not wish to show forth superlatively. Her view of professional life was basically Puritan. She hated failure because it was a sign of incompetence. Man had it in him to do well; to fail was not only a sin but an offense against nature. Failure left her baffled and offended in her function as a representative person. When she attacked Dad, and she was always the attacker, she was protesting not only a family indignity but a racial insult.

Mama was terrible in an argument because she was so good at it. In that Dad was steadily, obviously failing, her position was strong; the question was whether he had it in him to do anything about it. Mama would not let herself face the thought that Dad might simply be a helpless victim of his nature. If it were true she would not forgive him for it. So she was right and she was implacable. In the way it took possession of her, and of a whole scene, her passion was awful; and her tongue devastating. Her principles were high and stiff, uncharitable, and her intelligence was acute. Anger did not choke her up, it released a marvelous bitter verbal energy, and her scornful wit flicked and cracked over my poor father's already welted skin. Her contempt was superb in its efficiency, and dreadful to watch. I could feel my father's suffering on my own skin.

I am ashamed now to think how automatically and unfeelingly we boys sided with our mother in these quarrels, how we always took her part, either silently or by actually chiming in on the attack. Dad must have felt an alien and a fugitive in his house, like a small wild pig ringed by yapping hounds. We loved our mother fiercely and admired her intensely. How could anyone so pretty, so high-principled, so intelligent, so articulate, be wrong? Our father was demonstrably failing us all; we were ashamed and resentful, and I grieve to say we reviled him. I am afraid, too, that we were good at it, for I in particular inherited my mother's bitter tongue. No more than Mama did we consider that Dad might be helpless in his failing courses; we did not forgive, or even try to understand. It was not till many years later, when Mama was dead and Dad was growing old and I myself was nearly middle-aged, that a juster view of the case washed over me with a wave of sympathy and shame, and I saw what a hell Mama had made of things for him with her implacable rigorousness, how pitiless we all had been, how sweetly he had borne it. In those early days our mother's suffering had been too deep and genuine, and we had loved her too much, to allow us to feel and show any even justice.

I can feel grateful now for the defenses Dad had built into his own nature, though at the time they simply multiplied our exasperation. I refer mainly to his pathological optimism, his weird faith that it was not failure but success that was his natural destiny. I can even be grateful now, because it comforted him and the rest of us survived it, that his illusion lasted him through a whole lifetime of failure. Dad's view was that any failure, whether it was a matter of days or of years, was a mere accident, an aberration of fortune, awkward but not serious, soon to be corrected. When a given mess did not straighten itself out, and even he had to give up hope for the time, he was still uncrushed; the next enterprise would naturally succeed. So whereas Dad suffered keenly for a while under Mama's attack, and defended himself as well as he could, he would simply subside and go silent after a time under the tide of abuse. He saw Mama, ultimately, as simply misguided; she had failed to understand that the problem was one of passing bad luck against which it was wasteful and unnecessary to rail. On the other hand this roused Mama's final fury: the fact that she could not penetrate his innermost optimism. After one of their bad quarrels she would weep in frustration and shame, hating our situation, hating Dad's incompetence, hating the cruelty of her own bitterness.

These quarrels were usually limited to words, though the words often carried the weight of blows. But after supper one night in summer, when Mama and Dad had been squabbling through the meal, she suddenly lashed out with the wire-handled fly swatter she happened to be holding and struck him a slash that sent his glasses flying and raised a white welt across his cheek. Dad got up and retrieved his glasses, sat back down in his chair, and burst into hiccuping sobs. I had never seen my father cry before, but I could see why he cried now. With her elbows on the table and her face in her hands, Mama began to weep herself. We children sat silent, appalled at the suddenness and indignity of the blow and the rage and disgust that alone could have brought it about, and crushed by the weight that could force humane people to behave in such a way. Though we were all too ashamed ever to speak of it again, that ridiculous cruel scene stayed in one's mind as a secret image of our true condition in the last year or so at Crestwood.

Another incident seemed to work in the same kind of lowering end-of-an-era way. This one involved our cousin Lowell, who was then about seventeen and had begun to affect a rakish thin black moustache, very becoming on his handsome saturnine face. As a popular high school student he moved in a circle the rest of us knew little about, and when he was at home he kept so much to himself that we rarely saw him except at meal times or when he went to church as a courteous concession. Lowell and Mama were fond of each other, though she kept at him for not studying and for "smoking and drinking and carrying on." We knew little of his real habits, though we believed the worst, vaguely, because we always assumed that Mama was right about things. We younger boys were still intrigued and awed by Lowell, especially as he got older, bigger, and generally more impressive. In our last summer in Crestwood he took a job on a small florist's farm near town that raised flowers and shrubs for the Louisville market. Most of his work involved digging in the earth with a spade for hours at a time under a hot sun. Week after week, when he would come home and strip to the waist to wash, we watched the amazing growth of the muscles lengthening and bunching under his skin burnt to a rich brown. We would have given anything to own such muscles; to the spectator they seemed worth any amount of sweaty toil. When I tried digging potatoes in a big field at the standard laborer's wage of a dollar a day ("another day, another dollar"), I quickly changed my mind and gave up on the muscles.

One warm evening when we were all reading in the living room and the air from the open windows was heavy with the musk of honeysuckle and the drone of katydids, Lowell suddenly came into the room looking agitated and queerly white. He called Dad out into the hall and they stood talking in low voices. Then the door slammed and they went out and the rest of us sat on till long past bedtime, wondering and apprehensive. Finally Dad and Lowell came back and we heard the story. A group of young people including Lowell had been driving about the roads, too many of them in a small car with an open rumble seat. A boy named Ingram had been standing on the rear bumper and holding onto the back of the rumble seat. In a swerve or dip of the car he had been tossed head over heels; his head was crushed and he had died instantly. Lowell still looked incredulous and horrified as he told the story, and indeed we all felt stunned and curiously contaminated by this first incursion of disaster, unpredictable and hopeless, in our lives. Lowell denied that they had been drinking, as Mama of course suspected; but the question hardly seemed to matter. He was shaken by having to face the fact that one's ordinary casualness could be criminally stupid, fatal.

It was little comfort to know that Lowell had not been driving the car; the whole group of young people had killed that boy, and we all felt that we shared in the guilt. The Ingrams were members of our church and we all knew and liked the son. That was excruciating enough, but almost worse than the event itself was the shock of its mere possibleness, as a kind of thing that could come out of nowhere and simply happen. One felt the contamination not so much of responsibility as of vulnerability. It was all so sudden, so senseless, so wasteful. By any grand measure the disaster was small and not even surprising; but our measure was not grand. For us it was the first thing of its kind, a general malignity personal in application, and in such a small community it seemed big, close, representative. It left the ground shaking under one's feet.

But the ground had been shaking for a long time anyway. We children knew that Dad was under attack in his congregation, that there was a faction that wanted him to go, for there was a great deal of talk about it at home. The attack was led by the economists in the church, the let-well-alone types. Dad had pushed hard for the remodeling of the old frame church building, and he had got the thing done, but it had left the congregation with a debt, and the penny-pinchers could then point not only at the debt but at how little they had all got for their money. Dad was also a great advocate of giving generously to foreign missions, and that too offended the conservatives who wanted their small charity to stay at home. Then these spendthrift pastoral policies were viewed as an institutionalizing of our family's own untidy financial habits; everybody in town knew that the Reids wrote checks that bounced and ran up bills they could not pay. The congregation disapproved of such behavior on principle; but they were embarrassed by it also because they saw that the town would (quite properly) view our poverty as evidence that the Christians did not pay their minister enough to live on.

The money issue was the tangible one, but I suspect the more general and dangerous objection to Dad was a subtler one, a matter of person and of personality, the way he looked and behaved in his public carriage. His people found it hard to like him and harder to respect him, to be impressed by him as they wished to be impressed by their minister. He was a decent, gay, friendly fellow, but nobody could feel he was a person of consequence. Dad had already survived one vote of the congregation, by no large margin, and he stayed on, lacking any visible alternative, but I suppose that thenceforward his position was basically untenable. It was simply not within his powers radically to improve people's opinion of him, and it is impossible for a minister of a religion of love and kindness to preside long over a congregation many of whom wish him away. He feels guiltily that he is doing more harm than good, that he is dividing a flock that ought to be united.

The whole family knew, or sensed, this state of things, but we did nothing about it. We were not the kind of people who tried to treat with a disaster before it struck. We were experienced enough to believe that if you ignored a thing it sometimes disappeared. Dad was sufficiently schizoid to carry on in such a course quite convincingly, at least to himself, and he went on leading the Crestwood Christian Church through its ordinary and extraordinary devices. The extraordinary ones were ordinary in their way, being annual affairs, at least during Dad's tenure.

One such was pledge time, when each family committed itself to a sum of its own naming for the support of the church for the year to come. This promissory tithing was carried out in a congregational meeting, in a highly visible way. Everybody tried to create an atmosphere of gaiety and unselfishness, but the occasion always turned tense and embarrassing before it was over, and it was impossible to keep out invidiousness. The sum that was the general goal for the year would be written on one side of a blackboard in the front of the auditorium, then as a representative of each family rose to announce its pledge, that would be written on the opposite side of the board, accompanied by murmurs equivocal in import, according to the amount. One was bound to think of each pledge as a bid of some kind, for admiration or sympathy, or as a proclamation of one's prosperity or poverty. Secretly one knew, furthermore, that a good many of the pledges were dreams or lies, unsupported by intention or capacity to pay up. Finally the pledges would be totted up and compared to the needed figure. Whoever was in charge of the show would then go to work on the crowd, exactly like an auctioneer, to increase their pledges and meet the arrears. My own family's role in all this was especially embarrassing and risky. We knew, for one thing, though the fact was never stated, that we were among the primary items being auctioned off. Moreover we always felt that it behooved the minister's family to set an example of generosity, whether they were overdrawn at the bank or not. When Mama or Dad would get up and name some visionary sum such as three hundred or four hundred dollars, my flesh would creep with wonder and fear; I knew how earnestly they meant their promise, how hopeless was their prospect of keeping it.

The other annual auction was one of souls, which took place in a week-long revival meeting conducted by an "evangelist," an itinerant preacher, often of considerable fame, who specialized in efficient enthusiasm. Such affairs were traditional in our sect, at least among churches that could persuade themselves that they could afford it. Dad was divided in his mind about the practice. On the one hand he wondered about its good taste, fearing that it smacked of Baptist blatancy; on the other side he saw the value of a special charge of excitement in the year's worship, and he felt an envious admiration for the kind of preaching talent that could generate it, even at the price of a bit of vulgarity. His own attempts at vividness in the pulpit always turned out embarrassing; he admired the trick and would have liked to learn it. Mama scorned the whole process but felt she had to remain loyal; she endured the week in a state of low dudgeon. The "meeting" had two main purposes: to energize or "rededicate" the existing parishioners and to attract new converts to the church. In such a tiny community the number of unclaimed souls was small, but there were always a few old sinners about, and a few lagging young, and if your evangelist was especially seductive you could hope he might draw people in from a wider periphery.

On the whole Buddy and I rather liked the "meetings," not so much for the preaching, though it was a relief to see somebody other than our father in the pulpit, as for the singing of the hymns, which took up half of a typical evening service. Most evangelists came in a package with a "song leader," male or female (sometimes the preacher's wife), and we loved to roar out the great old revivalist songs as led by the flailing arms of this person of powerful voice and contagious energy. The service would end with the pracher's final exhortation to the uncommitted to "come forward and take the right hand of fellowship," as the rest of us (saved persons) sang softly and enticingly:

> Why not now?
> Why not now?
> Why not come to Jesus now?

The greatest year of all was the one when we had a Negro quartet, superb singers, a different sort of musical animals from the rest of us. We had not dreamed of voices so rich or of rhythm at once so strong and so complex and subtle.

But our days at Crestwood were numbered, and we all knew it, though we boys at least did not know how to count them. There came a day when Dad's ministry was put to another vote and this one he did not survive. He was forced to resign, and we had no place of our own to go to. We could only fall back on the hands of Dad's parents again, for what he characteristically interpreted as a mere breathing spell during which he would look round and choose among more glorious opportunities. None of us knew that we were entering a wretched interval that would last fifteen years, that would kill Mama, confirm Dad in failure, and see us three boys into inauspicious maturity. Buddy was thirteen, I was eleven, Paul was six. It was the late summer of 1929 and the Depression was waiting for the whole country.

FOUR

City Folks

Rather than creeping back to Louisville with his head hanging, Dad chose to handle the retreat from Crestwood as a mere outing, a family holiday: we would all go to Cincinnati to visit its famous zoo, something we boys had never seen, then head back for Louisville and arrive in dignity. So we packed up the Star, crossed the Ohio, and tooled east through southern Indiana for an hour or so along a wide road covered with a skim of loose gravel. We three boys lolled in the back seat, leafing through magazines and chatting drowsily. Suddenly the world whirled and bounced with a loud confused noise. We learned later that a car approaching us from the rear and about to pass us without warning had skidded on the gravel, hooked our rear bumper, tossed us head over heels, and driven on without stopping. The next thing I knew I was standing on the shoulder of the road looking down at the dusty corpse of the Star; one back wheel was spinning slowly to a stop. Soon we were all standing on the shoulder in a kind of communal daze as people collected about us. None of us boys had so much as a scratch or a visible bruise, but Dad was holding one arm oddly and Mama was holding a handkerchief against her bloody forehead; both of them looked badly shocked.

A nearby farm family took us all in and got hold of a doctor who set Dad's broken arm and stitched and bandaged the deep cut precisely in the middle of Mama's brow and extending well back into her hairline. Then our hosts gave us a meal and tried to help us sort out the mess we were in. The Star, uninsured of course, was smashed beyond hope and Cincinnati was out of the question. We had taken our tumble in a little Europe, near Vevay, Indiana, which was directly across the river from Ghent, Kentucky (pronounced "Veevie" and "Jent"), and connected by a small ferry. It was decided that our only feasible course was to take the ferry across to Ghent, and there catch the paddle-wheel steamer that traveled from Cincinnati down to Louisville; and that is what we did. In better circumstances we would have been enchanted with such a trip, but that night we were a sick and gloomy crew. Mama under her bandage and Dad in his sling were in real pain, and indeed we all felt bruised and stiff as we huddled on benches in the cold dark dampness of the deck. I had never seen Mama look so dazed and defeated, and I think we all felt the working of an abstract justice getting back at us for the false gaiety with which we had set out that morning to evade our real destination.

At least our condition eased our movement back in under our grandparents' roof; they had to see us as pitiful and interesting for the moment, and not merely as chronically incompetent and exasperating. I suppose we were all of those things. Our state was bad but we thought of it as temporary. It was lucky that we did not know we would be sliding lower and lower for a long time to come. It is hard to delimit and divide the next long movement of our lives. It really lasted more than fifteen years, through the war and beyond, until the time when Buddy and I made a struggling and unlikely beginning in careers as college teachers and began to stand more or less firmly on our own feet. Yet there were fairly distinct intervals within the long movement, some rising and falling along the downward tending plane, before it began to tip hesitantly upward at last. The new family fact was a deeper poverty than we had ever known, grinding and chronic, and the despair and recrimination that followed from it. That Buddy and Paul and I survived it and grew up and found ways to live still seems to me remarkable.

Like Thackeray's Rawdon Crawleys, we were now living on nothing a year. Though it took us a long time to recognize the fact, and longer still to reconcile ourselves to it, Dad had run permanently out of luck, even the moderately bad kind he had had heretofore. His latest comparatively dignified failure had happened to coincide with the onset of the Great Depression, and the general economic collapse and the abrupt shrinking of opportunities found in him a creature of perfect vulnerability. Trained in a small, highly specialized genteel profession, in which he had invested twenty years without accumulating a negotiable record of success, he had little to recommend him for the few professional positions that might appear, and no other capacities to offer at a level higher or lower than his now empty dignity. "Listen to him out there, kicking up his heels," Mama would say bitterly as the old swing on the front porch grated on its chains. Dad was willing enough to work, but she could not see that he was a man with almost no options.

So we settled uncomfortably back into the ugly chocolate brown house we had left five years before to go to Crestwood. At first we crowded in with our grandparents on the second floor; then, after it had grown plain that Dad was not going to find a new church anytime soon, Dutch Kessler, our old friend the ice man, and his wife, Inez, now parents of small twin boys, decided to vacate the ground floor and we moved down there, into five small rooms and a bath arranged shotgun fashion. The lot was narrow and fairly shallow, running from Eighteenth Street back to the alley, with a tiny front yard between the cement porch and the sidewalk largely filled by a big "Indian cigar" tree, a mere strip of side yard, and a small backyard mainly of beaten earth. A little screened back porch was almost filled by a big copper-tub washing machine used by both branches of the family. As there was no car, the ratty frame garage on the alley served as a coal shed and general dumping hole.

I am surprised when people I know come to Louisville for the first time and find it "pretty" or "handsome." My parts of it are not so. It is true that certain parts of the city have some natural beauty or man-made elegance, and somebody had the great good sense to preserve a wide scatter of big green well-wooded parks named after Indian tribes: Cherokee and Seneca on the east, Iroquois on the south, and Shawnee on the west. The parks were lifesavers for active boys and harried parents. But the old commercial part of the city on the Ohio had been left to decay into a tangle of railroad yards and warehouses after spoiling the river setting, and the main body of the city had agglomerated over the years to the south and west in gridiron patterns filled with close-packed featureless frame houses. There remained a sort of backbone of domestic elegance, slowly going seedy, in the old streets of red brick town houses, from First to Sixth, running south from downtown; and the older affluent neighborhoods such as the Highlands and Crescent Hill did show many signs not only of wealth but of taste. But it was years before I made acquaintance with any of that kind of style.

At 1516 South Eighteenth Street we were situated in a nondescript lower middle class neighborhood in the southwestern quarter of the city.

Eighteenth Street was also called the Dixie Highway, for a few blocks south of us the houses petered out and the road continued on, past tobacco warehouses, distilleries, and untidy suburbs, toward Fort Knox and Elizabethtown and on into the deeper South. Only the churchyard separated us from the corner of Gaulbert on the south, and on the north only a house converted into a dry cleaning establishment stood between us and the corner of Hill Street where the Eighteenth Street "car" made its loop at the end of its run from the central city. The noise and smell of steam and hot wool from the cleaner's, the whine and clatter of steel wheels grinding round the curve of the loop, and the pounding of trucks heading out the highway dominated our atmosphere and kept our black and white dog Buster in a state of tense nerves and loud protest. Eighteenth and Hill saw heavy traffic from four directions, and the east side of Eighteenth Street in the block diagonally across from us had got pretty well filled with small business places, beginning with a little old fashioned Quaker Maid store on the corner where we did our basic shopping for provisions. If it was not basic, we didn't buy it. The Quaker Maid chain soon got swallowed up by the A&P.

For some years we lived in the neighborhood rather than in the city; our parameters were few and close and within them we moved in a crude Z pattern. We almost never went farther south, for there was nothing to do out there. And we rarely went due east, except when Buddy or I got hold of a dime, when we would sometimes walk up Hill Street to Fourteenth where there was a crude lunchroom that sold big hamburgers, delicious if a bit greasy, with a thick slice of raw onion. If we had fifteen cents we sometimes, especially on Saturday when the serial was playing, walked a half-mile north to the Oak, the nearest movie theater. Going downtown meant taking the streetcar north to Broadway and transferring to another line running east to Fourth Street; but that was a rare trip for us and it usually signified either an emergency or a celebration. Our true habitual line of movement was due west for a half-mile down Gaulbert to the point where it terminated at the J. B. McFerran schoolyard. A bit south at that point was Algonquin Park, really only a makeshift playground on waste land with a softball diamond, a pavilion, and a few picnic tables. A line running north from the schoolyard formed an important axis, for that led to Parkland Junior High School (a year or so later) and the Parkland branch

library. If you went on north through Parkland you came to West Broadway, where you turned west again for about a mile to Shawnee Park and
the Ohio River.

For us country boys asphalt streets and concrete sidewalks opened up
new and interesting modes of locomotion. Almost everyone owned roller
skates for play, and they were also a thoroughly practical means of travel,
much faster and more interesting than walking. One could skate to school,
for example, and I soon formed the habit of skating to the Parkland library,
about a mile and a half, and back with a half-dozen books under my arm. (I
suddenly recall one terrible day when I forgot to go to the toilet before I
started home.) One got expert at oiling and repairing skates, and when one
skate went beyond repair you could still make a scooter out of a mere two
pairs of wheels, set at either end of a scrap two-by-four for footboard, with
a vertical piece of the same lumber at the front and a crosspiece for the
hands. That, too, was faster than walking, and it opened the way for a
show of personal style in the design. But you could take a nasty tumble on
skates or on a skate scooter, costly to knees, elbows, teeth, and nose, when
a wheel struck an unnoticed pebble at full speed. We nearly always carried
a few healing scabs.

At a couple of intervals Buddy and I got control of a secondhand bicycle
which we shared, riding it by turns or both together, one sideways on the
bar. With a bike we could go as far as Shawnee Park, to watch a big sandlot
baseball game or to play baseball or tennis ourselves. One of the saddest
shocks of my childhood occurred when I leaned the bicycle against a big
tree while I walked over to watch a game from the third base sideline, then
turned round to find our bike gone forever. It had never dawned on me
that people would steal a bicycle, though the policeman to whom I reported assured me it happened all the time. In Crestwood nobody stole
bicycles.

Lowell had come to join us in Louisville now, crowding us more tightly
in our quarters. He had stayed behind in Crestwood to work out that first
summer, living with friends. He had also salvaged the chassis of the
crumpled Star from the ditch in Indiana and had tried to make a "racer"
out of it by adding a bright red cigar-shaped body; but the scheme had
proved unworkable mechanically, and so we had to write the Star off as a
total loss. Counting on a financial miracle as usual, my parents planned to

"send Lowell to college," and so he was entered for a final two years at the Louisville Male High School, Dad's old academy. He came home after his first day in Latin class, where he had been told that "the Latin alphabet is the same as the English except that it has no *J* or *W.*" "You mean to tell me I have to learn a new alphabet?" he asked Mama in outrage; and he refused to have anything more to do with Latin. That was the day Mama gave up on Lowell as an intellectual possibility, though she appreciated the fact that his stupidity took entertaining forms. I remember going with Dad one day down to the famous corner of "Brook and Breck" (Breckenridge) to meet Lowell after school. Watching the stream of boys bounce confidently down the wide stone front steps, I was amazed and awed at how old, how self-possessed they looked. They seemed young men, and I wondered if I would ever feel the kind of assurance they exuded. They seemed to know exactly where they were going, and why.

Gaulbert Street was the main beat for Buddy and me, for that was the track to school, and nearly all our friends lived on it or near it. We liked to start for school in time to pick up our friends along the way, and we would arrive finally in a chattering group of eight or ten boys, occasionally with a girl or two on the margin. Most of those young people have gone from my mind, but I remember Ed Heckel and Chester Merrifield, whom we called "Check," very clearly. Ed was a big powerful boy with a red porcine face. He had huge muscles covered with a layer of fat, and he was ponderous but still efficient in his movements. He could hit a baseball, as we said, a country mile, and carrying a football he came at you like a locomotive. Later he became a star athlete at St. Xavier ("St. X."), the big Catholic high school, and after that I lost sight of him. Ed's nature was like his body, rather brutal. We did not like him much, though he was useful for games, and he used to keep us posted on details of the physical maturing of his red-haired younger sister, which we found fascinating.

Check Merrifield was an exactly opposite type, in body and temper: short and slight and chirpy, exactly like one of the dusty brown English sparrows that still survived in flocks following the trail of horse dung about the streets, picking out the seeds. He was so thin that he might have been put together out of dowel rods. In those days we still wore knickerbockers to school, pulled on over long mercerized stockings and fastened by a buttoned band below the knee. Check's stockings sagged in folds about his spindle shanks and could only be held up by a wide extra elastic band above the knee, like a girl's garter. He was charming company, bright and chatty and ingenious. Him, too, I lost sight of after we moved away from Eighteenth Street. Then about twenty years later, returning to Louisville on a visit, I saw his picture on the front page of the *Courier-Journal:* sentenced to death for killing a man in a tavern holdup. None of it made sense; nothing tallied with my experience of him but the name.

The only girl I remember from Gaulbert Street was Louise Brunger, tall, pretty, and dark-haired, who lived just round the corner from us. She was not a part of our group for school or play, being several years older than ourselves, fifteen or sixteen and a high school student; but she was friendly with Buddy and me in a frank, uncondescending, good-fellow fashion, and I think we were both a bit in love with her. We used to sit talking with her on the front porch, feeling shy, impressed, and libidinous. But the sight of her I still recall gratefully occurred one day as I rode past her house on the bicycle; it made me slow abruptly and I would have stopped if I had had more nerve. Louise was helping her mother wash down some pieces of furniture above me on the porch; her back was to the street, she was bent at the waist to reach something on the floor, she was wearing a short skirt, and I could see the whole length of her lovely long slender white legs to the hip. "Heavenly God!" as Stephen Dedalus exclaims when he sees the bird-girl on the strand. Today's young, when nakedness has become a commonplace if not a bore, will scarcely credit how rare, how informative and heartening, was such a vision to a shy moral boy in those days of female modesty.

As in most city neighborhoods, the street was our common playground. It was our track for skates or bicycles or footraces. We threw or batted or kicked balls about in intervals of traffic. We played a game we called hockey, confused and sometimes bloody, using a tin can battered into a knobby ball and sticks made of tree limbs with a crook at one end. When we were tired we sat on the curb and talked or bickered aimlessly for an hour. At night after supper we played hide-and-seek or run-sheep-run, racing about under the street light until bedtime, while the citified bats zipped and flapped softly in the gloaming air above our heads.

For games such as baseball or football that needed more space we were hard put. We could use the school playground after hours, but it was really too small and cluttered. More often we walked a half-mile out the Dixie Highway to a big waste field by a factory railroad spur. It was ugly and punishing to the eye and body, of dry red clay as hard as brick and dotted with clumps of straggling weeds, but at least it was spacious and reasonably level. We resumed in a slightly more populous form the old pickup baseball games we had played in Crestwood, and I was surprised to discover that I had accumulated skills in throwing, hitting, and fielding actually superior to those of most city boys my own age.

Finally some young entrepreneur organized a real game, of two full teams of nine each, to be played on an actual diamond in the adjoining neighborhood of Parkland. I suppose our team vaguely represented J. B. McFerran School. We hoped not to disgrace ourselves but we had no hope of winning, for the opposing pitcher was to be the famous Boogie Schupp, a lean dark dangerous-looking boy who was considered unbeatable. He was the younger brother, moreover, of the more famous Cotton Schupp, an authentic citywide sandlot hero who actually broke into professional baseball a couple of years later. He lasted only a season or two but he had at least temporarily reached the apotheosis for which we all yearned—even I, now that I was about ready to give up on the cowboy life. I came to bat against Boogie in the bottom of the ninth with the score tied and two men on base; when Boogie sent up a fat one I was naive enough to line it over second base for the hit that won the game. Our other eight men and the several spectators cheered me loudly and I went home savoring my first taste of heroism.

That night in the dark after supper there came a knock at our front door and when I answered there stood our chunky freckle-faced catcher Puddin' Duffy and a tall saturnine young man shaped like a buggy whip whom he introduced as Riley Harrod. Riley was the manager of the Junior Colonels, a real team in the junior city league; he had heard of my fame and he had come to invite me to join his club. I'm afraid what I said was, "Gosh, I'm not *that* good"—which I realized at once was silly from all angles. We soon agreed, in any case, that I would try out for first base. That evening was an important one for me, for it marked the beginning of my involvement in team sports, organized competitive athletics, that would occupy more of my time and passion than any other single motive for the next dozen years. That old ghost is even now unlaid for me; I still, heading into old age, have an occasional absurd baseball or basketball dream in which I play my old not very glorious part—a superannuated dream but an honest one.

The prospect of being on a real team brought to an acute point my chronic preoccupation with equipment. Buddy and I still spent hours salivating over sports catalogs, and a shop window full of "sporting goods" such as Sutcliffe's on Fourth Street would bring on a kind of slavering trance. If I was to play first base for the Junior Colonels I obviously had to get hold of a first baseman's glove, the big webbed mitten worn by any worthy occupant of the position. But there was no money in the house for such an expensive item. I managed it by a coup. A little variety store several blocks north of us was running a "chance" punchboard with a first baseman's glove as grand prize for the person who bought the last chance on the board—obviously hoping to con a greedy lad into paying out more for a last big bloc of chances than the glove itself was worth. I haunted the shop for days, keeping a sharp eye on the board, until at last I could run home and tell Mama that there was only a dollar's worth of chances left. Staggered by the bargain she gave me the dollar and I ran back and cleared the board and came home with my prize. It wasn't a very good first baseman's glove, but it was the right shape and it looked fairly convincing.

Caring for one's equipment was as complicated and preoccupying as getting hold of it in the first place; there was a large folklore on the subject, such as the notion that a baseball bat should be rubbed with a beef bone. Everybody worried about keeping his glove flexible, and spent hours pounding and molding a "pocket" in the palm that would be deep and attractive to balls. Having heard that one should "oil" one's glove, and assuming that one oil was as good as another, I set to work with some linseed oil I found in the shed. I rubbed in a good dose and things looked satisfactory; but when next I picked up my glove it felt stiff, so I rubbed in some more oil. When it dried it was stiff again, so I applied more oil, and so on for several days. By the time it dawned on me that I had got hold of an oil of fatal properties I had ruined the glove forever; it was stiff as a board and could only be thrown away. In the state of our family economy a mistake like that was a real crusher.

The exact sequence of things at this period in our schooling has got confused in my mind, complicated by several factors. For one thing, Buddy, being nearly two years older than I, was about to begin preceding me into different kinds of schools. Also both of us had got somewhat out of phase with our years because our verbal facility had led to our "skipping" grades at Crestwood. In fact I had skipped two grades (to the ruin of my mathematics), but I believe I had lost some part of that advance owing to an illness, real or imaginary. I do know that I was eventually to graduate from high school nearly two years early. Though I did not think much about it at the time, I must have been handicapped in school sports because I was competing with boys who had a couple of extra years of experience and physical maturity. I must have spent about a year and a half at J. B. McFerran School, but I remember very little about it, except that I seemed to spend most of my time under the baleful eye of a classical elderly schoolmarm type, Miss Crutchfield, whom we privately called Crutchbutt: gray, spectacled, and cross, repressed and repressing. When she was especially irritable one of my friends would remark scornfully that she must be "having her monthlies," but I had no idea what he was talking about. I can still taste and smell our school lunches, which I enjoyed thoroughly. Most of the children scoffed at the school food, but it was better than I got at home and I looked forward to it, particularly a watery but savory "chili" that you could buy in a big enamel cup for two cents.

Slowly, as the city could afford to build them, Louisville was in the process of inserting new junior high schools, covering the seventh, eighth, and ninth grades, between the traditional elementary schools and the four-year high schools. A new junior high had just been completed in Parkland and it was decided to open it at once to the seventh and eighth grades, and I moved into Parkland Junior High School in the middle of my seventh grade. The shape and size of things immediately opened out so much that life suddenly seemed a good deal more complex and interesting, and one felt more adult and at least tentatively more daring. My walk to school doubled in length and became more tiring but also more varied than the old track straight down Gaulbert. After McFerran the spanking new red brick building with tall white "colonial" columns seemed enormous and elegant. There was a big auditorium with a stage and padded seats, a shiny cafeteria with a new menu, well-equipped shops for wood or metal work or printing for the boys and sewing and cooking rooms for the girls. But what dazzled me most was the gym with two full size basketball courts and

dressing rooms and showers, and outdoors a huge playing field with football and soccer areas and a cinder running track. I felt as if I had moved
into a big country club—not that I had ever seen a country club. Everybody had a personal locker on a hallway and an open-work wire basket in
the gymnasium dressing room, which soon smelled sweaty and stale as any
boys' club.

After years of sitting all day in a single classroom, studying everything
under the same bored and repressive all-purpose teacher, it was exhilarating to have one's work divided into "subjects" and to move every hour to a
new room and a teacher who was a specialist of sorts, not a mere dragon
squatting in her den. Our new teachers were a younger, brighter, happier,
dressier lot than those we had known, and the presence of men among
them was surprising and challenging, if only to a different order of un-
ruliness. I fell in love at once with my shy, pretty homeroom teacher, and I
grieved when she was killed after only a few weeks, in an automobile
accident on her way home from a teachers' meeting. It seemed shocking
and unfair for something so violent to happen to one so gentle and
harmless. I felt a different and disturbing sort of passion for my Latin
teacher, Miss Givens, an ivory-skinned, black-haired beauty whose en-
chantingly curved body sent me into sinful reveries; but she betrayed me
by marrying a tall mathematics teacher who struck me as obviously unworthy of such a treasure.

Our social studies teacher was also a young woman but of the standard
schoolmarm type: bespectacled, round-faced and round-bodied, tortured
by a chronic shyness that she tried to hide under a mask of stony dignity.
One day she emerged from the teachers' restroom and when she turned
down the hall we saw that she had unconsciously tucked the whole back of
her skirt and slip inside the waist band of her long pink bloomers, leaving
them completely exposed. Not one of us tittered or made a sound as she
marched the whole length of the hall, her plump pink thighs pumping in a
stately rhythm, and turned into her classroom. We were appalled to think
of the shock about to strike that fragile composure when she discovered
what she had done.

The move to the new school also meant a sudden access of new acquaintances. Most of my old friends from Gaulbert Street had moved along with
me, but they had got scattered into divergent patterns in the new school

and I was thrown with an unfamiliar group. Most of them came from the Parkland area north and west of my old neighborhood and somewhat more elegant. I found the new kids bright and knowing and friendly and on the whole I liked them very much. There was an oddly blighted tall, sallow boy named Leroy Drane (called by my friend Hal Maynor "Pipey," for Drainpipe), who had a queer skin disease that had jaundiced his skin and taken every hair from his head and even his eyebrows. He wore an unconvincing wig, and every so often, with a sardonic grin, he would snatch the wig off his egg-smooth skull and wipe his face with it. At the opposite extreme was Buford Mitchell, a small beautiful boy with blond hair and blue eyes and perfect manners. Somebody was paying fanatical attention to his clothing, for he came to school in one set after another of sweaters and trousers perfectly matched in color, often pastels—an incredible elegance. He was so pretty that we could see the teachers were in love with him. Buford should have been intolerable but he wasn't so at all; he was a manly, good-humored boy, wearing remarkably lightly the burden of a doting and ambitious mother. I counted him a friend; but Hal Maynor was a closer one. Hal had a brown moon face and big round brown hounddog eyes, and he could look incredibly solemn, but in fact he was a natural clown and so good at it that he seemed almost professionally funny. He became one of my few steady joys. Hal and I shared a great deal of comedy as well as some very sad times over the next dozen years, and he helped me to survive my adolescence.

He took me home after school one day to meet his family, and then I began to sense some desperation behind his clowning. It turned out that his parents were divorced—the first such case I had ever encountered. Hal and his mother and his pretty blonde older sister, Sarah, shared a shabby little flat on a side street in Parkland. Mrs. Maynor was in a pathetic shape, yet one soon found her charming and even impressive. Fast in the grip of a strange glandular illness, thyroid I think, that had not then been diagnosed, she was barely able to move about. Her face and hands were puffed and stiff, her eyelids sagged nearly closed behind her thick lenses, and her words came out slow and slurred. Yet she was cordial and kind, and in the labored way her illness allowed, witty and funny. That first visit shook me badly, but I was also curiously heartened by it—to see people in a home situation as poor as my own, complicated by divorce and serious illness, yet surviving even with gaiety. I saw a good deal of the Maynors after that, and Mrs. Maynor and I grew very fond of each other. A few years later an intelligent doctor got hold of her, saw what was wrong, and gave her treatment that changed her into a new person almost overnight—the old crippling symptoms all gone and her natural liveliness of mind and body set free. It was the closest thing to a miracle I had ever seen, intensely exciting to witness.

Two of my new friends in this period in the early thirties I associate with "plus-four" knickers, a kind of morbid efflorescence of an English golfing style. Plus-fours were a much more comprehensive garment than our old skinny knickerbockers, cut fuller throughout and blousing out extravagantly down and around the calf with an effect that would have seemed almost Turkish had it not been so heavy and stiff. I could not afford plus-fours but I admired them enviously on boys whose fathers were better fixed. Frank Sheldon Anderson, known as "Shel," was the heir apparent of a prosperous woodworking manufactory, and I think his plus-fours of heavy Donegal tweed must have been custom-made to accommodate his tall, heavy, flatfooted frame. Shel was blond and rosy and handsome in a jowly fashion—a nice kid, though he seemed rather frighteningly marked for power and success. Billy Mossbarger, a warmer and more vulnerable person and a much closer friend, also looked well in his tweed plus-fours. He was a short square boy with a thick chest, shy and good-humored, full of laughter and blushes. His big mouth was so full of teeth that one wondered if his dentist father might not have installed a few of his spares. I usually managed my walk to school so as to pick up Billy on the way, and we often walked home together too when I didn't have to stay for basketball practice.

In the second summer of our friendship a terrible thing happened. Billy had gone off to a summer camp, an institution I had never heard of. When I went by his house one day to ask when he would be coming home, Mrs. Mossbarger told me tersely that Billy was sick at camp and closed the door in my face. I was puzzled by such rudeness but went back stubbornly a day or two later. This time I was told equally tersely that Billy had died, and again the door was abruptly closed on my stammered questions. Later I learned that Billy had got "blood poisoning" from a trifling injury such as an insect bite and the infection had galloped him straight to death. It was the first time I had lost a friend to death and I was staggered by it, especially by its swiftness and mysteriousness. Almost as disturbing was his mother's way of treating me, as if I had had no stake in Billy's life—for I had loved him. I think I understand that now: she had not been able to bear the sight of my good health.

The gymnasium naturally brought me other new friends, notably George Marr, a bright, self-assured boy who later made a success in business in Louisville. Parkland's big bright well-equipped gym was a paradise after Crestwood's poor little crackerbox. Even calisthenics could be fun in such a setting; and I made especially rich use of the showers, a phenomenon entirely new to me: a dozen or so exposed shower heads, adjustable as to texture and temperature, arranged around the walls of a big tiled room. After I got past the shock of bathing together with ten or twelve naked boys, some of the older ones remarkably hairy, I began to luxuriate in the new experience. No time limit was placed on showers, at least following afterschool sports, and sometimes I lingered for a half-hour after everyone else had gone, experimenting with various effects, until I was almost faint with wetness and warmth.

Directing all the boys' gym classes as well as the "varsity" teams in football, basketball, and track was a busy young man named Lee DeWitt, whom we all called "Coach," chunky, muscular, curly-haired, exacting and sometimes sardonic in manner, but not unkind, not a bully like so many of his trade. He obviously knew what he was about, and as a bona fide letterman in football at Indiana, he was a hero to us aspiring athletes. I suppose I admired him more than anyone else I knew. George Marr had chummed up to Coach and achieved a kind of satellite relationship in which, for example, he was given a whistle and allowed to direct groups of younger boys in some of the simpler games and drills. He had also been given permission to eat his lunch in Coach's office, whether he was there or not; as a satellite of George's I was invited in too. I greatly enjoyed those sporty, man-to-man conversations with the two of them, or with George alone, especially because he sometimes gave me one of his sandwiches, much classier than mine, of thick ham sprinkled with black pepper on buttered bread.

In one of those sessions I got a rude shock. George remarked that he knew where he could get hold of some Bourbon whiskey, "Bottled in

Bond," and Coach closed with the offer on the spot. These were still Prohi-
bition times, and the whiskey was bound to be illegal. It was staggering
enough to hear my admired friends speak so casually of breaking the law;
it was worse to see the man I thought of as a trained athlete and a moral
person snapping so eagerly at a chance for some booze; most shocking of
all was to hear my friends making chatty sophisticated distinctions among
kinds of booze. I had thought of the stuff as all one, and all awful. At home I
had never heard alcohol mentioned without fear and loathing, as one of
the most deadly and iniquitous vices open to man. Steeped as I had been
all my life in the folklore of the Temperance movement and the Anti-
Saloon League (of which Dad had been a state secretary), I viewed a person
who could choose blithely among grades and kinds of vice as almost unim-
aginably knowing and corrupt. I tried to put the whole episode out of my
mind, but my ideal image of Coach in particular had undergone a hard
shaking.

I had been playing as much basketball as possible, and in my second
year I actually made the team and won a varsity letter—my first, and
certainly my proudest prize in life to date. It was literally a letter and
nothing else: a block P in pebbly grey wool—the Parkland budget did not
run to a sweater to mount it on. Part of the fun of being in an early class at
the school was that we had to make up the paraphernalia of a "tradition" all
of a sudden: choose colors, write songs, start a newspaper and name it, and
so on. I think we chose our colors, navy blue and silver grey, lamentably
dull as they seemed, because we understood those had been Lee DeWitt's
colors at Indiana. My entry in a competition for school "fight song" was a
direct steal in sentiment and rhythm from a college song I had heard
somewhere, Washington and Lee's, I believe. It began:

> When Parkland's blue and grey men fall in line,
> We're going to win again, another time.

Even I had to admit that was pretty flabby, and I was relieved when somebody else did a good deal better.

Between poverty and ambition, I kept getting into messes over my athletic equipment. Now at twelve and thirteen I had begun to grow to a
promising height, but I had put on a sort of layer of puppy fat at the same
time, and I felt myself embarrassingly heavy and cumbersome. (I used to

pray at night that I would come out at what I considered the perfect size for an athlete: six feet four and 220 pounds). Perhaps, I thought, I could run that fat off—but then a real runner ought to have spiked running shoes, which I could not afford. I took a cast-off pair of leather oxfords, bored a dozen holes through the bottom of each shoe with a red-hot ice pick, stuck a steel bolt through each hole from the inside and snugged it against the outer sole with a nut, and finally filed the protruding ends to a point. Every morning for several weeks I got up at daybreak, walked out to our old field by the factory siding, put on my running shoes, and pounded around the hard clay for as long as I could stand it. Those shoes made a noise like running shoes but they felt like the wrath of God. The concussion of the bolt heads against the bottom of my feet was sheer torture. When I weighed myself on the gymnasium scale and found I had actually gained weight I was relieved, for I knew I could not bear those shoes any longer.

My other shoe crisis was more wounding because it was basically spiritual. When I survived the cuts and made the basketball team, I felt entitled to a really good pair of shoes. I had already ruined one cheap pair with my hot-poker treatment, trying to give a suction-cup effect to the hard rubber soles. I had spotted the shoes of my dreams, high top canvas of a handsome rusty brown. But they cost seven dollars and Dad said we simply could not afford that much money. Then Lee DeWitt said he could order the shoes through the school for about four dollars, and I bullied Dad with that figure until he gave in; he said I could tell Coach to place the order and gave me his personal check to cover it. The shoes arrived and they were all I had hoped, but a day or two later in one of our office lunch times Coach handed me Dad's check with a grim look: it had bounced. I could only creep off with the dishonored check, feeling I could never look Coach in the eye again. I didn't really blame Dad, who I knew had meant well as usual; I blamed my stars, the design of the cosmos as it apparently intended to treat me. We did finally pay Coach his four dollars, but it took weeks to manage, and I never ate lunch in the office again. Coach had failed me with the booze and I had failed him with the money, and the old friendliness was gone for good. Every time I laced on my new shoes I cringed inside.

As usual I can recall very little about my ordinary academic work. I enjoyed woodworking shop under Mr. Roessler, a swarthy and sweaty German who would say earnestly, "Now, poys . . ." and I was able to take home a white pine footstool that sat almost straight on its legs. In the well-equipped printing shop it was probably significant that I took most pleasure in the simplest process of all, "setting" or composing a few lines or a paragraph of prose in the "stick," the little metal pan held in the palm of the left hand and filled, one tiny lead integer after another, with the letters, punctuation marks, and spaces that slowly formed a sensible sentence. I have often wondered if the clean spare prose of old printers like Ben Franklin and Mark Twain may not owe a good deal to the typesetter's tactile knowledge of words as occupying physical space and weight.

I had begun to see dimly that divisions of subject matter corresponded in a rough way to compartments in the conduct of life, and to be interested in each in that pragmatical sense, though my own gifts were unevenly arranged. I had made it through long division, fractions, and decimals in reasonably good order, but I could already see that anything subtler, more analytical or logical was going to muddle my head. Subjects in which the medium was verbal gave me no trouble, and I was good at things like English and history. I won a prize for writing a short story, and mainly on the strength of that I was made editor in my ninth grade of the school newspaper. I wrote a solemn editorial exhorting my schoolmates to conduct themselves so as to leave a worthy example for following generations of Parkland Junior High students. I'm afraid my metaphor was that of leaving footprints on the sands of time. I was hurt to see my father smiling as he read it.

In the ninth grade, too, I had my first date with a girl, and the last for a long time. For a year and a half I had been watching with a mixture of respect and lust a dark-skinned, brown-haired, brown-eyed, intelligent girl named Elsa Brauer. She was not only the brightest but the most athletic of the girls I knew, and her neat bosom and slender brown legs looked ravishing in her blue gym suit. In class she was at least as clever as I was, and I admired everything about her modest and frank and good-humored ways of conducting herself. Elsa's prettiness was marred only by a large brown mole at the inner corner of one eye, just where the eyebrow curved toward the nose. She paid no attention to the blemish, and I decided with some sense of magnanimity that I could overlook it too. After weeks of scheming, nerving-up, and family conferences I asked Elsa to go with me, or, as it turned out, with us, to the May Music Festival, and she accepted with one of her pleasant frank smiles.

The May Music Festival was quite a grand affair by our standards, a long-established annual ceremony put on by Louisville Male High School in which the orchestra and chorus, conducted by a fine German musician named Marzian, performed an elaborate more or less classical program in the biggest auditorium in town, the Jefferson County Armory, before an audience of several thousand people. Buddy had begun to be interested in music when he entered Male, and he would be playing a second violin on his pawnshop fiddle in the orchestra at the festival. Naturally we all wanted to go to support him and hear the program, if we could scrape up the money for tickets and transportation. We did manage to get five tickets and I invited Elsa. The natural thing would have been for Dad and Mama and Paul to take the street car downtown and for Elsa and me to go the same way on our own. But Mama, taking her usual aristocratic view, decided that a street car was too inelegant for my date: I must take Elsa in a taxi. That being settled, we characteristically determined that since the money had to be laid out anyhow, we might as well all make use of the taxi. Poor Elsa ended up with a date with the whole Reid family, and we never had a moment alone.

I collected Elsa, looking her prettiest, from her mother in her parlor. "People say we look like sisters," said her mother brightly, and I murmured agreement: it was true, and the cliché was one I had never met. I installed Elsa between Mama and me in the back seat of the cab and we rode downtown to listen soberly to "The ErlKing," "Mighty Lak' a Rose," and excerpts from *Tannhauser* and *Lohengrin*. Then we rode home in the same order and I gave Elsa back to her mother with a polite good-night. It had been an anticlimactic and deflating experience, and I was horribly aware that I had subjected the poor girl to a flat and unromantic evening. In class over the next days I imagined myself to be the subject of sly and scornful comment among the girls, though in fact I am sure Elsa was too good a sport to tell a tale that would embarrass me. I felt typed, accurately, as an inept courtier, and I never dared ask her for another date. I couldn't afford girls anyhow, I told myself bitterly, and I had better stick to baseball and basketball.

My other attempt at Parkland at gallantry of a different kind also turned out badly. I had long admired the stoical and stylish athletic performance of a tall, slender, hard-muscled boy named Lincoln Ellington, known as "Link," who was the nearest thing we had to a star in football and basketball. Probably recalling the impressive and graceful effect with which such occasions were handled in the Frank Merriwell books and *Stover at Yale,* I resolved to pay him a personal formal tribute at the time of his graduation. I composed a short, solemn speech and got it fixed in my head. At the end of the graduation exercises I followed him out of the auditorium, stopped him in the hallway, shook him by the hand, and began to deliver my salute to the distinction and dignity of his career. Halfway through, he muttered something, scuffed at an old chewing gum spot on the floor, and set off down the hall, looking back once, apprehensively. I saw that I had made a fool of myself as usual.

At last I can begin to date events a bit more precisely again, for my entrance into Male High School as a sophomore coincided with the family's removal to Thirty-fourth Street, and as I was graduated from Male in June 1935, just after my seventeenth birthday, we must have made the move in the summer of 1932, when I was fourteen. We moved without our noble Buster, for he had died the preceding summer. For a time we had had another dog as well, a curly-haired black mongrel who had adopted us, but he had been killed by a poisoner. (Have you ever seen a dog who has been poisoned with strychnine? Avoid the sight if you can. The limbs, all the muscles of the body, go absolutely rigid, stiff as steel rods. The animal's agony is terrible; but fortunately it does not last long.) As a sensible country dog Buster disapproved of the noisiness of Eighteenth Street, and he had developed an unbreakable habit of chasing cars. He had been hit once but had survived, without learning anything from the experience. On the Fourth of July, between firecrackers and cars he had got into a hysterical state, barking incessantly and pursuing one car after another up and down Gaulbert. Late in the afternoon he ran into the backyard barking backward over his shoulder, reeled in a half-circle, fell to the ground, and died on the spot. We could find no mark on him, and we concluded that his heart had simply failed. We felt we had lost our oldest friend, and our last link to the country purities.

Just what we had been living on in the three years since Crestwood is a continuing mystery to me. Dad had laid hold of any desperate expedient that came his way, such as selling life insurance or encyclopedias, but these experiments always left us worse off than before. The truth can only have been that we were all living on the small rents from Granddaddy's old remodeled brewery in the West End, and we of Dad's family had drifted into the position of confirmed and unwelcome dependents. The only rent of any real consequence came from the filling station on the busy corner of Thirty-fourth and Market, which had been doing well for some years in the hands of a small, dapper, arrogant man named Stallard, who had tarted the place up with a lot of bright paint and signs offering Stallard's Sudden Service. But Stallard had apparently overreached himself, and he fell an early victim of the Depression. There followed a ghostly short interval in which Dad tried to run the station himself, and Buddy and I went down to "help" him—to do nothing, as it turned out, for nobody came in; which was just as well, since none of us knew what we were doing. This fiasco probably coincided with another in which Granddaddy was trying to set up a "hardware" business in one of his vacant store rooms with a small shoddy stock he had picked up in a bankruptcy auction. Times were hard, then, and they stayed that way. A couple of the small flats in the building were standing empty, and my grandfather decided that he would put the brown house on Eighteenth Street up for sale and move the two branches of the family to Thirty-fourth Street.

The move could only be read as another step downward in our general descent. We would be moving to an entirely different and equally un-distinguished neighborhood, not only a mile farther west but several miles farther north, quite across the city gridiron. We would be part of a large flat featureless lower middle class area known vaguely as the West End. The Market Street car line ran loudly past the corner, traveling downtown to the east and terminating on the west a mile and a half from us near the river at Shawnee Park and a shabby but interesting old amusement park called Fontaine Ferry (pronounced "Fountain"). On school outings from Crestwood in more innocent days we had thought it a highly glamorous place. There was a lot of car and pedestrian traffic on Thirty-fourth Street as well as on Market Street, and most of a block in all four directions had filled up with shops and small business establishments. Our filling station sat on the southeast corner and the rest of the building, two stories high, ran south another hundred feet or so to the alley. Across Market Street one corner was occupied by a small Piggly-Wiggly food store, the other by an A&P. Across Thirty-fourth Street was Mr. Miersch's yellow brick drugstore with the family living quarters above. What was to be our church, West End Christian, stood a couple of blocks northwest of us. But there was a large Catholic population in the neighborhood, mostly of German and Irish descent, and the parochial establishment of St. Columba's stood a block down Market Street: a church, a school, a rectory, a dormitory for the teaching nuns, and a fair-sized playing ground including, blessedly, a cinder-topped outdoor basketball court.

Our building was the eyesore of the neighborhood, and the knowledge that we inhabited the shabbiest place within a square mile was a shaming penalty of our poverty. Mentally one cringed every time one entered or left the building. Like much of the nineteenth-century red brick commercial architecture that fills American cities, the little old brewery had possessed integrity and an unconscious sense of style; but Granddaddy had got rid of that for all time. He had angled the filling station across the open corner, covered the two-story fabric of red brick with a layer of ugly pebbled stucco that had since peeled off in large patches, and filled the old shell of the structure higgledy-piggledy with a warren of impracticable storefronts and awkward, uncomfortable flats. The original conversion had been handled in a styleless, grudging, cheapjack fashion, and subsequent repairs, when they were made at all, had been done in the same penny-pinching spirit. The place was really a self-contained slum, entered by a series of four crude concrete stoops of varied heights falling directly onto the sidewalk. It was a wretched place, and we were to spend ten increasingly miserable years there.

My grandparents were even more uncomfortable than the rest of us, in three dingy airless rooms in the middle back of the ground floor, where the only daylight came from windows across the kitchen wall on the alley: a horrible place to finish off a life. Our flat, at 207, above the largest of the three stores, at least received light and air from front and back. Everything was small, flat, and rectilinear. We had a narrow living room with two windows onto Thirty-fourth Street, two toy bedrooms dividing between them the length of the living room, a dining room in the middle, the length of that shared between a dark kitchen and a dark bathroom. Across the whole width of the back was the only reasonably pleasant feature of the apartment, an unscreened open porch above the alley. Here one could occasionally achieve a brief illusion of privacy and peace. In winters the flat was drafty and cold, the only heat coming from a small gas stove in the living room and the gas range in the kitchen. In the summer we sweltered, particularly in the tiny bedrooms, and one stifling summer we got so desperate for air that we simply knocked out a big square hole in the thick brick partition between the two rooms. Off the back porch a ramshackle stairway fell down into a dirt-floored areaway. We also rigged a ladder up to the flat roof, and one of our cats used to climb up there and catch bats. The apartment was a cramped, tasteless, dispiriting place. I never entered it without loathing and I could not bear the thought of inviting a friend in. I still think of it with hatred. The place and the life we lived there killed Mama, and it certainly wounded us all.

We rather liked the unpretentious neighborhood Christian church. It was homely, earnest, struggling, the kind of barebones establishment we had known all our lives. I suppose we must have passed for fairly classy people there, except that we were not much use at collection time. It occurs to me now that Dad's steady unemployed presence in the congregation must have been a nagging embarrassment to the minister in place. The fact that I had not thought of this till now suggests that Dad did not let it become a problem, and I am sure he behaved well in the position of resident prophet chronically without honor: Dad was a sap but a gentlemanly one. As a matter of fact our minister, Brother Nutter, reminded me somewhat of Dad. He not only had the pince-nez but also was a poor preacher in the pulpit and abstracted and strained in his way of meeting people; a good man but marked for failure—like Dad one of the world's losers. After a few years he was succeeded by one of the nicest men I ever knew in our faith, Brother Blankenship who came up from a Kentucky country parish and lasted out our time in the church. Modest, quiet, intense, he looked colorless, but he was both winning and formidable because integrity and generosity of spirit washed out of him like a positive energy. Unfortunately he came accompanied by an ugly, jittery wife and her son by an earlier marriage, a boy a couple of years older than myself who had been christened Julius but traveled under the name of Chocolate, which had been attached to him by his country hooligan friends. There was much kindness and some charm in Chocolate, but I'm afraid he was a hopelessly bad apple: a raucous, stupid, amoral boy, not only a clown but a fool, and a bit of a crook.

For Buddy and me the only positive advantage of the move to the West End was that it brought us much closer to Shawnee Park, which was now within walking distance, though by no means an easy distance, especially after a hard day. Shawnee was essentially a large level plateau, falling down on its long west side to a bend of the Ohio River. On that lower side the circumferential road ran past cottonwoods and outdoor fireplaces and picnic tables set in rather ragged grass where lived the world's hungriest chiggers. (The chiggers' strategy was to climb one's body until they met an obstruction, then go underground. One found oneself with fiery itching welts, sheer torture for ten days or so, in the groin, about the waist line, in the armpits.) Dotted about the park were flower gardens, wading pools, an elegant little bandstand of neoclassic design, and in the middle of things a dozen clay tennis courts, a refreshment stand, a "recreation" building, and a concentrated play area with swings and seesaws. I once saw there a sight I wished could be painted by Henri Rousseau: the whole long row of swings, perhaps a score of them, occupied by frolicking nuns in long black habits, kicking up their high black boots in the happiest kind of way.

But more essentially Shawnee Park was an immense open-air temple of baseball where most of the city's amateurs came to perform or to worship. As I remember it, there were eighteen complete baseball diamonds, each with a number on the backstop, and on a summer Saturday there might be hundreds of players watched by thousands of spectators. Some of the diamonds overlapped a bit, and outfielders in adjoining games might find themselves face to face; occasionally a game had to be held up for a moment when a player from the adjoining field came panting, sweaty and chagrined, after a ball that had gone over his head, or worse still, through his legs, and picked it up and heaved it desperately toward his own infield, while spectators at the invaded diamond craned to see "who the heck hit that one." Steady fans knew most of the players in all the games going on at a given time.

FIVE

Male

In Louisville schools at this time, and for years thereafter, blacks and whites were segregated as a matter of course and hardly anybody (white) thought twice about the matter; but the white high schools were also segregated according to sex, and boys and girls went to separate schools, except for Ahrens Trade School, which admitted both. This meant that boys like Buddy and me, who really had no social life apart from school, lived in a basically male society and came to know girls only in church; they would be girls from one's own neighborhood and not numerous or necessarily desirable. In practice students were separated also on religious and cultural grounds more complicated than those of sex—if anything is more complicated than sex. Young whites almost never met blacks of their own age; their paths did not cross. Louisville was a city with a large Catholic population and a fairly large Jewish population and these groups tended to cluster clannishly in certain neighborhoods. Until we came back to Louisville from Crestwood when I was eleven, I had never consciously met a Catholic or a Jew; I had lived in a WASP world of middle or low middle grade. On Eighteenth Street we had known a few Catholic children, but they were a minority and religion created no issue in our play. On Thirty-fourth Street we suddenly found ourselves outnumbered by Catholics and for the first time began to feel in a mild way the discomforts of minority status. And now at Male High we suddenly knew a lot of Jews.

Boys like us could choose among three high schools: Male, Manual, and St. X. Nearly all the Catholics went automatically to St. Xavier on Broadway. DuPont Manual Training High School offered a traditional education with an extra "practical" emphasis less narrowly vocational than Ahrens Trade. At Louisville Male High School the program was strictly academic, with a "classical" or college-preparatory design. Hence Male attracted most

of the non-Catholic boys who had, or whose parents had for them, intellectual ambitions and a general notion of going on to college. Such distinctions obviously involved class divisions: Male would get nearly all the
Jews, from rich to poor, most of the well-to-do boys from the "better"
eastern and southern neighborhoods, and a scattering of the hopeful gen-
teel-poor like Buddy and me from all over the city. Buddy and I were
certainly poor by any standard and we were genteel at least by instinct and
expectation. None of the family doubted that the three of us boys would go
to college and become professional men of some sort, though nobody had
any notion how it was all to be arranged—the Lord would have to provide. Our parents' college ambitions for Lowell had foundered decisively
by now on the rocks of poverty and his own unambitiousness. In fact he
had put himself into a "barber college" and was now cutting hair in Bob's
Barber Shop on the corner of the alley behind our building. He was turning into a disappointing and rather pathetic person, poor in prospects and
losing his good looks along with his black Indian hair. (I am happy to say
things improved for him later. He married a quiet, pretty girl, went into life
insurance, and became head of a Metropolitan agency in a fair-sized town
in central Kentucky. We never saw him again after he moved away from
Louisville.)

At Male a few boys lived within walking distance and a few elegant types
came by automobile, but most of the two thousand students came by bus
or streetcar from all over the city. The street railway company sold "school
checks," brass tokens for students at half price, and before and after school
the cars and busses were crowded with us. The effect was often raucous,
especially before a big game; but we were not really badly behaved or
destructive. Buddy and I would board the eastbound Market Street car in
front of Miersch's drugstore, carrying our books, and he usually burdened
with a violin or trombone case, or both. Talking or studying we rode the
clattering drafty vehicle straight up Market to its junction with the Second
Street line, where we transferred to a southbound car. At Broadway the St.
X. crowd got off, at Breckenridge the Male High crowd, while the Manual
boys continued another half-mile to Oak Street. We walked the two blocks
east to Brook Street, where the school and its grounds filled the whole
block from Brook to Floyd and from Breckenridge to Kentucky. Behind the
school building was a football field surrounded by a cinder running track

and bordered along one long side by concrete stands. The high school building fronted the length of the block on Brook Street, a structure of two high stories that looked low because of its length, built of dark red brick with doors and windows framed with sandstone. It was a handsome, comfortable, old-fashioned building, reasonably well appointed except that the athletic program had outgrown its facilities, the crackerbox gymnasium being particularly inadequate, too small even for decent practice sessions.

As homerooms were assigned on an alphabetical basis I joined Buddy's group of R's. I was surprised and comforted to see that in his quiet way he had made himself liked and respected by the R's and had many friends among them. That helped smooth my way when I entered Male as a beginning sophomore or "English III": as English was the only universal study, students were designated by their place in the English sequence; a last-half senior would be at English VIII. It was local practice among teachers and students to call boys by their last names only, at least until closer intimacies formed; hence Buddy and I were simply "Reid."

Perhaps the oddest element in the Male High program was the presence of an ROTC unit, generally known as Rotsy, presided over by several Regular Army men of low brain power and no charm at all. Maybe a third to a half of the students "took Rotsy," for one motive or another. It was an official alternative to gym classes, for one thing; and for poor boys the free uniforms, ugly World War khakis though they were, were a godsend because they solved the problem of clothing. And some simply liked the drilling, the military lingo and paraphernalia, and the chance to rise to be an officer and shout commands. The cadet colonel, for example, was a grand figure, like a field marshal in his tailored two-tone uniform, glossy high riding boots, and long glittering saber. Buddy and I could have used the free clothing, but we scorned the military mumbo-jumbo on aesthetic, intellectual, and moral grounds.

Basically the two of us followed the same line of study, though of course I was two years behind him. He went farther in science and mathematics than I did, being much better at those than I; and where I took French he took German, largely for the sake of his music. He picked up an instrument fairly easily and now played the piano and the trombone as well as the violin; but apparently he lacked real flair as an instrumentalist, for in each case he soon reached a point where his hard work ceased to pay off.

Before long he turned to singing, and that proved to be his true metier. He turned out to have an excellent baritone voice, very pleasing in timbre and modulation, though not big enough in the long run for high professional performance. Buddy's concentration on music, and mine on sports, began to make the main differences in our lives, which otherwise ran on very similarly in these years. He was as good an athlete as I was, which is to say not quite good enough, but he had determined to give up team sports and really work at his music.

The academic tradition at Male High was an old one and still sound. It was a place where learning was honored and one could work hard at one's studies without being considered freakish or effete. There were dullards and laggards and vulgarians about but they did not set the tone; it was they who were odd, and even they knew it. The general level of work was high, and there were an extraordinary number of boys who possessed something close to brilliance. The Jewish boys as a class were bright, intense, hard-working, concentrated on an objective in a way that sometimes seemed almost fanatical. There were equally good brains among the WASP types, though they liked to pretend to lesser ambitiousness and greater non-chalance. The faculty, too, was a distinguished one, though again it included a few incompetents or nonentities. To teach at Male was a profession honored all over the city, and the faculty included a high proportion of university-trained men, as good as most college teachers, and many of them had given their whole professional life to the school.

Some of them had their difficulties with me. I was hopeless in algebra beyond the simplest problems. Oddly, perhaps because so much of the formulation is verbal or pictorial, I did rather well in geometry under Jim Elam, a big dark monolith of a man, stiff and kind, who also coached football. But chemistry defeated me entirely, once the problems turned mathematical. Mr. Allen, an elderly, jovial, fatherly man, tried hard but it was no use. Of his class I remember most clearly spending a whole hour watching a tall thin girl in a backyard across Breckenridge Street as she faced our windows and went through an endless, hardly varied high-kicking dance that seemed quite mad, expressing some queer mixture of defiance, contempt, and sexual invitation.

For Latin I had Mr. Wetherell, who introduced himself to the class by quoting his English father on the spelling of his name: "Three he's and two h'ells." I should have done well in Latin but I did not. Part of the trouble was that the grammar defeated me. English had always come to me so easily and correctly by ear that I had got by without learning any formal grammar. Now, when the ear could not carry me, I lacked the patience and application to work out the logical distinctions that made sense of Latin grammar. The same reluctance stood between me and the sheer labor of memorizing noun and verb forms. Only two things seemed to me worth that much time: reading and sports. Hal Maynor did help by making up a Latin song to be sung to the same tune as another of our folk songs:

> Oh, the women wear no pants
> In the southern part of France,
> And the men dance around
> With their johnnies hanging down.

Hal's version ran:

> Videbam-bas-bat
> Videbamus-batis-bant,
> Videbo-bis-bit
> Videbimus-bitis-bunt.

I feel no need to apologize for my poor work in mathematics and science; my brain just would not take the stuff in. But I am ashamed of my abandonment of Latin, and I prefer to blame it on laziness, naivete, and confused values rather than on stupidity. It left a disgraceful gap in my education, one which, because I never repaired it, became permanent and seriously hampering to me intellectually.

In any case I did work at the subjects I liked and for which I felt an aptitude—English, French, history, even economics—and I did well enough in those to form a total record that put me not far from the top of our big class at graduation time. My three English teachers were very different men but all interesting and I liked all three. Mr. McCreary was tiny and fey, said to be a poet, and so dreamy and detached that he hardly seemed present in the classroom at all. He did not teach literature so much as commune with it privately; we could overhear the process or not as we chose. He directed a reedy monologue at the ghost of Shakespeare or the ghost of Edwin Arlington Robinson that grew less and less audible until it went altogether silent and interior; then he would take off his big horn-rimmed glasses and stare off blindly into space for two or three minutes while we all watched and tried to imagine what the ghosts were saying to each other. It speaks well for us that we never found him ridiculous. In his small dry outlander's way he was of the tribe of Coleridge.

Mr. Teague was a popular figure in the school, and I entered his class with misgiving, for I mistrusted glamor and easy competence. He was then about thirty-five, a handsome curly-blond man of medium height, with a brisk vigorous body, beautifully dressed. He was locally famous for his wit, and admired for that and for his invigorating enthusiasm for the school's athletic teams. I had privately put him down for a poseur and a charlatan, but in his classes I soon changed my mind. It was even instructive to find oneself so wrong. His manner was gay but it was not frivolous; he honored his subject matter and led us to work willingly at it. His wit turned out to be the real thing, not mere verbal smartness but the energy of a quick ironical intelligence, and he never used it to punish the earnest dullards among us. Mr. Teague was a character but he was also a real talent, an example of the kind of men who gave distinction to that faculty.

My great favorite was the third of my English teachers, a very different kind of man, of subtler personality, less justly appreciated by the students. Mr. Robert was a tall slender man of about forty, very dark of hair, eyes, and skin, soberly dressed. Between classes he would stand at the door of his room hunched and brooding like an unhappy hermit at the mouth of his cave. I cannot recall ever seeing him really smile, though occasionally you could see a little twisting at the corners of his mouth that seemed to express a certain melancholy derision that arose inside and stayed there, pointed mainly at himself. I do not know why he was so sad, but I am sure his reasons were profound. His abstraction was different from Mr. McCreary's; it worked deep in the spirit. Where Mr. McCreary communed with Muses, Mr. Robert talked with God. When you spoke to him directly, his bright dark eyes swung up at you from under the black bony ridge of his brows, a gaze that seemed to come from a place deep inside where there was smoke as well as fire. He was a very kind man who found it hard to unbend and make a simple contact. I became a favorite of his (I thought— he gave no outward sign) after a day in class when he asked if anyone knew what an allegory was, and I answered promptly that it was an extended metaphor: I had chanced to look up the term the evening before. His head flew up and his gaze flashed at me in startled approbation. It was years before I recognized the sophistication of mind involved in the definition I had parroted. I thought Mr. Robert a splendid teacher, an absolutely serious intelligence, grave, concentrated, intense. He made one wish to be a wiser and better person.

Apparently I was also a favorite with my French teacher, Mr. Gardiner, again an altogether different kind of personality. I suppose I was a fairly toothsome object at that time, though I had little confidence in the fact. I did not know what I was except inexperienced and shy, easily embarrassed and horribly given to blushing; I would blush and then blush at my blushing. I had a lot of blond hair that fell in a single wave over my forehead, and I had lost my puppy fat and got fairly tall and slim. I assumed that I would keep right on growing to my dream size of six feet four inches and 220 pounds; but in fact I had already reached my full height and the weight I would keep for the next ten years: an even six feet and 155 pounds. My friend Hal Maynor assured me that Mr. Gardiner was a "fairy" and that he lusted after me, but I pooh-poohed the idea, both halves of it. I had never heard of homosexuality until I went to Male and began to hear a good deal of sniggering gossip about it. The whole concept seemed so improbable that I could hardly believe in it as a fact. Heterosexuality, which was still only a glorious dream to me, gripped my imaginings so fiercely that I could hardly take in the male-male image at all, once it was described to me; it all sounded absurd, ugly, a grotesque waste of time as compared to my male-female fantasies, which were spectacular. A couple of "queer" boys were pointed out to me, and I could see they were odd in their manner, but I really could not believe in the rest of it. I could see too that Mr. Gardiner handled his rather heavy body in ways that could be called effeminate, but I put that down to awkwardness and bad luck. I liked him fine as a person and a teacher, and thought him bright and humorous and charming, though I suspected that he got by rather lazily on cleverness and good manners.

In my last year at Male the whole issue came to a head in a manner that remained happily undramatic. Mr. Gardiner asked me to have dinner and spend the night in his apartment on Oak Street. The idea sounds distinctly suspicious now, and to any family but ours it would have had a nasty air at the time. But I had put down Hal's insinuations entirely, long since, and it seemed to me simply that a nice man wanted to give a treat to a poor kid he liked. My parents read the case the same way, and it seems to me now that our innocent instincts were sound. There was nothing secretive about it: Mr. Gardiner issued the invitation, suggested that I clear it with my parents, and met them when he picked me up in his car in our shaming quarters on Thirty-fourth Street. He lived as a bachelor on the second floor of an old red brick house with decent shabby furniture, lots of books, and a Negro houseman who came in to cook and serve his meals—a kind of functionary I had never encountered before. We had dinner, Mr. Gardiner went out for some errands and a meeting. I found a copy of Balzac's *Droll Stories* with the lascivious Doré illustrations and read that hungrily. He came home, we chatted a while rather awkwardly, and then we went to bed—in the same bed. That did not bother me; it was the only bed in the house, and I had often shared a bed with another male, of my own age or older. Because I was nervous and slept badly, I can testify that he slept soundly and never laid a finger on me. In the morning the houseman came back and fixed us a delicious breakfast that included half-green tomatoes dipped in cornmeal batter and fried, a delicacy I had never tasted before and a favorite of mine ever since. Then Mr. Gardiner drove me home. A slightly mysterious occasion, I suppose, but surely not a corrupt one; perhaps he had been waiting for me to make a move. As it was, we could not have behaved in a more genteel fashion. I was still a virgin and for all I knew, so was Mr. Gardiner. My only regret was the feeling that as usual I had been pretty dull company.

Athletic rivalries among the three boys' high schools, particularly between Male and Manual and particularly in football and basketball, were very old and very fierce. The annual Thanksgiving Day football game between Male and Manual, for example, agitated the whole city for weeks in advance, and the tension in the schools themselves reached hysterical levels, culminating at Male in an orgiastic pep rally in the auditorium in which the band played marches, mad enthusiasts from the faculty like old Mr. Glenn gave ranting speeches, the varsity players were paraded like gladiators, and we all stamped our feet and roared in response to gyrating cheerleaders:

L-M . . . H-S!
Will we win?
Hell yes!

As a matter of fact we lost most of those games, though they were always bitterly fought. The brawny football players were heroes to me, and some of them were my friends, but the game itself rather frightened me. I felt no drawing to the violence of it, and I was not big enough in any case. In both high school and college I chanced to come along in an interval of generally poor athletic fortune, and I was a marginal member of even those subpar teams—not that that diminished my passion. I had concluded that basketball was my true metier and that it was there that I must make my push for fame.

In my first year at Male, as a sophomore aged only fourteen, I felt too shy and unready to try out for the team, but I followed their season with a tense admiration. That year's team was an impressive one, and I was dazzled by the style of their movement, its intricacy and economy, so different from the hectic hithering and thithering I was used to. Players like Jim Goforth and John Helm, tall, muscular, beautifully coordinated, awed me with the poise and power of their play. They did not seem like boys at all but men a generation beyond me in capacity and cunning. Then there was a dashing new star, Lefty Swearingen, who moved toward the basket like a mad meteor. These men made me feel proud but terribly small and young.

So I went to work more or less in private on the fundamentals of my game, making use of the outdoor court at St. Columba's a block west of home on Market Street, where the teaching nuns took brisk constitutionals in another part of the playground, forming long arm-linked lines in their black and white habits and executing a fast-walking crack-the-whip accompanied by many giggles. Every afternoon I put in a couple of hours practicing dribbling and shooting, often alone, sometimes with Buddy, sometimes with a few neighborhood friends with whom we could organize a pickup game and use the whole court. This would go on all through the fall and winter. Nothing stopped me except a rain or snow that made the terrain impossible. In cold weather one's hands would go cracked and raw or so numbed that they would not hold the ball. But l discovered that one could get by even in bitter cold by wearing close-knit brown cotton work gloves; they held a ball fairly satisfactorily, especially after they got dirty enough to be sticky. I went through many a pair of those gloves. Luckily they were cheap. Balls were a terrible problem. We really could not afford the expensive cowhide balls, the only satisfactory kind, and the cinder surface at St. Columba's was murderous, roughing the leather and soon wearing it through. When one did get hold of a good ball it seemed a desecration to subject the beautiful leather to that kind of treatment.

Then a minor miracle occurred. A local creamery began to offer a free basketball to anyone who sent in a stipulated number of their butter cartons. We saved butter cartons passionately, but we could not afford butter any more than basketballs. Then Mama had an inspiration. In her susceptible friendly way she had made a crony of a frail old colored man of courtly manners whom we called Uncle Virgil. He had shown up on Thirty-fourth Street, pushing a rickety two-wheeled barrow in which he collected rags, bottles, iron, paper, anything that could be sold for a bit of cash. As nearly everything we owned was junk in some sense, he posed a problem for us. But Mama invited him in and gave him something and found him conversable, and he formed the habit of calling on us every month or so when he was in the neighborhood. Mama always tried to save something for him, a castoff of some kind or a few nickels. His Uncle Tom ways got on one's nerves after a while, but he was gentle and needy, Mama was kind enough and lonely enough to find his company welcome, and the two of them would sometimes sit mourning softly together for an hour or more over the gas stove in the living room. Finally it occurred to Mama to put Uncle Virgil on the watch for the right kind of butter cartons, and the results were astonishing; he would labor up the stairs chuckling, carrying a couple of dozen cartons at a time. We began to harvest basketballs and before long we had two or three at a time. They were not very good basketballs, being inclined to develop wenlike protuberances, but they were a great deal better than none.

Our habit of hanging about the St. Columba's playground had got Buddy and me into an odd situation. I think we were the only Protestant boys who did so, but it never occurred to us that we might be unwelcome. Having grown up in knockabout societies where everybody was pretty much in the same shabby boat, we had simply never learned to think in terms of the cliquishness that we were about to meet among Catholics, Jews, and the classier sort of WASPs. But in fact Father Voll and the Catholic boys we met at St. Columba's raised no objection to us and we became tolerated acquaintances; it would be too much to say we were friends. We began to hear specifically Catholic talk for the first time, and to realize with some shock how specific that could be. We found ourselves rather inhibited and straitlaced as compared to the Catholic boys. They appeared to allow themselves liberties in speech and action that felt close to immoral to us; we rather resented their privilege of confession and absolution, which we felt dangerously lax—self-indulgent and illogical. We seemed to take a straighter view of sin and responsibility for sin. I remember feeling outraged as I listened to an older boy describe how he had timed a night's outing, vaguely alcoholic and sexual in content, to end at the right hour for early mass so he would not have to make a separate trip. That struck me as morally grotesque.

But the odd thing for Buddy and me was that we got drawn into the St. Columba athletic teams for several years, basketball in the winter and baseball in the summer. All of us felt it just a trifle strange, but it seemed to happen very naturally at the time; we needed a team to play on, they could use some extra players for their teams in the city leagues, so we got together. One summer, for example, Buddy played second base and I played shortstop for St. Columba's, and I had one of my few moments of glory as an athlete when I saved big Ed Schoenbachler's no-hit game in the eighth inning by tearing out into left field to take a soft liner over my shoulder. Of course we lost the game in the ninth. St. Columba's also introduced me to a ceremony I did not like: the custom of players' clustering before a game, laying their hands in a pile, and praying silently for victory, with or without a priest. I laid my hand in the pile with the others but I declined to pray. It seemed to me pretentious and shocking to ask God to intervene in a secular contest far too small to interest Him, and in which one side had no more claim on His favor than the other. Years later I felt offended in the same way when I heard preachers praying for the success of our armed forces. Why should God favor us any more than the enemy, who was undoubtedly praying at the same time? And why expect God to take a hand in a mess of men's own making?

In my junior year at Male I got up enough nerve to try out for basketball, and though I did not finally make the team I survived several cuts in the squad, and I believe I did play in several junior varsity games as one of the honorable rejects. I had enjoyed the long hard practice sessions and the drills; even the exhaustion of it all was nourishing to the spirit. I felt I had learned a good deal and that at least I now had a clear idea of what was expected of one. And it made me feel older, more a part of things to be recognized as a respectable individual by the coach, Frank White, whom I liked very much. Mr. White was a small chunky man who was said to have been an All-American at Butler University. He knew his business and he was a clever teacher and a hard-driving man, though by no means an inhumane one, not the paranoiac tyrant one encountered so often in his trade.

Next year as a senior I tried again and this time I seemed to be succeeding. During the weeks of hard preseason practice I was very happy, enjoying the work itself and for the first time the freemasonry of friendship with skilled equals. When I was named to the team it was delicious actually to be given official equipment, first practice clothes and finally real game uniforms. I felt like stroking those elegant objects of purple and gold. Mr. White had decided to try out a new kind of basketball shoes that resembled those worn by professional boxers, with extra high tops of fine lightweight black leather and white rubber soles with a thin but distinct built-up heel. With my susceptibility to style, I loved those shoes. We were also issued "sheepskin" coats for general wear, stenciled with the name of the school. They were somewhat battered from having been worn on the sidelines by the football players, but that was all the better; the coats were big and loose and warm, and above all they spelled, visibly, distinction and status. I wore my coat back and forth on the street car with what I hoped was modest nonchalance, but I felt marked as a man on his way to Olympus: a varsity letter at Male High.

The trouble was that we were not a very good basketball team—though it took a while to demonstrate our inferiority to recent Male High teams. Size was one serious problem. The tall agile boys all seemed to have disappeared. We did not have a single big man, and that was a severe handicap with the rules still calling for a center jump after every basket. At six feet I was actually one of our taller players. Even more hampering was our lack of aggressive shooters and scorers, boys with a ruthless homing instinct for the basket. I, for example, was a skilled shooter, especially on set shots and rebounds, but I was also a skilled passer and really took more pleasure in good passing than in scoring. I was afflicted with a notion that shooting was egotistical and with a chivalrous image of myself as an unselfish man who maneuvered the ball around until somebody else got a chance for a good shot. Our team tended to pass and pass until we were intercepted or tied up in a jump ball or lost the ball out of bounds. We simply did not possess an efficient offensive energy; our style was too static even for those low-scoring days.

We won our first game, but only barely, over a country high school that was supposed to be a mere breather for us. We all felt the ominousness of that, though I had had my first small triumph in leading the team in scoring. We took a road trip up into Indiana, during which I slept in a hotel for the first time in my life, and I believe we lost all three of those games. When we came home we won a game then lost another. We were floundering in unsuccess and not even improving our style of play; practice sessions turned frustrated and gloomy. Then arrived the merely personal disaster. Sitting watching a junior varsity game, waiting for time to dress for the main game, I was approached furtively by our student manager who brought orders from Mr. White: I was not to dress for play that night. I was shocked but as yet simply too mystified to be deeply hurt or angry. Looking around me after a bit I saw that two other senior players, Elwin Horine and Irv Goldstein, had apparently received the same instructions. They understood, as I had not, that the message was a real quietus: we were fired, finished. They were talking in sullen and rebellious terms, but I was too crushed and dispirited to feel angry, too shy in general and too mistrustful of my capacities to feel unfairly judged. What I felt was sick.

Apparently Mr. White had concluded that there was no hope for a successful season and was determined to start working for the future by getting rid of his lame-duck seniors and bringing on younger players who would have two or three years of eligibility. I could see the logic of that, once it was explained to me, but it was cold logic, and Mr. White himself

never bothered to explain it. He simply wiped us out with an underling's
message, with no personal word of thanks or regret or good wishes. What
hurt almost worse than the shock of losing my last chance at a Male High
letter was his discourtesy, amounting to something like contempt, so unworthy of a man I had admired. It is terrible how one's early traumas linger
in the spirit. By any mature standard the issue was a trivial one; who cares,
after all, about a high school basketball team? Obviously I cared a great
deal; by my standards at that moment the issue could hardly have been
larger. The fact that after fifty years I am tempted to maunder on about it
shows how deep the wound had been.

Socially Male High School had been
full of surprises and instruction for me. I was young for my class in school
and no doubt young for my own years, naive, my experience limited to my
own not very complex kind of person. The school formed by far the most
varied and complex society I had known, and I met whole classes of people
that were new to me. Male High attracted so many Jewish boys that we
were sometimes referred to by Manual and St. X. as Louisville Male
Hebrew School. I found the Jewish boys impressive as a group and most of
them very likeable as individuals. A few of them seemed as hard up as I
was, but most were prosperous; yet neither sort paraded its condition, and
I liked that. I admired the Jews' unapologetic seriousness about learning,
their air of competence and concentration, their clear-headed attack upon
real objectives. They seemed to have a clearer notion of what they were
about in the real world than I did. On the other hand I disliked their
clannishness, once I began to recognize it. For me it was easier to forgive
than Catholic clannishness. It seemed to have a sounder reason for being;
and they were subtler about it, more graceful, less blatant, confident at
what seemed a profounder level of belief and experience. But I disliked
exclusiveness of any kind, and though I had apparently warm daily friend-
ships with boys like Allen Linker, Max Davis, Irv Goldstein, I saw that they
did not finally penetrate to the level they reserved for their own kind.

The classy WASP types were fairly numerous and very influential in the
school, and they were also a new breed to me. In Louisville such boys
rarely went off to private schools, they came to Male as their fathers and
grandfathers had done; and more than any other group they set the tone of

the place. Though certainly there were parvenus among them, most were the sons of the town's older families who were likely to be the wealthiest families. Theirs were the names one kept seeing in accounts of professional and financial doings and public affairs, or in the "society" pages of the *Courier-Journal* accompanying photographs of females gracefully posed about glass-topped tables on stone terraces in front of French windows. They were the members of the Pendennis Club downtown and the Louisville Country Club out on the River Road, places of which I had only the dimmest conception.

One soon learned to recognize these boys by the look and sound of them, their carriage and the inflection of their voices, and of course by their excellent quiet clothing. There was the usual sprinkling of dark and fat and ugly and sickly, but the norm was handsome and healthy: fair, tall, well formed, "clean cut." Anglo-Saxon types, I suppose. The real aristocrats among them served to define traditional gentlemanliness for me; by enacting good manners not in a set of forms but in a general and natural considerateness, they showed that there was real content in the idea of noblesse oblige. These elegant WASPS numbered many fine students and excellent athletes, and in games, too, they seemed to me to perform with a special tone of their own, a gallantry of nerve and style that gave shape to the idea of sportsmanship I had carried about from my childhood reading. I admired these boys and as with the Jews I had good daily friends among them; but again it never went beyond the routine of the school day. We really did live in different worlds; I was divided from them by money and class as I was divided from the Jews by religion and culture. These boys went to tea dances and debutante balls; I had never gone to a dance in my life, and never would do so. They would soon go off to places like Princeton and Yale and Washington and Lee, and then they would come back and marry girls like themselves and live in big houses and join the Pendennis Club. That was a kind of civilization I could never hope to know. After a good while it dawned on me that I was not really sorry. There turned out to be an odd Spartan pleasure in deprivation and the need to struggle, in having to fabricate a life.

The class of nondescript poor boys like Buddy and me drifted into Male from all over the city, drawn by family culture or ambition and the fact that it offered a good education with which we hoped to begin improving our lot in the world. Among the poorer Jewish boys from struggling downtown families I made several good friends, especially a funny moon-faced boy named Irving Potash who had just moved to town from Brooklyn and whose accent amused us by its occasional freakish proximities to southern speech, and Harry Cohen, a scrawny witty boy with sandy hair and a big nose, whom we called Little Harry to distinguish him from a tall black-haired boy with the same name. Harry was too small for competitive team sports, but he was an excellent tennis and basketball player, and I saw a lot of him over the next ten years. He became my only fully close friend among the Jews.

I also took an interest in a strange pathetic boy named Herbie Maas, the son of a downtown undertaker, whose assorted handicaps had delayed him in school until he was several years older than any of us. He was a tall, thin, pale boy with bad eyesight and a lame arm and leg from a polio attack that had also affected his speech so that he slurred his words and sometimes threw out a little spray of saliva. Herbie was generally regarded as simple and some of the cruder boys made a butt of him; but I did not think he was stupid, and I liked him for the good-humored way he responded to his treatment by God and man. One day in history class I heard a commotion in the back of the room—a chair knocked over, an awful loud indrawn sucking moan. "Herbie's having a fit!" somebody called. We all gathered around him where he flopped and gasped on the floor, his eyes closed, his teeth clenched and horribly grating. As we watched, a pool of urine formed about his body, thick and foul smelling. When his convulsion ended he lay unconscious for a minute or two, then he began to struggle to get up and groped about for his glasses that had been thrown off. When he was finally helped up and sat resting on the corner of the teacher's desk, it was curious how dignified and intelligent he seemed as he looked blindly about, dirty, rumpled, and smelly, holding his bent spectacles, and apologized for making a scene. It was my first encounter with epilepsy. One kept on learning the facts of life.

During the three years I spent at Male, from the fall of 1932 to the spring of 1935, the country was supposed to be groping its way slowly out of the Great Depression; but it did not work that way for my family: we groped in the opposite direction and got poorer and poorer. Buddy and I went to school shabby and many days we went without lunch. You could get a decent hot lunch in the school cafeteria for fifteen or twenty cents, but when the choice lay between carfare and lunch we had to choose carfare; that at least got us to school, and it was much too far to walk. Textbooks were a terrible problem every term; we could not even afford the cheap used copies one could buy at the two dusty Jewish book shops downtown. But then we learned of a new scheme to issue free books to needy boys and we were able to qualify for that. The books were to be turned back at the end of the term, unmarked, and the name of the school was stamped in black ink on the unbound edge, proclaiming the poverty of the bearer. I am afraid I did not bear such stigmas with much dignity; I went through agonies of humiliation. We had all taken over Mama's equation of poverty and shame. Her sense of outrage was less social than intellectual. Poverty was a form of failure; it put you among the world's incompetents. She could have tolerated belonging to a class that was naturally poor, a situation in which she could have struggled to surmount her destiny. What she could not bear was the stigma of belonging to a class of failed professionals, people who had no business to be poor. I think it was this family sense of aborted destiny that made us all flounder so long and helplessly, and made us so slow to do anything effectual about the mess we were in.

My old chum from Parkland, Hal Maynor, had entered Male with me and remained my steady friend, and his family fortunes had followed the same dull downward path as mine. He was the only person with whom I could talk confidentially about my misery as an equal in suffering and sympathy, and he was a great comfort. He was a cleverer bankrupt than I. It was Hal who discovered that you could buy candy or even cigarettes (after I got fired from the basketball team and no longer had to "train") with "car checks," and that a certain kind of candy mint wafer would work like a nickel in a slot machine. It must have been Hal who turned up the Student Loan Fund, a municipal charity very politely and considerately titled; its loans were gifts, and nobody ever said anything about paying them back. It was a simple and humane idea. Students from all over the city, boys or girls, who could demonstrate their need, could go down once a week to an office in the old Board of Education building at Seventh and Chestnut and receive from a nice lady named Miss Napier a little brown envelope containing a week's supply of car checks and two dollars in cash; hence one could not only travel to school but eat lunch. It was my family's first resort to outright charity, and I skulked about it shamefully, my back-bone being unequal to the logic and dignity of the operation; but there is no doubt that it saved my life academically by getting me through the last two years of high school. Hal and I used to take the long walk down to Seventh and Chestnut together, and he took the view that our dutiful submission to embarrassment entitled us to a small spree. He always pro-posed that we walk over to Eighth and Broadway and blow twenty cents apiece on two hamburgers for each of us at the White Castle. I went along with this for a time but gave it up because it seemed too ignobly self-indulgent.

Two new friends at Male were also to last me for a long time. Bethel Ream showed up out of phase in my junior year, having just moved to town from Versailles, on the Kentucky River near Lexington in the Blue-grass. Bethel was in my English class and also, by accident of alphabet, in my homeroom. He was a tall slender boy with a small head and straight blond hair, rather patrician looking in spite of currently bad skin, and made immediately interesting by the fact that he was walking with a cane. He explained that he was recovering from a broken ankle suffered in a baseball game at his former prep school, and this at once gave us much to talk about. He was mad on the subject of baseball, the kind of boy who keeps the records of all the stars in his head; it was only a matter of time, he was certain, before he would be pitching in the major leagues. I liked Bethel quickly and I found his personality and his history strange and fascinating. He was a casualty of the Depression like myself, but he had fallen a great deal farther. He had grown up in something like luxury, with a very wealthy father whose fortune had been made in mining. Mr. Ream had evidently been wiped out fairly completely in the crash and its after-math, and Bethel had been removed from his private school and sent to live with his sister Frazier, who was married to a Louisville doctor and living in the Puritan Apartments out on Fourth Street near Central Park.

It was the first time I had known a rich boy close up, even a lapsed one, and I studied him with much curiosity. He made it very easy to be a friend; I think he was lonelier than I was and in some ways even more wretched. Aside from baseball, his interests appeared to be in recovering the family fortune and in writing. Outside literature he had no serious academic in-terests that I could see, but he was a thoughtful boy with whom one could converse philosophically, and he and I used to take long walks after school talking soberly about life and letters. It was really Bethel who started me reading serious modern fiction, especially Hemingway and Faulkner, and thereby raised the level of my taste by several degrees. Our talk was often gloomy when we got considering our hard condition and murky prospects. His depressions were sharper and more intellectual than mine, less merely habitual, and I used to worry that he might be actually suicidal.

"Why don't you two guys get married?" asked my friend Julian one day, seeing Bethel and me so much together. Actually I spent more time with Julian, though I never felt so close to him as I did to Bethel. Julian's deepest motives were always selfish ones, so that one did not give him one's ultimate trust; but he was generous when that was not costly, and he was enormously entertaining. I owe him a long debt for that and for other reasons. Julian was rather undersized, about five feet six or seven, and that was a trial to him because he was vain of his appearance in a more obvious way than the rest of us. He had beautiful wavy red-blond hair, but his eyebrows were so light and thin that they were hardly visible and gave his high-colored face a slightly naked, parboiled appearance. Still, I would have agreed with him that he was quite a good-looking fellow. Julian had three main interests in life, which amounted to obsessions: golf, girls, and genealogy. They were all put to work in the service of his overriding motive, which was snobbery. He was the first dyed in the wool snob I had ever known, a snob by instinct and cultivation. It was tolerable because its workings were often amusing to a spectator, and because he was willing to be laughed at, up to a point.

Julian's father and mother had come to Louisville from Paris, Kentucky, and he argued that this Bluegrass provenance was enough in itself to indicate blue blood. He had determined that his lineage was Scottish, and he was resolved to prove that he was descended from the Scottish kings. One day soon after I met him, as we were starting home after a day of high school, he suggested that we walk by the main library, a half-mile away at Fourth and York; there were some things he wanted to look up. I idly agreed, having nothing pressing to do. In the long reference room I sat down to leaf through the *Britannica* and bound volumes of the *National Geographic,* leaving him to go about his chores. When I sauntered over after a while to see what he was up to, I was startled to find him taking notes from a fat volume of genealogy. When I asked him about it as we waited for a street car, he said he was working out the history of his family. He had reached the Scottish nobility and he was now on the track of royalty. My derisive laughter did not shake him in the least. The library trip was one we often repeated thereafter.

Julian was willing to pursue any girl, of any class, who seemed to him to offer a prospect of amorous gratification, but his serious energy was directed at aristocratic types. He dreamed of marrying a girl of perfect configuration: a good name, an ancient family, money, good looks, sensuality, an interest in golf. But he was ready to consort experimentally with a girl who offered any one of these credentials, and over the next few years I watched him go through several of these odd episodes: with Polly Nesbitt, a neurotic moon-faced girl who had nothing obvious to recommend her but a good name; with Nell Roper, a stiff, dark, intense girl who was pretty, had a good name, and played excellent golf but turned out to be an uncomprehending and offended snow maiden when he tried to get sexy; with Sue Morton, who had a good name, some money, good looks, and played excellent tennis and a bit of golf, but who was much too tall for him and also thought him frivolous and absurd. Julian was excellent company for anybody, but I suppose girls found it hard to take him seriously for a long haul.

His great attraction for me, speaking seriously, lay in his propinquity. I suspect he would have said the same of me, for neither of us had ever had a really congenial confidential friend in easy reach before. We met when we found ourselves riding the same Market Street cars to and from Male High, and it turned out that he lived only a couple of blocks south of me on Thirty-fourth Street. I cringed inwardly the first time I had to turn off at my ugly doorway and I would not have dreamed of asking him in, but he invited me to his house, and over the next few years I was to spend many hours there. He lived in a decent small two-story house of grey stucco on a narrow lot, and he was the only child of parents whom he scorned as unworthy of their aristocratic lineage, indeed almost unconscious of it. They were decent undistinguished people whom I liked, though Julian's father went through surly spells that could be difficult. He was a very small, bald-headed man universally known as "Shorty," generally quiet, practicing a sort of defeated irony after being stuck for years at a very minor executive level in the head offices of the L&N, the Louisville and Nashville Railroad. Julian's mother was named Lola, and he despised the vulgarity of both his parents' names. She was a small, dark, pretty woman running a bit to fat, chatty and friendly and very kind to me. All three of them played golf, but they belonged only to the L&N company club, which used a flat little nine-hole course on the southern edge of town. Julian looked forward to the day when, probably through marriage, he would come into his deserts as a member of the Louisville Country Club.

Most of our time together was spent in aimless brainless ways that were still comfortable to me after my crowded shabby home. We would sit idly talking of girls or friends or school affairs with the radio playing jazz or walk across the street and do the same thing with Julian's friend Jake Wommer, several years older than we, an enormous squatty youth of over three hundred pounds, a student in chemical engineering at the University of Louisville. Or I would hang about as Julian practiced his golf swing, calling out the distance he was driving each imaginary ball. In bad weather he practiced putting into a tuna can set inside the drain in his basement floor. (He would also urinate there, to save himself a trip up to the second floor, creating a distinct odor that the family did not seem to notice.) Once in a while I would ride out to the course and walk the round with him, but I never played myself, not being able to afford the equipment and being busy enough already with two warm weather sports, baseball and tennis. Julian had reason to be vain of his golf; he was shooting in the low eighties fairly regularly, and his eye was set on par.

Our family had no car, of course, and I had never even had a chance to learn to drive; but Julian's parents owned a neat little dark green Plymouth coupe, and it was that we used for golf trips and for our grubby small-time amorous pursuits. I really knew almost nothing about girls, having been kept innocent by a combination of shyness, scruples, and poverty, and I hardly ever spoke to a girl except at church. My sexual life was composed of dreams by night and fantasies by day, but those were lurid and engrossing. I often think how lucky it is that girls cannot see into the inferno in the mind of the adolescent male; they would stay home with their doors locked. I conceived of only two ways of behaving with a girl: friendly and polite, or a complete orgiastic indulgence. I practiced the former and dreamed of the latter. Like Stephen Dedalus I prowled in my mind like an animal and longed to sin with one of my own kind; but if by some miracle a girl had offered herself to me I would have declined—ashamed of my ignorance, afraid of consequences, horrified to offend against my mother's morality.

Now I was staggered to learn from Julian that there was a way of behaving with girls, between chastity and unchastity, between nothing and everything, that was called necking: an established ritual with conventional gestures and rhythms but slightly vague limits. The heart of the matter was kissing, Julian explained. I was skeptical of that as a sufficient satisfaction, never having tried it, but I was more than ready to give the whole ritual a try. For weeks Julian and his obese friend Jake had been plotting a more extreme event. I thought it was all fantasizing, but it turned out I was wrong, and I followed the whole scenario with fascinated revulsion. Jake had told Julian of a desperate older girl down near the park who would "go all the way," and he proposed that the two of them take her out in Jake's family's car and do the deed. The evening arrived. Next day Julian described Jake's toadlike performance in the back seat in derisive detail. When his own turn came, he said, he had simply refused out of fastidiousness: the girl was too ugly, and he was revolted by her wet hairy crotch. I suspected he was repelled more socially than aesthetically; his snobbery had come between him and a girl who was willing to copulate with fat Jake. I pitied her need and admired her generosity.

I almost never had any money, and Julian was jealous of what he had and surly about providing not only the car but most of the gasoline for our girl-hunting trips. But he knew a filling station that would sell him as little as a quarter's worth of gasoline and we often got by with that inasmuch as the girls he had in mind to attack all lived in our end of town. It was no part of the plan to spend any money on the girls. The car was the whole theater of action. Julian supplied the girls as well as the idea, the transportation, the energy; it was hard to see why he bothered with me at all, unless he thought I might form a buffer between him and a possible irate father. As much as anything else, I think he enjoyed setting up a scene that we could discuss derisively afterward. I don't know how he got hold of the names of those girls; in a sort of underworld gossip with other boys, I suppose. Most of them were girls he had never seen before. I suppose that was part of the general venturesome but noncommittal exploratory logic.

Starting out with nothing but a name and an address, Julian would pull up in front of a house, kill the motor, beep his horn, and wait. Sure enough, to my repeated amazement, a girl would open the front door in a moment and stand looking curiously at us; then nearly always she would trot down her steps to the car and stand chatting with us at the open window in a preliminary mutual sizing up. If the girl did not look hopelessly repugnant, Julian would propose a ride, and about half of them would accept. The other half would refuse with excuses; but I can't remember that any girl showed offense at the vulgar directness of our approach. Evidently they felt entitled to remarkably little consideration by the male; at any rate they had learned not to expect it.

What ensued had a curious formality of sequence about it. With the girl wedged warmly between us in the seat of the coupe, Julian would drive down to the park or simply to a dark side street where he would pull up. After a bit of more or less sexy banter, there would begin an unsatisfactory sort of lovemaking for which necking was a fairly accurate term, in that most of the action was confined to the area of the head. You would pull the girl to you and apply your mouth, which she accepted willingly enough, and while that was going on you put your hands to work, aiming at breasts and thighs. Before you had got far, the girl would apply her hands and elbows to deflect your hands, which ended up on her back, where you slid them down as low as she would allow. After a few minutes you drew back for a breath and perhaps a bit of persuasion; then you attacked again, with exactly the same results. Julian and I would take all this in turn. Most of the girls seemed to find nothing odd in dividing their limited favors between two lecherous but fundamentally harmless boys. I was baffled by the morality that let them be so free up to a point, so adamant beyond it. Probably it was a matter of instinct; morality was a name given to common sense.

I felt a mad wish to touch the female body in all its secret places, but I was utterly unwilling to accomplish it by any brutality of force or deception. There was a girl named Dorothy in our own neighborhood, nearer home than Julian and I ordinarily worked, whose beautiful round firm bottom I had long admired in motion, especially the lovely triangular delta at the base of her spine and the enchanting declivity where her buttocks began to separate, which one could make out as hooded outlines under her skirt. One summer night Julian and I had advanced to the point of actually taking out a whole girl for each of us, and we parked down near the river with Dorothy and me all alone in the rumble seat. She kissed me sweetly and I poised my hand over that mystic point on her rump and brought it down, but she slapped my hand away with an angry offended roughness that made it clear that the delta was forbidden land. Another time, though not with Dorothy, I actually touched pubic hair, and it set me tingling all over. I suppose the rules in these contests would have changed if Julian or I had shown any signs of serious intentions that would have made us either dangerous or desirable. These girls gave one harmless freedoms rather than be left out of things altogether; but they were not going to give up anything crucial without a prospect of real romantic return, potentially domestic. I always went home after one of these evenings with an unpleasant sticky wetness in my jockey shorts and feeling tired and disgusted with myself. About all one got out of the ritual, finally, was a more explicit accuracy of detail in the imagery of one's dreams.

At home, life was going on in its increasingly wretched way during my high school years. From time to time Dad tried his hand at some marginal bad-paying job, but that accomplished nothing other than getting him out of the house for a while and giving him a passing illusion of usefulness. Basically our family and Dad's parents were all surviving, barely, on the rents from the stores and apartments, and those were small and unreliable. These places rented for sums like ten or fifteen dollars a month and often stood empty. All were so shabby and inconvenient that nobody would take them who could afford a decent alternative. We kept getting tenants who could not or would not pay their rent, and as we were too soft-hearted to evict anybody, we were sometimes owed as much as a full year's rent, while we got so hard up ourselves that we were at times driven to beg our solvent tenants to pay us something in advance.

Our own apartment was barely endurable. Mama was growing more and more bitter and dispirited, losing her good looks along with her health, suffering especially with bad teeth that she had no money to fix. Her dark eyes still shone, and her humor remained ready to flash. But she

Isaac Errett Reid, Sr., with his parents, Joseph Kendrick Reid and
Katherine Errett Reid, about 1890

Benjamin Lawrence Reid, Margaret Lawrence Reid, Isaac Errett Reid Junior and
Senior, and brother Joe, about 1918 in Texas

Mama and her mother: Elizabeth Butler Lawrence, Margaret Lawrence Reid

Ben and Buddy in early years

The author as a Crestwood
schoolboy, looking up from
(probably) Zane Grey

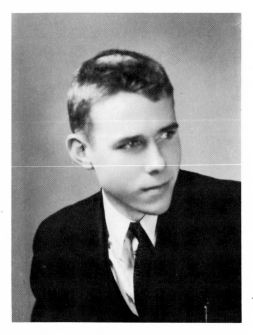

The author at sixteen as a senior
at Louisville Male High School

Morris and Frances Davidson with the twins: Ruth standing,
Jane seated, about 1922

The Davidson twins with their mother, Frances, and Grandfather Coleman, 1919

Virginia Austin as clothed dryad in
Shawnee Park, Louisville, fall 1939

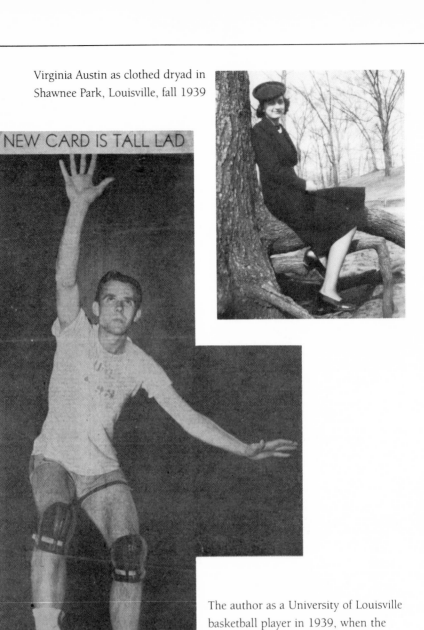

NEW CARD IS TALL LAD

—(By Times Staff Photographer.

Ben Reid.

Six-feet-one without stretching, Newcomer Reid threatens
to win a regular job with the University of Louisville varsity
five, now that basketball is getting back in full swing after term
examinations. This versatile fellow, who is almost equally adept
at all positions on the court, becomes eligible with the start of
the second term, when he moves up to the sophomore ranks.
Coach Laurie Apitz expects much help from him since his height
is sorely needed by the Cardinals. Reid played with the freshman
team the first half of the season.

The author as a University of Louisville
basketball player in 1939, when the
team never beat anybody

Paul Carey Reid in Navy V-12 uniform, with girlfriend (Ruth McGill?), 1942

Buddy at Bonnie Gardens in
Williamsburg, Massachusetts, 1950

Ben, Laurie, and Jane on South Birchwood, 1943

Ben with grumpy Colin at Sweet Briar, 1953

was drawn and tired, and she hated our cramped rooms so much that she could hardly bring herself to do any cleaning. The place smelled of cats and dirt. We could not evict cats any more than tenants. We had started with a coal black female whom we called Omohundro in honor of Grand-daddy's name for oleomargarine; but she bred, and her children bred, and soon there were cats everywhere. One day I was amazed to see a cat produce three kittens on top of a chest in a bedroom. Buddy and I helped do the washing in the old electric machine downstairs in our grandparents' kitchen, and we usually ironed our own shirts and cotton trousers. We also scrubbed out the kitchen and bathroom from time to time and swept all the rooms with a broom, but you felt you were only moving the resident dirt from one place to another.

Soon after we moved to Thirty-fourth Street it dawned on us that we had bedbugs. None of us had ever seen a bedbug before and it took us a while to put a name to the creatures. One would wake up at night scratching, or feel something small and tickling crawling on one's legs or belly. If you caught it and squashed it with your fingernails you got a drop of your own blood and a foul fungoid odor. If you turned on a light you might see three or four bugs hustling off across the sheet toward their secret daytime lairs. Where had they come from? Had the previous tenant left them behind for us, or had we brought them in somehow or generated them by our filthy ways? Mama was inclined to believe that they had crawled up the walls from the store underneath us, where a chicken merchant was running a small wholesale business in live broilers. In fact his operation was remarkably clean and he was forever hosing his place out; but inevitably his birds were noisy and their odor joined that of our cats in thickening the air of the neighborhood. The bugs were a nuisance and a shame to us and we did not know how to fight them. For the better part of a year we attacked them by dripping kerosene into the cracks of the bed frames and burning them out of the coils of the openwork springs with matches. Then one day somebody idly pulled off a loose strip of wallpaper and there in a space about a foot square were several hundred bedbugs, a whole army lined up hip to hip on the white plaster. Clearly we were being outgeneraled, and Dad said our only hope lay in poison gas. So one day we sealed the doors and windows, set a fumigating candle going, and vacated the place for several hours. To our amazement the tactic succeeded; we never expected anything to work. We never saw another bedbug, and we could concentrate on our other disgraces.

Downstairs in my grandparents' rooms life went equally badly. Both of my grandparents were well along in their seventies now and Granddaddy in particular was showing his age. He had got very thin and stooped and unsteady on his legs and forgetful and vague in the head. He would totter down the crooked front stoop and stand meditating for a moment before starting off in one direction or another. If he turned right there was usually no problem; he would recognize our entrance and mount the stairs and sit with us for a time. But if he turned left he was soon in trouble, for he quickly lost track of where he was going or where he had come from. Nearly everyone for blocks around knew the old man and usually somebody would recognize him and lead him home; but sometimes we had to turn out and search for him. I remember one occasion when he set out on his leftward journey, walking gravely along with his hands crossed on his spine, wearing nothing but his tattered grey long underwear and a pair of carpet slippers. He was very quiet in these days of his helplessness, easy to pity and easier to like than when he had been younger and more forceful and spiteful. Even Mama softened to him.

My grandparents had now given shelter to a pale, frail pair of elderly sisters who had been their friends in one of Granddaddy's early pastorates. Miss Fanny (Skene) and Mrs. Jolly must have been hard up indeed to need the charity of people like us. Mama tended to scoff at the two old ladies, especially at Mrs. Jolly, because Dad had told her that she and Grandmother had once had a scheme to mate him with Mrs. Jolly's daughter Marguerite. Mama thought of the idea mainly as a good joke; she had long since given up thinking that Dad was a prize. It was impossible not to pity the gentle, well-mannered old sisters in their helplessness, especially after a sad accident that soon happened to Mrs. Jolly. Our old-fashioned copper-tub washer with its hand-turned wringer had been replaced by a more modern machine with an automatic wringer mounted on one side. One day Mrs. Jolly's hand got caught in the folds of a sheet and drawn completely through the wringer before anyone could release the rollers. No bones were broken, but in pulling against the action of the wringer she had torn loose all the flesh on the back of her hand so that it hung down in a great bloody flap. It was an ugly wound and horribly painful, and though the flesh was put back and stitched and bandaged, it healed slowly and left the poor old hand forever livid and pulpy in appearance.

The only real amenity in either of the family apartments was the old upright piano downstairs, and it was mainly Buddy that made use of that. He played the piano a bit himself, or Grandmother played to accompany his violin. Very often Buddy would be joined by Harold Welch with his violin, and the two of them would play duets for hours with immense patience and little skill. Harold was a friend from our church, a good friend to all of us but a particular crony of Buddy's. He was several years older than Buddy, a brisk short chunky blond fellow with a round red face, very shy, polite, good-humored. Physically Harold resembled his father, an elder in the church, so precisely that the effect was comic. Both Buddy and Harold sang in our church choir, and in the soirees in our slum music room they sometimes put the violins aside and sang to the piano. Soon they were joined by a funny solemn elderly man who had just joined the church and its choir. When in French class I translated a line from Victor Hugo's *Hernani,* "Hark, from the tomb a voice is heard!" I thought at once of Mr. Coleman. He looked like a man impersonating an undertaker, or perhaps his most recent client.

He was the last man I ever saw wearing a wing collar, which with a little black or white string tie propped up a long white hound-dog face with a voluminous grey moustache under a bald dome. I never saw him smile. He was not bitter or censorious or even sad; he just never saw anything funny in anything. He simply did not understand the idea of humor. As a matter of fact he was a thoroughly nice man, gentle and generous, with beautiful Victorian manners. When we first heard him sing we were electrified; we had never had a voice anything like his in size and accuracy in any of our churches. It was a real basso profundo, and it went down, down, and down, always full and always under control. It took a while to recognize, or rather to accept, the fact that the voice, like the face, was dead. When he sang Mr. Coleman was conversing with Lazarus. The voice had immense range and volume and it hit every note on the head; but it had absolutely no color, no shading, no animation. He was a singing machine. He never tired of singing, and he and Buddy and Harold would go at it by the hour. Mr. Coleman's resonant monotone made even Harold's nasal tenor seem interesting, and it turned Buddy's flexible baritone into music of the spheres.

Most of the boys I knew as a senior at Male had occasional dates with girls and the air was full of lewd talk of their conquests. We all knew it was mostly fantasy, necessity conventionalized. I had not had a date with anybody since my stiff little evening with Elsa Brauer at the May Music Festival in junior high school, though I met girls at church with a chaste institutionalized friendliness. There were a half-dozen girls of about the same age as Buddy and me, and miraculously they were all so pretty that during service one's mind tended to wander to alien gods. Even Harold Welch's slightly squatty younger sister Margaret was pretty in her way, and she later made a very good marriage. Harold himself dangled hopefully after Viola Powell, a tall, dark, elegantly made girl, the older of two sisters who looked like Thomas Hardy heroines transposed by divine dispensation for which one gave thanks. Viola (accent on the second syllable) was the organist, that is, pianist, of the church, and it was a feast to watch her move to and from her instrument. One could see that she tolerated Harold for his proximity and devotedness, and mainly out of politeness. It was clear that she qualified for a classier man and that sooner or later she would get him.

Dorothy, my Venus Kallipige of the beautiful and untouchable bottom, was a casual member of our congregation, but our relationship really came to nothing. Basically we did not like each other; I could see she was fundamentally a rather stupid girl of vulgar instincts, and she could see I was a boy of poor fiscal promise. I was more attracted to another pair of sisters, the Austin girls, who lived several blocks north of us on Thirty-fourth Street. The younger sister Jane was the more obvious beauty of the two, a strikingly handsome girl of middle height, with a dark-skinned version of the Myrna Loy face and a body of disturbing precocious voluptuousness. Virginia was handsome in subtler ways than Jane, alongside whom she tended to go a bit pale to the eye. She was very tall and slender, almost gangling, and young enough to carry her body with a certain self-conscious awkwardness. She was fairer than Jane and wore her wavy brown hair rather short on her small well-shaped head. Her eyes gave Virginia her real beauty, deep brown doe eyes exquisitely fringed with black brows and lashes. The lower part of her face, the chin and jaw, went a bit vague and small; but she had a pleasant scoopy nose and a pretty red mouth. Virginia is a subject I approach with tenderness and trepidation, for she is still often in my mind, especially in sleepless nights: she was so generous to me, and I liked her so much, and I ended up treating her so badly. She is almost the only person I am conscious of having in a manner betrayed. I got myself into a position where I had to hurt somebody, and she was the one I hurt. She deserved better of me, much better.

We had known each other for two or three years in a friendly, undistinguishing sort of way, paying no special attention to each other. Then suddenly we became much more intimate. It all happened in a way I found very odd and invigorating. We were going to an evening affair at another church, and Harold was driving Virginia and me and another girl, not Viola, in his family's car. Virginia and I sat in the back seat, and on the first curve we were jostled together a bit. She laughed happily. Soon it dawned on me that she was using every turn and bump of the car to apply her hands and her body to mine in a systematic way. I was dumbfounded but delighted; it all felt lovely, and I responded as well as I knew how, which was not very well. When Harold brought us back at the end of the evening we asked him to let us off at the church, and in the drab and incongruous setting of the church basement we went on with our serious and exhilarating play, talking and laughing and kissing and stroking. It was clear that Virginia had definite prohibitions in the matter of touching, but within those limits she wanted to be as intimate as possible.

I was still trying to understand what was happening, what she was up to. It had never really occurred to me that a nice girl could let herself go this way, or take so much frank pleasure in doing so. Yet I did not feel that she had left off being a nice girl. I saw nothing lewd or wanton in her manner, nothing but free enjoyment of something she wanted very much to do. She obviously liked to kiss, and I soon began to understand why: for her a kiss was not something one did with the outside of the face; it involved the teeth and the tongue and even the throat. It was an exuberant if symbolic sexual penetration. She had no intention of going beyond the surrogate, but she meant to enjoy that to the utmost. I was sure this was not a way Virginia commonly behaved with boys. The details of her behavior were a matter of pure sexual instinct, a kind of genius. Her general performance that evening had been sweetly calculated. She had decided that she wanted to be my intimate girlfriend and she had taken the steps necessary to get things started. I felt no lack of dignity in her action, only an admirable candor and generosity.

I walked home that night in a sort of daze. Aside from sheer sexual excitement, I felt mainly gratitude and relief. It was lovely to be *chosen* this way, to be trusted with the kind of confidence Virginia had offered me; and it was an unspeakable pleasure to have, at long last, a decent, handsome, and hospitable place to put some of my awful sexual tension. Virginia and I were to be intimate friends for the next several years, and her friendship was as sweet to me as her love.

SIX

Life and Letters

My graduation from Male High School came at the end of May 1935, the month I turned seventeen. We scraped up the few dollars needed to have a picture made for the annual and to buy a copy of the book. My picture shows a slender boy in soulful half-profile with very short hair lying flat (I had been trying for a crew-cut effect). The face looks sensitive, brooding, not so much weak as unsophisticated, tentative, vulnerable. It was an accurate photograph. My mind had never been one that conceptualized naturally or well, but it had done well with congenial subject matters, one at a time, with little awareness of connections or patterns. Mama felt powerfully that graduation was an occasion calling for a new dark suit, and I agreed, but it was out of the question. I got by with a borrowed double-breasted jacket that was too short and tight and not quite matching trousers. Nobody seemed to notice. When we seniors filed solemnly up the aisles of the auditorium between the rows of younger students, my eyes went wet and I was afraid I would break out in a loud sob. I had loved the school.

My friendly French teacher Mr. Gardiner, knowing how hard up we were, had found me a summer job tutoring the young son of friends of his who lived in one of the elegant old red brick town houses down on Second Street. He hinted that the boy might be a bit difficult, but I was optimistic that I could manage him, especially if there was money in it. I was to receive ten dollars for two hours of teaching five mornings a week, and I reasoned that that would still leave my afternoons free for baseball and tennis. I took the street car down to Fourth and Magnolia and walked up two blocks to meet the boy and his mother: a thin, fidgety, suspicious boy of ten and a dark, supercilious, equally nervous woman of forty. My spirits dropped but my need had not diminished. The struggle lasted two weeks and it was close to a fiasco. One problem was that I was supposed to teach the boy some mathematics and I knew little more of the subject than he did. But the real difficulty was that I could not deal with the boy himself. I doubted that anyone could have controlled him, and I soon saw I could not. He did not intend to let me teach him anything at all, and I saw that he was taking a sadistic pleasure in creating my failure. After a couple of days' acquaintance I did not know what to call him except mad. He was an only child and a classic spoiled brat, completely out of rational control and immune to any discipline available to me. If I tried sternness he went sullen and silent, refusing to speak or even to look at me. If I tried patience and humor he turned giddy and giggling, with a complete flight of ideas. He was dead set on evasion and of course he succeeded. His mother paid me off with bare civility that left no doubt that she blamed the failure of the enterprise on my immaturity and ineptitude. I felt she was half right.

Had the University of Louisville not existed I could not have gone to college at all. It was a queer place, but it saved the lives of a whole genera- tion of the Reid family, and I don't mean only the intellectual lives. Fees in the liberal arts program at this time were absurdly low; tuition was a mere sixty-five dollars for a semester. But even so small a sum was large to people who found it hard to pay for three meals a day. I applied for a scholarship and was notified that I had been awarded a grant to cover tuition; so it looked as if the university might be as barely feasible as high school had been. The institution I knew in the late thirties and early forties was a small, quiet, homely place where one knew practically everybody on the main campus, at least by sight or name. It is one of the oldest munici- pal universities, going back to 1837, and catered almost entirely to local students; there being no residence halls, everybody lived at home and came to campus by street car or automobile or on foot, as at Male. (Later I was the only one who arrived in a milk truck.) Three small professional schools, of medicine, dentistry, and law, were situated downtown in the business section. The main campus sat at the southern extremity of the downtown area, and it was mainly the home of the College of Liberal Arts, though Speed Scientific School stood at one corner and a shabby little Music School was tucked away in the middle of things. Within the eight broken years it finally took me to get a degree, the Law School moved onto campus in a small handsome new Georgian building, a new School of

Social Work was established, and a year or two later the School of Music moved out to a mansion it had been given in Cherokee Park.

For me the early omens seemed good. I found my teachers both impressive and likeable, and willing to like me. Most of my good friends from Male High were entering the class of 1939 along with me, so I had plenty of cordial company: Julian, Hal, Bethel, Harry Cohen. My fellow casualties from the Male High basketball team, El Horine and Irv Goldstein, were both there, and we looked forward to a new career beginning with the U. of L. freshman team (freshmen were not then eligible for varsity sports). It seemed natural and most pleasant to have girls in class again at last, and this lot struck me as friendly and nice to look at. People took their academic work seriously but not solemnly, and the atmosphere outside the classroom was relaxed and unpretentious. It all made a pleasant, hard-working, serviceable way of life; yet I managed to mess it up shamefully. As usual the heart of the matter was money.

I discovered to my surprise and silly outrage that my scholarship was a "work" scholarship—not a free grant but an appointment to earn a sum of money by working at thirty-five cents an hour paid out of one of President Roosevelt's Depression "recovery" foundations, the National Youth Administration or NYA. The scale of pay was not so grotesque as it sounds now; thirty-five cents was a sort of standard hourly wage for unskilled labor in Depression times. I was willing enough to work, and at that rate. I chose to find myself insulted on other grounds: because the "scholarship" was a tricky misnomer; because it was an unworthy way of recognizing my excellent work in high school; because the nature of the grant had not been made clear to me when I accepted it. I don't know why the message had not got through to me; I'm sure the incomprehension must have been mainly my own fault. At any rate, though I had little enough dignity to pretend to, I chose to find myself deceived and insulted. Instead of reflecting that the university was chronically broke, with almost no largesse to offer, and thanking my stupid stars for a chance to earn a wholly necessary pittance, I reported to work in an aggrieved and sullen frame of mind.

By that time the only work assignment left open to me was on a team of students doing a complex kind of statistical study being conducted by a woman in the economics department. Almost anything else would have been better for me. I stuck it out for a couple of weeks but I hated it: the hours of claustrophobic sitting, puttering with figures and charts I did not understand in the service of a purpose I could not comprehend. The real problem was that I was unequal to the fairly simple mathematical principles involved, and I lacked the nerve to admit it. Finally I simply threw up my hands and abandoned the scholarship. The family now had to find cash for tuition as well as carfare and books and lunch money and clothes. Somehow it was managed, and I finished out the term in good enough order, doing fairly well in my courses and playing freshman basketball in the first half of the season. But it was an unhappy time in which I moved under a cloud I knew was of my own making. For the first time in my life I had acted out a dangerous bit of silly arrogance, and I was ashamed of myself. I had begun by feeling betrayed and ended by betraying.

I think it was that winter that our family finances hit absolute bottom, and it became clear that college was an impossible luxury for people who were not eating. We had got by for years on chronic hopefulness and pastiche, but those poor ruses were wearing thin. A grim day arrived when we had no money, no credit, and no food in the house except a box of spaghetti. The first day we ate nothing. The second day Mama boiled the spaghetti but there was nothing to put on it but salt, and none of us could eat more than a few mouthfuls. The third day we had nothing again. That evening I walked down to Julian's and hung about until he got hungry and offered me a sandwich, which I did not refuse. Next day somebody's rent came in and we started eating again. Three days of starvation had made us feel foolish and degraded, which we were, but at least they forced us to face the reality of the abyss: unless somebody started bringing in some regular cash we must either go on relief or starve. It was the Welches who got me a job, as "head of the packing department" in the furniture factory where Harold and his father worked as upholsterers. My title sounded resonant but the job was really small potatoes and the pay wretched. But it was better than starving. Jimmy the foreman gave me a vague explanation of my duties that left me pretty mystified, but I reasoned that I could learn my job by doing it. I found the work of the floor interesting from the outset, and I quickly came to respect the skill and toughness of the workmen.

The Louisville Chair and Furniture Company was an elderly, seedy family business with few pretensions to style or elegant craftsmanship. It aimed at a mass market on the lower margins of the middle-class range, offering "breakfast sets" of a table and four chairs in oak and a line of standard upholstered "occasional" chairs, plus several conventional styles of living room "suites" of a sofa with one or two chairs. The shabby old red brick factory building on Twelfth Street stood five stories high, with each floor given over to one or two distinct stages in the manufacturing operation. Orders came in from furniture stores all over the country, and in the main office an order card would be made out for each piece of furniture, the card including many small "tickets," separated by perforations, for the piecework operations the chair or sofa would go through, the tickets to be torn off by the persons doing the various tasks, the workers to be paid according to their accumulated tickets.

My floor was the second, and I punched my card in the time clock and climbed the steel stairs each morning at eight o'clock. Our floor was given over primarily to the upholstered furniture, its upholstering, packing, and shipping. The fabric cutter at one end and the shipping clerk and I at the other received copies of each general order because we had to deal with all the pieces involved. For some odd reason the floor also contained a sort of liquid hell known as the "filling booth," a big square steel cubicle with one open side, protruding into the great barnlike room alongside the big open freight elevator that served the whole factory. Here labored three or four poor devils whose duty it was to "fill" the open-grained oak used in the breakfast sets. This they did by slopping over the surface with large brushes a dark brown liquid that contained a pigmented paste filler in solution, then wiping the stuff off again with big rags, leaving the filler in the pores of the wood. The men wore skull caps and long rubber aprons and throwaway clothes, but they still spent the whole day coated from head to foot with a thick layer of the filler solution.

The upholstering began with the "spring-up boys" who took the bare frames and nailed in strips of strong webbing and then either a prefabricated spring unit or a series of separate coil springs that had to be sewed down to the webbing and tied into a unit by a spiderweb of stout twine; then a top sheet of burlap was added to seal off the springs and form a base for the upholstering. After that the chair or sofa was pushed along the floor to the real upholsterers, who were the aristocrats of the operation. (Mr. Welch was the best of them, having spent his whole life at the trade; Harold, who had been at it only three or four years, was still considered a bit of a tyro.) They would have received the proper "cover" from the cutter, with any necessary sewing, such as piping, already done. They filled and shaped the unit with the necessary padding, of cheap tow or the more expensive moss or hair, depending on specifications, topped with a layer of coarse fluffy cotton batting, and finally fitted and tacked the cover itself, holding the tacks in their mouths and "spitting" them onto the magnetized tips of the small tack hammers, working with a speed and precision I found incredible. Then the piece was pushed along to the "trimmers," women who tacked on the plain back panels of the cover and applied any specified ornament such as braid (known as "gimp") or decorative brass nails. Then the finished piece passed along to the inspector, a big friendly tobacco-chewing jokester named Jonesy, who brushed it off and examined it skeptically. If he did not like any part of the ensemble he pushed it back to the guilty workman and ordered him to put it right. Finally everything came to my department for packing in preparation for shipment.

My duties were mostly straightforward and simple, but I managed to make a mess of them for some time, until I developed some skill with my tools and caught on by trial and error to the processes in which I was given no instruction. The department consisted of me and two, three, or four "girls" in my charge, aged anywhere from eighteen to fifty, the number of girls depending on the state of business. We occupied a working space of about twenty by sixty feet, plus an equal area given over to great piles of knocked down cartons of heavy cardboard, awaiting use. The girls or "wrappers" did their work on a wide low bench running along the wall under the windows. I had a work space at the end of this bench, and a "desk," which was a mere slanted shelf with a drawer underneath fixed to a pillar, where I handled the orders and the shipping labels.

When a chair came to me from the inspector, I upended it on its arms on the padded end of the wrapping bench. If it was a straight chair I knocked into the tip of each leg a fat round-headed nickel-plated tack known as a "glide." If the chair was a rocker I applied the "runners," dabbing glue into the two sockets of each runner, tapping them onto the legs with a rubber hammer, then driving the four long screws into the legs from the bottom with a big Yankee ratchet screwdriver. I was so inexperienced with tools that even these simple operations took some learning. When the stock of runners got low I fetched a new supply from the fifth floor, bringing them down on the elevator on a big wheeled push truck. Occasionally an especially heavy or delicate or costly piece had to be crated, and that too was my job. Once I got the fairly tricky knack of it, I enjoyed designing and building a crate that would outline a carton snugly, or carry a single uncartoned piece riding on a sort of homemade palanquin inside a frame. If a chair was to be wrapped only, I passed it on to one of the girls, who whipped a smock of heavy brown paper over the back and another over the seat, then tied paper-covered excelsior pads to the outline of the back, the arms, and the legs, leaving the tips free to slide on the floor. The girls were clever and quick at their job, and I saw that the piecework system was a great animator.

If chairs were to be "packed," only the paper smock and the arm pads were applied; then I picked out the right size carton, opened it up, sealed the bottom with glue and heavy gummed tape, put one chair in on its feet, folded a heavy cardboard divider to fit over the arms and back, upended a second chair and put it in with its arms on the divider, sealed the top as I had the bottom, and wrote out in blue crayon the order number and the numbers of the style and covers of the chairs inside. Often cartons had to be cut down with a sharp knife to make a tight package, and eventually I got pretty good at that. I was also responsible for making out the shipping labels and glueing them onto the wrapped or cartoned chairs. When an order was complete I notified the shipping clerk at his desk in the corner, and often helped him push the chairs down the big steel chute to the platform below where they would go into a truck or a freight car on the siding. Across the narrow roadway and the single line of the railroad spur was another factory that made molasses. It filled the general air with a rich caramel essence that could be sickening on a hot day, and some machine at the factory emitted in a rhythmical pattern a loud round spurting noise that always made me picture a huge bulbous face spitting out a swollen mouthful of thick brown molasses.

Aside from my routine work in packing and assembling the orders I was supposed to oversee the work of the wrappers and to tidy up our space at the end of the day. I actually enjoyed sweeping the place clean, and I soon felt I knew every nail and knot in the rough board floor. The exhausting realities of factory labor, indeed of a full day's hard work of any kind, were a brutal shock for a boy who had led a life as physically easy as mine. At first I could hardly believe the length of the working day, the working week. We worked from eight to five with a half-hour for lunch from Monday to Friday, then a half-day on Saturday. For the first week or so I was so tired that I could hardly stay awake to eat my supper. But quite suddenly I realized that I was developing the necessary muscular and stoical resources; and then I began to take a grim quiet pride in being equal to the job and in knowing that I was making the family at least barely solvent.

In the factory I was again coming to know a new class of people, the blue-collar wage slaves, men and women, southern branch, and they struck me as surprisingly instructive and in many ways admirable people. Most of them were country folk, a few months or years away from farms and rural towns; few of them had gone beyond grade school, and most of them would spend their working lives in factories. There were stupid or surly or dispirited ones among them, but most were bright and cheerful in their ways, shrewd in their general management of life, and steady conscientious workmen. The piecework system meant that they had to work hard and fast to make a living, but I saw that most of them still tried to honor their crafts and their consciences by doing work of the highest quality consistent with speed. Socially and intellectually I stood a cut above any of them in spite of my young years, but I felt humbled by their toughness and skillfulness: they did their job so much better than I had ever done anything. The big room on the second floor was a surprisingly gay place, full of banter and teasing and country humor, much of it profane or bawdy, with the women taking a hearty part that shocked me at first but later came to seem natural and healthy. One kept learning the facts of life. I worked in the furniture factory for more than a year, and I might be there still, perhaps as an ageing broken-backed foreman, had Dad not suddenly found a job in the public housing office under the city government that carried us through the next winter.

Less luckily for many, this turned out to be the winter of the great flood of the Ohio River, which struck in February 1937. Floods were a more or less annual commonplace in low-lying sections of Louisville near the river. They never did much damage and nobody paid much attention to them. But the flood of 1937 was another order of experience. It came after many days of rain in the whole long valley of the river, from Pittsburgh down past Cincinnati to Louisville and on to the junction with the Mississippi at Paducah. There was plenty of warning, but most people simply did not credit the potential size of the thing. The sheer volume of the spreading water passed belief. Among other things the flood was a lesson in topography. It found all the flat parts of the city and covered them, and it surrounded everything it could not quite reach up to cover. Slowly the water rose and rose, and the higher it rose the wider it spread. Motorboats ran about at Fourth and Broadway, a half-mile from the riverfront. To the south, east, and west it spread for miles, the depth of the water determined solely by the height of the land. The whole huge plain of the West End was under water, ten feet deep in spots.

That was our part of town. At Thirty-fourth and Market we could walk out for a block or two and watch the brown tide coming slowly nearer as it rose and spread. As we watched it approach from east and west on Market Street and from north and south on Thirty-fourth, we saw a dramatization of something we had never realized: our shabby corner was the highest point for perhaps a mile in any direction. We had been warned that food would be short, electricity cut off, water contaminated. We had filled all the big pans in the kitchen and even the bathtub with water for drinking and cooking. Now the manager of the A&P on the corner unlocked his doors and told people to help themselves to the stock. We were late in getting the word, and by the time we got to the store we found nothing worth taking but cookies and peanut butter, so we carried off a large supply of those. There was water in the street now, and from our upstairs windows we watched it inch up the curb and spill slowly over the sidewalk. Finally, when we saw that it had quit rising, the level stood an inch below our lowest doorsill. Our ramshackle old building was not going to take a drop of water.

The scene was strange but peaceful; no movement of automobiles or street cars, no noise except for an occasional shout somewhere in the neighborhood. Buddy and I sat upstairs playing cards with the two scrawny whining girls from across the hall and eating oatmeal cookies spread with peanut butter, an indoor picnic that soon turned into a simple bore. There was no place to go, nothing to do. After a time two men came around with a side of beef in a rowboat and cut off chunks for anybody who wanted it. After a couple of days the water began to recede and the city slowly drained itself back into the riverbed, in reverse order, the last areas to fill being the first to empty. So we were among the first liberated.

When we could move about again Buddy and Paul and I reconnoitred the neighboring watershed. Aside from the water damage, the shocking thing was the mud that covered every surface, in some places several inches thick. One suddenly realized why the floodwater had looked so brown—all that sand and silt in solution. Most people who lived in two-story houses had tried to carry all their furniture upstairs, but some things had been too heavy or bulky to move, and in some houses water had climbed even to the second story. Low-lying one-story cottages had been completely helpless. Overstuffed and veneered furniture had been the most vulnerable; sodden sofas and chests and tables with crazy hanging sheets of veneer sat in pools of mud in front yards. Everywhere people were laboring with a curious hopeless stubbornness to deal with the coating of mud on their floors and walls. As persons who had been spared all this we felt an obligation to lend somebody a hand, and we settled on Brother Blankenship, our pastor. In his little white house on Vermont Avenue we found him barefoot and with his trousers rolled to his knees, trying to swill out the mud with mops and brooms and shovels, and we worked with him for two days.

The oddest consequence of the flood for us was that we came out of it with a car. Hundreds of cars had been caught in the floodwaters about the city, some of them completely submerged for as much as a week. Any car that had had its engine under water was generally taken to be a total loss; aside from what the water did to the upholstery and the electrical system, there was the problem of the silt and sand that invaded the cylinders and crankshaft, every moving mechanical part. Buddy spotted a black Ford sedan that looked abandoned a couple of blocks from us and traced down the owner, who said he would sell the car for a hundred dollars. By some process that I cannot now conceive, the money was got together and Buddy had the derelict towed into the alley behind our building. Except for its sodden interior the car looked very good to us. It was a '34 model, one of the very first of the Ford V8's, handsomely designed with a long rakish low line in the hood, fenders, and running boards.

We took out all the seat cushions and dried them in the sun and brushed them down. Being the only one of us with any mechanical sense, Buddy set to work on the moving parts, and he spent many days, working with begged and borrowed tools, taking everything apart, washing all the parts with kerosene, and putting the machine back together. When the great day came and he started her up she sounded just fine, the eight cylinders growling with a low steady rhythm that we thought very sensual and heartening. We drove that car for several years, and we certainly got our hundred dollars' worth. The only problem was that the engine simply drank oil. You could not drive it across town without adding a quart. Before long we began to use "re-refined" oil that had been drained from crankcases and cleaned up a bit. You could get that for ten cents a quart, and we reasoned that it did not stay in our engine long enough for the poor thing to tell that it was being mistreated.

A further consequence of the flood was that Dad found another temporary job. For many years the basement of the main library at Fourth and York had housed a cranky little museum of natural history, full of Kentucky artifacts and relics of amateur archeologizing from all over the world. Partly because it was next door to the men's toilet, I often went into the museum and moused about for half an hour, usually all alone in the room. The basement room had been completely covered by the flood and all its fittings and collections had been afloat for days. The curator, a kindly, bald, owlish old savant named Colonel Lucius Beckner, was left with the mess of restoring order and salvaging what was not hopeless; probably because he had chummed up to the lonely old man in his chatty way, Dad was hired to help him. The job amounted to a confused, concentrated, inundated archeological dig, with relics of many cultures jumbled into a common sodden heap; everything had to be excavated, cleaned off, identified, reassembled, and newly labeled. It was a perfect job for Dad. He admired Colonel Beckner, and he liked nothing better than poking about in a detailed mess with its endless occasions for speculation and chat. His pay did not amount to much, but we always felt that anything Dad contributed was a pure bonus in our economy.

Both of my grandparents were dead now. Granddaddy Reid's heart had run down at last and he had died slowly and peacefully at eighty-two. Grandmother died soon after of Bright's disease. I can't remember that their deaths made much difference to anybody, even to Dad. Any love that had ever passed between the generations had been cooled for a long time, and the old people had simply been waiting out the end of their empty span. That long preceding emptiness was the only sad thing in their deaths.

I don't know what to call my relationship with Virginia, which was the other thing that had been going on for the past year or so. It was not a pursuit, or a courtship, or an affair in the usual sense. Call it a sensual friendship. I am afraid Virginia was in love with me, and I was half in love with her; but we both recognized the dangers in the word and we did not use it. At this time she was not seeing any other boys nor I any other girls, and we saw a great deal of each other; yet we could not have been called lovers. Had things broken differently, had she been more acquiescent sexually, for example, or had I felt more nerve or decisiveness, I might well have married Virginia and lived out my life fairly contentedly in some undistinguished job in Louisville. She would have been an easy person to be happy with—a gentle, straight, practical girl, a sweet, bright, strong presence in the landscape or on the doorstep. I hope she has been happy.

The factors other than luck that kept us from coming together in any conclusive way were cultural and economic, joined in my family in an odd way. Whereas in our poverty and general shabby style of living we looked a disgrace not only to our own class but to our lower middle-class neighborhood, in our private and personal being we were more cultivated folk than those we lived among. Virginia recognized that, as I did, though we did not talk about it. The situation made a difference between us, for the present and the future. After high school Virginia had gone not to college but to business school, and she now worked as a secretary in an office downtown. That defined an intellectual level. It was actually higher than mine when I was a laboring wage slave in a furniture factory. But nobody assumed that such a job defined my nature or my destiny; they were more nearly defined by the fact that I talked well and read a lot of books and had a few rudimentary ideas. Virginia was not stupid in the least, but she did not read and she did not worry about ideas; she was an admirable and immensely likeable citizen of what Carpentier calls the Kingdom of This World. It mattered, for example, that her grammar and diction were and always would be a little bit shaky. I remember her describing a man "going through all the emotions," when she meant "motions." No great matter, of course, a trivial confusion; but it expressed the sort of cultural tone-deafness that could be fatal to a relationship unless circumstances intervened to cancel it out. In our case, circumstances tilted things the other way; they worked to affirm the cultural difference and to undercut the powerful appeal of nearness and familiarity and warm liking.

In the short view there was the intersecting problem of my poverty, my interrupted education, my vague determination to work through to a career that would be in some way intellectual. I hardly put names to my dream, but I suppose I saw myself as a writer or teacher in a future hardly discernible in the mist. I think Virginia would have taken me on the spot, in my joblessness and ignorance; she was that loving and generous. But I was not willing to impose my incapacity, or to accept such a mediocre definition of myself, end-stopped at such a point. Moreover, I saw that I, or Buddy and I, needed not only to get on with our education but also to plan on supporting the whole family for years to come. I see I am making myself sound much more thoughtful, more systematic and analytical than I was. In fact I was a gloomy, confused, pessimistic kid of nineteen, my head full of vague stubborn dreams, living from day to day, hoping for a miracle to take me over and make something out of me. More than any other single thing I wanted the power to make Mama proud of me and to make her life happier.

So Virginia and I went on with our amorous companionship, a more satisfying thing than one might suppose. I was still chronically broke, and we never went out to dinner or to dance. I was not only too broke but too shy, and I never learned to dance. Fortunately we both loved movies and they were cheap; we could take a street car downtown or walk to the neighborhood theater at Thirty-eighth and Market. I would pick her up at her family's little house at the north end of Thirty-fourth Street where it gave way to open ground. After the film we would find a dark spot somewhere and kiss and talk till bedtime. Buddy's resurrected Ford improved our style as well as our comfort, expecially on cold nights, for now we could park and neck systematically like any respectable couple. Some nights we merely rode slowly about and talked, and one night I got so engrossed that I ran smack into the median strip on Western Parkway and blew out both front tires. But usually we would stop in a parking area in Shawnee Park that was patrolled by forgiving policemen, and stay in the car or get out and stroll about on the dewy grass in the dark.

As Virginia saw it we.were there to talk and kiss, both of which she enjoyed heartily; but for nothing more. We talked by the hour, simply as good friends, which we were; but we kissed like consummating lovers, which we were not. Her kisses were so nearly orgasmic, long and deep and hot, and she gave herself up to them so completely, that for a long time I could not understand the logic of stopping there, the logic of her prohibitions, which were absolute. She was happy to give her kisses, but she would not give another shred of anything. She made it clear from the beginning that I was not even to touch any part of her anatomy not involved in the kiss, and most emphatically not her breasts or her thighs. She was perfectly willing to tease and argue about the issue, but give in she would not; and I liked her too much and honored her sense of rightness too much to force her or even to try seriously to persuade. In any case her kisses were nourishing things in themselves, almost literally; one had a sense of feeding.

Tactically she was wrong, no doubt. She could have had me if she had been willing to grant the favors that would have bound me to her by lust and gratitude and commitment. I think Virginia understood that, but she was simply too high-minded to trade on those terms. Only once did she make a gesture that was a relaxation of her rules. We were walking about in the park one hot moonlit night and we stopped by a fountain for a drink of water. As I looked at her body against the moon I saw that she was not wearing any brassiere. I realized in a flash that it was not the kind of thing she would do without intention. It was an invitation; an incomplete one, but for her enormous. She stood perfectly still as I ran my hands slowly up under her blouse and cupped her two breasts. They were bigger, heavier, firmer than I had imagined, and there were those hard points in the middle that seemed to work a strong purpose of their own against my palms. I suppose I had imagined a woman's breasts as something like balloons, round and soft and insubstantial. I found them formidable and beautiful, and I stood that way a long time in a sort of *liebestod*, a sensual swoon. Then she moved and we walked on. I can't remember that we said a word about the episode; it seemed too magical for talk. She never repeated it. Why had she offered her breasts to me, things so beautiful, so private? It was as if she might be saying: "All right, perhaps you do have a right to know what my body is. Try it. Now you know. Do you want it badly enough to love me?" The answer, when everything got finally counted in, turned out to be no.

It was settled that Buddy and I would make a new assault on education at the university in the fall of 1937. I was now nineteen, the time I had lost in the factory and in idling having brought my actual age into phase with that of my classmates. As usual it was unclear where the money to keep us in school was to come from. Buddy and I had applied for NYA work "scholarships" again and they had been granted. I made it clear that this time there would be no nonsense, no spoiled-brat stuff: I would do any work assigned to me. Looking back at this period now, I can see it was the time when I commenced whatever growing up I was going to do. I felt a good deal more at myself, firmer in purpose and clearer in my head, though by no means free of doubts and fears. I would never lose those. One's sense of one's own age is a very queer thing. I sometimes wonder if I have ever grown up in any sense but the chronological. Here at sixty and more I still feel very boyish in myself. A few years ago I realized that I had been thinking of myself for many years as fixed at a single age, which seemed to be about twenty-eight. I talked to my colleague Joyce Horner about that sensation, and she said, yes, she herself had been thirty-five for a long time. When I turned forty-nine it came over me that I had now been twenty-eight for twenty-one years, and I wrote a poem to celebrate that queer coming of age. It turned out to be a poor idea, for I suddenly began to feel, at least intermittently, a good deal older.

Buddy and I would both be pursuing straight B.A. degrees, though he would be doing much of his work in the music school. English seemed the only logical major for me, though I was almost equally interested in history and later in art history. Being still officially a freshman, I was taking mostly required courses in "general education" and finding them sensible and plenty demanding. The natural science "survey" baffled me, of course, but I sturggled and survived it. The history of civilization course was overwhelming in its sweep through space and time, but its mere immensity of view made its own necessary point; one saw how much one needed to know more. My lecturer there was a man with a Hollywood joke–Englishman's name: H. Sherwood Warwick. He looked and sounded "English" too: a tall, spectacled, square-jawed man whose classroom manner was formal and formidable. Actually I think he was just a bright middlewesterner who had had some British training. Later when I got to know him better he turned out to be a straight, kind, rather shy man.

After many years of academic experience I still marvel at the quality of the faculty in that small struggling provincial university. Harvey Webster and Richard Kain in English, Justus Bier in art, Broderius in languages, Kutak in sociology, Vinsel in political science, Williams in economics, Warwick and Jim Read in history were a learned and humane lot of men who made it a pleasure to be their students. Most remarkable of all was Ernest Hassold, head of the English department and later for many years head of the humanities division. Hassold not only conceived but begat and nursed the humanities program in the college, and he really thought more naturally and happily in those big interdisciplinary terms. I met him now in the first year of my return when I was placed in a special experimental section of freshman English that he had designed. I think it was Dad who heard about the course and got me into it; he did have occasional attacks of such prescience. The class was a small elite group most of whom seemed much smarter and more learned than I. Hassold himself was dazzling, and his conception of the course as an introductory history of ideas was far over my head. One of his devices was to bring in experts from several disciplines, philosophy, psychology, science, to talk generally about their fields of study and submit to our questions. (I remember with an old blush that I asked the philosopher what was the *use* of his subject.) I felt fascinated and lost, and again I struggled and survived. Hassold had impossibly high intellectual ideals, but he also had a forgiving temper. He asked extravagant things of students, as an obligation to the ideal powers of the mind, but he was able to fall back and admit at last that we were mortal. Over the next years he became the strongest intellectual influence of my life; and when I finally published a book I was fairly pleased with it seemed natural to dedicate it to him.

My old friends Julian, Bethel, and Harry Cohen were still on the scene at the university, but in my absence a new crop had appeared among whom I soon formed new intimacies. Closest of my new friends was Jess Cusick, the chunky untidy son of a well-known local photographer. Jess was a Male High graduate but I had not known him there because he was several years older than I. The fact that he too had had a broken academic career was probably one of the things that brought us together. Like me he was hard up and a bit shabby. He rolled cigarettes for me, and he showed me how we could pool our cash and make a bet as small as fifty cents at a bookmaker's down an alley near campus. He was a shrewd handicapper and we sometimes won a dollar or two. Jess brought me other new friends of his own, especially Bob Lotspeich, Bill Woosley, known as Whizzer, Charlie Hough, Bill Pate, Tommy Thomas. Jess and Pate and Thomas, as well as my friend Elvis Lane, were all interested more or less professionally in writing and journalism, and all of them worked on the campus newspaper, the *Cardinal*. I used to sit about the newspaper office with them and listen to their vaguely Marxist talk, the going thing in those days, which gave them a line.

My own political innocence was absolute. I did not know what was going on, or why, and I was too busy surviving to think much about it. The serious Marxists were involved in European issues, and they were years ahead of me in sophistication. I was completely dumbfounded to learn, for example, that two boys I knew slightly were going off to fight for the Loyalists in Spain: Bob Leopold, a bright, elegant Jewish boy from Male whom I had always thought of as a natural succeeder in the conventional way; and a strange older boy whose name I can't recall who had always set me giggling inwardly because he looked like an identical twin of an actor who played mad-anarchist types in the movies—tall, scrawny, myopic, uncoordinated, with long wild kinky hair. Neither of them was conceivable as a soldier, and the notion that anybody could care enough about a political idea to go off to Europe and be shot at for it was beyond my comprehension. The next thing we heard was that they were both dead in Spain. It made one feel awfully young, and glad of it.

There were pretty new girls all over the place, and I was in love with so many of them that I began to fear that poor Virginia was not going to survive my resumed education. There was Anne Falast, a slender, boyish, red-haired girl; Ewing Arne, a beautiful pale blonde snow queen; Mary Fishback, a merry brown-haired good-fellow; Marian Cardwell, tall and handsome and far too elegant and ambitious for the likes of me. In several classes that we shared I began to know the Davidson twins from the Highlands, chubby and plain, but very intelligent, and gay, generous, companionable girls. Like Jess they brought me other friends: Jessie McCracken, Ann Tyler Fairleigh, Sue Morton and her older sister Henrietta, or Henri, both tall blonde tennis players, and two other handsome athletic girls, Stacy Hall and Helen Jennings. All of these girls came from families far above mine economically and socially, but there was very little "side" about them, and they made themselves pleasant and easy to know.

The whole atmosphere of the university, at least of the parts of it I knew, was homely and friendly. Nobody pulled rank, nobody dressed to kill, none of my new acquaintances raised an eyebrow when they came upon me between classes, stacking lumber or stinking of brass polish as I worked at the edges of the stair treads as part of my NYA job; they were more likely to stop and chat. A group of us, usually including Ruth and Jane Davidson and Sue Morton and Julian, got into the habit of walking in decent weather down to lunch at Brooks's delicatessen on Third Street, a few blocks off campus, where you could get freshly cut sandwiches for a quarter and stand to eat them at long trestle counters covered with shelf paper. I see now that I hardly realized how quickly and pleasantly my range of acquaintances was expanding. I had far more friends than ever before, of a more varied and interesting kind. I was happier than I had been for a long time, though the situation at home weighed on my mind so chronically that I was hardly aware of the fact.

Most of my other friends came from among the athletes. I had by no means given up my old dream of playing varsity basketball, and I suppose the game was my strongest passion aside from sex and survival. Being still officially a freshman, I played freshman basketball again in the first semester under John Heldman, who was the varsity baseball coach and with Laurie Apitz, the varsity football and basketball coach, ran the whole athletic program at the university. Heldman was a big, bearish, genial midwestern German—what was known in Louisville as a Dutchman or

Squarehead. Oddly enough his head was rather square, flat on top and straight on the sides. I liked him fine and he approved of me as the rare kind of athlete who got comparatively good grades and created no problems of eligibility. Among the players I got particularly fond of Elvis Lane, a tall red-haired boy who wanted to be a writer, and Bob Weber, known as "Cup" because of the way his ears stuck out, a tall, blond, skeletally thin boy, a mere rack of bones, who also played good tennis. Both were straight, modest types and serious students and both became good friends of mine. With the second semester I was taken onto the varsity basketball squad and played out the season with no great success. We seemed hardly ever to beat anybody, though we had a wonderful time trying. I loved the game itself so much that I took a voluptuous pleasure even in the long daily practice sessions: the late afternoon ritual of dressing, taping ankles, the sweaty drills and scrimmages, the long hot shower and locker room banter, the long ride home by dark on the street car feeling tired and wonderfully clean inside and out.

The University of Louisville has become a national power in basketball, but in my years the athletic program was small potatoes and our amateurism was simon-pure. Nobody at U. of L. ever heard of an athletic scholarship; we gave our time out of simple love for one sport or another and perhaps some hope of local fame. No doubt these conditions showed in the quality of our play. The athletic department, as the Heldman-Apitz partnership was grandly known, did try to find summer jobs for its athletes, preferably something outdoors and muscle-building. That summer the best they could do for me was a queer assignment to solicit new students for the YMCA Day Business School. As I was never able to see anybody about except the director and his secretary, I had some doubt that the school existed at all. I was given, on separate cards, the names and addresses of all the girls who had graduated from all the city high schools in June, and I was supposed to call on them, inquire about their plans, and present the charms of our school to anyone who looked like a reasonable prospect. For this I was given fifteen dollars a week and a promise of a commission for each student who finally enrolled. I rather enjoyed the work, rambling about town on foot at my own pace and chatting with the girls and their mothers, making no arduous effort to sell my product, which I knew nothing about anyway. Most of the girls knew what they were going to do with themselves with no help from me. As I began to suspect early would be the case, my commissions came to nothing at all, and the whole school soon folded—if it had ever existed.

In the fall of 1938 I was back at the university for my second full year. Essentially it was to be more of the same, courses, friends, sports, all dug a little bit deeper. I was beginning to get into the main line in several studies now, in English, history, and art history, and was finding it all very engrossing. In modern European history we had a splendid new teacher, James Morgan Read, who had a brand new Ph.D. from Marburg and a head full of ideas. He was then at work on his book on anti-German atrocity propaganda of the Allies in the first World War, a touchy subject in 1938, with the Germans coming on again. Jim was an excellent scholar and a stylish, energetic performer in the classroom, a tall, black-haired young man with a scoop nose and long expressive hands. He liked to assign short papers that involved concentrated reading on a small subject, and I got very expert at writing those. Some of us, especially Sue Morton, the Davidson girls, and I, soon got to know Jim more personally when he began courting Sue's older sister Henri, a gentle, pretty, level-headed girl almost as tall as he was and somewhat storklike. A sweet girl, dead now, alas.

The departments of art and music had been lucky enough to attract several of the German Jewish scholars who fled Hitler in the thirties and who brought a wave of pure excellence into higher education in this country. In music we had little Gerhard Herz, with whom I never studied but whom I came to know later as a friend of my friends. I remember his account at a party of how, when the registrar telephoned him and began a long harangue, he put the receiver in a big bowl in the middle of the table and went on with his work. In art we first had Richard Krautheimer, but I sat under him for only a few lectures in a general humanities course. He soon went on to higher things and made a distinguished career at New York University. I preferred his successor, Justus Bier, who became one of my favorite people on earth. Bier had been head of a famous museum in Nuremberg, a specialist on late medieval sculpture, and as such I suppose a retiring, private kind of scholar. I scarcely realized at the time what a shocking and exhausting change his new life must have made for him; not only separated from his wife and small son but also required to become in middle life an entirely new kind of professional man: a bustling all-purpose academic, lecturing in a strange language to ill-prepared students on the whole range of art history.

How hard he worked and what a good job he made of it! Bier taught practically everything, all the periods and all the forms, even architecture and photography, and he was always absolutely convincing. It was dazzling. Ultimately I think I took every course he offered, and when I graduated I had at least as many credits in art as in my major in literature. I loved the seriousness of the study and the tangibleness of it, the fact that there were always *things* to take hold of. Bier was an enchanting person: a little roly-poly figure with stiff grey hair and thick black eyebrows, bouncing briskly back and forth between his lighted lectern and the image on the screen, absorbed in the need to find words for what he wanted us to see and feel. One soon caught onto his thick accent, in which *th* always came out as *s* ("sis" and "sat" for "this" and "that") and in which appeared occasional hilarious locutions such as "snapshoots." He bubbled with gaiety and he was always ready to join in our laughter even when he was its object. We all knew he was a long way from absurd, and we sat alert in the dark room, learning how to look.

In literature courses in humanities and English we tended to read a great deal of fiction in translation. We read fair amounts of Flaubert and Balzac and Zola, but much more of the Russians and Germans, a bias probably determined in the main by tastes of Ernest Hassold. Sooner or later we read and argued our way through most of the major texts of Tolstoy, Dostoyevski, Kafka, Thomas Mann. I was gripped powerfully by works such as *Crime and Punishment, The Trial, The Castle,* "Tonio Kröger," "Mario and the Magician," *Buddenbrooks, The Magic Mountain*—fascinated by the way their vision intersected what I was learning about modern movements in painting but more deeply shaken by the haunted, phantasmagoric quality in those imaginations that seemed to speak of the dislocations and unpredictables I had been feeling in my own life for the past ten years. They seemed to address me with great familiarity; I knew what they were talking about. They made my own experience seem no more comfortable but a good deal less peculiar.

I am afraid I managed my studies in English in such a way as to avoid a systematic acquaintance with the real discipline, the central tradition. I came out of my "major" with no conception of literary history, of roots and range and relationship. There were whole centuries in which I never willingly read a word, and my mind was so ignorant and narrow that I was incapable of seeing how badly educated I was. I knew nothing of the classical tradition and I was so anti-Romantic, or thought I was, that I rejected anything of that coloring out of hand. I proceeded as if literature had begun about a hundred years before, and in fact I thought almost everything more than a generation older than myself was too primitive to bother with. I saturated myself in contemporary fiction and poetry.

My literary judgments were passionate and untrustworthy, indeed often not literary at all. I fell in love with things that spoke to my own confusion and self-sorrow, and blindly condemned other things on grounds that were absurdly inartistic—sociological or political or merely solipsistic rather than aesthetic or even humane. I thought of my standards as tough and objective when they were really soft and subjective. For example, I wrote a long hudibrastic paper attacking Shakespeare's loving farcical treatment of the "Athenian" workmen in *A Midsummer Nights Dream,* so offended by his condescension to his rude mechanicals that I could not begin to make my way into the magical world of the play. In a modern novel class I provoked a violent quarrel with a more enlightened student over what I saw as the triviality and snobbishness of Henry James's *The Ambassadors,* my stiff pragmatical biases having made me immune to the subtlety and profundity of what James was doing. It was years before I realized how my touchy have-not economics were blinding me as a student. I thought of myself as a political radical, perhaps even a communist. But there was no content in that either; I had read no Marx and really knew nothing about political theory or economics. All I had was a parcel of angry deprivations, giving rise to prejudices that I thought were judgments.

Meanwhile my appetite for anything I thought was "modern" and preferably "experimental" was bottomless. Here again my literary taste was confounded by my fascination with modernism in painting, a medium where the movement took deeper, more objective, more classical shapes. It was respect for Picasso and Matisse and Cézanne and Henri Rousseau that drew me, for example, to a shoddy writer like Gertrude Stein, who caught me first by the charming audacious arty gossip of *The Autobiography of Alice B. Toklas.* It was not till ten years later when I was writing an M.A. thesis at

Columbia University that I finally had to admit that the main body of Gertrude Stein's work, the parts on which she wished to stand, was self-indulgent and unreadable, a closed solipsistic system. My fixation on E. E. Cummings was equally characteristic though a bit more soundly based. I got caught not only by his bright pictographic gadgetry but also by his whimsical and funny fracturings of language and his sardonic defiances *pour épater le bourgeois*. I admired his artistic nerve and inventiveness, his impertinence, his anger at hypocrisy and his affection for simplicity—so much that I wrote an independent-study paper on Cummings that ran to nearly a hundred pages.

The mere massiveness of my papers in those days showed my basic insecurity of judgment and of spirit, my need to prove something to my teachers and to myself. All the time the truth was that my love for such works as Cummings's *The Enormous Room* and Gertrude Stein's *Three Lives* was really an emotional reaction, founded less on their announced modernism than on their old-fashioned softness at the core, the sentimentality of hurt personal feelings that any of us then would have been shocked to be charged with. I was a romantic who thought he was tough, a disciple of other unconfessed romantics. It was a long time before I began to catch up with the real hardness that is classical and feels no need to attitudinize.

Like most students, I suppose, I was finding my homes less in subject matter than with teachers I liked. I took as many courses as I possibly could from Justus Bier in art and from Harvey Webster and Richard Kain in English, and above all from Ernest Hassold in English and humanities. Webster and Kain were then young teachers of thirty or so with new Ph.D.'s from Michigan and Chicago, respectively. I found Kain highly competent but a bit cool and stiff, and it was not till some years later, after he had done much of his work on Joyce, that we got to know each other better and became friends. Webster and I were friendly from the beginning, and over the next several years I often visited him and his pretty wife Lucille at home and no doubt made myself a bit of a nuisance. He was very contemporaneous in his tastes, full of Freud and Marx, and of course that appealed to me; but I liked him personally as a warm, friendly, humorous man, very easy for a shy person to know. Jane Davidson and I began taking his classes in creative writing, and that brought the three of us closer together, particularly because he praised Jane's and my stories and poems and professed to think we had talent. It was also under Webster that I wrote my endless paper on Cummings.

Ernest Hassold was a different order of experience, and I think it was Jane who made me understand how extraordinary he was, for she was really in love with him, in a dissolved, hero-worshipping way. Hassold was the first pure type of the all-around intellectual man that I had encountered, and he remains the most impressive example in an experience that has now grown long. He was a tall, fair, burly man, bearishly stooped, with a grave abstracted air. In time one was surprised to realize that he had both much humor and much common sense, and was a man quite able to deal shrewdly with personal and professional problems. He was no Casaubon. Hassold knew so much, of so many kinds, that it seemed mere chance that he had landed in the English department: he could have functioned admirably in classics or German or philosophy or history or theology or art, or even in basic science.

For one who knew nothing it was terrifying to meet a man who knew everything. He had not only read everything but remembered it, and that was dazzling to my leaky mind. Hassold was capable of dealing in straight, detailed, literary-critical terms with a text, but a single text or even a single discipline tended to bore him quite soon, for the whole bent of his mind was interdisciplinary, conceptualizing, patternmaking. Whatever he picked up quickly turned into a unit in the history of ideas. To sit in his class was to watch that process occurring in his head, as he paced bearish and flat-footed past a bank of windows, his fine deep breathy voice following his thought as he gazed out at an air-hung blackboard scribed with learning and speculation, then turned to flash a smile at us that expressed his amusement at an odd conjunction he had found there. Half the time I did not know what he was talking about or how he had got there; but I did not doubt it was a good place to be, and I staggered panting behind him.

When I got up nerve enough to propose an independent study under Hassold and went round to confer, he laid out a subject and said what I must look for was "the unstated assumptions" moving within the work. I nodded bravely and went away, but it was weeks before I even began to see what his phrase meant; I was having a hard enough time with the stated assumptions. I'm afraid I was a disappointment to Hassold, though he was kind enough to give me good grades in his classes. Jane kept up with him better, having a better brain. Later he gave her his highest praise. But Hassold's most visibly authentic stars at this time were Kent Hieatt and Joe Duncan, two natural-born academics who later went on to excellent careers. Kent was especially dazzling because he seemed to think easily in Hassold's conceptualizing style, and he talked the lingo fluently not only in English but also in German. Listening to him chatting companionably in German with Hassold or Bier or both, cracking incomprehensible jokes, I felt myself turning green inside.

                         In 1938–39 I played a full season of varsity basketball for the first and last time in my life. Our coach was Laurie Apitz, and he was a strange one, a tall, bespectacled man whose face usually showed a tense buck-toothed grimace. He was high-strung, ill-paced, spasmodic in his thinking and acting, a neurotic personality who seemed to me nearly mad at times. He was misplaced in his job—tense without being concentrated, unfocused, overcomplex. Like everybody else on the faculty Apitz was underpaid, and his head was full of odd schemes for making money, one of which was to harvest and market the stones from abandoned farm walls in Kentucky. A sight of New England stone walls would have perfected his nervous breakdown. He was not a good coach; at least he aroused little respect in his players, and he was never able to give much force or shape to our style of play. But perhaps he was as good as his material deserved. The fact that I was a starter most of the year was a pretty good measure of our quality.

Our chronic problem was lack of size. Our two tallest men, Monk Meyer and Cup Weber, stood only about six feet two, and Cup was so frail that he got knocked about badly under the basket. Monk Meyer was an engaging country vulgarian who had come to town from the coal mining hills of eastern Kentucky. He was so entertaining that on road trips players were offered a choice between the car with a radio and the car with Monk. He was a good-looking rosy blond, muscular and strong and by no means slow afoot, a good shooter and a powerful rebounder; but still he was constantly being overmatched against men several inches taller. Western Kentucky, for example, had a center named Red McCrocklin who stood six feet six, a size that seemed to us grotesque. We assumed that McCrocklin must be a flat-footed goon—until we played against him and found him fast and graceful. But I still don't understand where all the big men have come from in the last few years, the hundreds of finely coordinated players of six and half to seven feet tall one now sees in college and professional basketball. They seem like a mutation in the race.

With the virtual elimination of the center jump and the invention of the fast-break offense, the tempo of the game was speeding up and scores were beginning to rise, but the basic style of play continued rather conservative and deliberate. A few teams like Western Kentucky were beginning to cut loose with jump shots and long flying one-handers, and whereas we considered such tactics vulgar and exhibitionistic, we had to admit they were hell to defend against and they scored a lot of points. Most of our games were with small college teams in Kentucky and we did reasonably well against teams such as Georgetown, Centre, Transylvania, and Eastern Kentucky; but Western was always a powerhouse and usually beat us badly. Laurie Apitz was ambitious and he overmatched us against teams like Bradley Tech, Cincinnati, and Indiana University who probably took us on as a breather. Bradley, his *beau ideal,* beat us by something like forty points, while Apitz salivated at their power and finesse.

For some reason I seemed to play better against the best teams, and I remember scoring respectably against Indiana and Western. But I was no star, only a mediocre player on a mediocre team. I lost my starting position for a time after a queer little confrontation with Apitz that I suppose was characteristic of both of us. We went to the locker room at the half, lagging in a game we should have been winning, and as we sat about, sweaty and exhausted, Apitz mounted a long rant denouncing our ineptness and lack of effort. He snarled at each of us in turn, demanding a mea culpa and a vow to fight to the death. When he got to me I remained silent and refused to grant either the confession or the vow. His whole exhibition seemed to me childish and unfair: we had played badly but not for lack of trying. Apitz was furious at me and benched me for the rest of the game, and he used me only as a substitute for the next several games. I was hurt but unrepentant.

Jane Davidson and I were drawing closer during this year, and that meant that Virginia Austin and I were moving slowly apart with confusion and sadness. I still saw Virginia for at least one or two evenings a week, for our routine movie or necking session at Shawnee Park, and those were still warm occasions, for I liked her very much. But I had begun to see that I was treating her badly, using her in this way when I cared less seriously for her than she cared for me. She could sense my slow withdrawing, and she knew I was seeing other girls at the university, and while she made no complaint I could see that in her quiet way she felt hurt and insulted. Virginia was a straight, simple person with a great deal of dignity. There was one painful, comic-pathetic day when she came out to the university library, totally alien territory to her, and posted herself at a table in the main reading room, pretending to read but obviously determined to see for herself what was happening to her love. All unworthy, I talked to her with a mixture of amusement, pity, admiration, and shame. She was the most impressive person in the room, the one with the wholly serious errand.

But Jane and I were together more or less constantly—taking many of the same courses with Hassold, Bier, and Webster, studying together in the library, walking down to Brooks's for lunch. I often took Jane and her twin sister Ruth to free or inexpensive campus plays or musical events or a football or baseball game. It was very pleasant to loll about in a round of friends in the sunny grass along the third-base line, fielding an occasional foul ball. I had been out to the Davidsons' house on Castlewood Avenue, overlooking Tyler Park, fairly often and had got to know the twins' parents, Morris and Frances Davidson, and their grandmother, Mrs. Jennie Coleman, who had lived with the family for many years. We sometimes got up simple evening parties that included Jessie McCracken, the pretty little dark bird-girl, and Julian who was pursuing Jessie in his opportunistic, uncommitted fashion. Jessie was also being courted by a sober-sided Louisville boy named S. O. Newman, or "So," and she dropped hints that she had a serious beau back in Nashville named Bill Booth. (It was he who came to claim her in a couple of years, and they were married and settled in Nashville.) Our noisy gatherings must have been a trial to the senior Davidsons, but I am sure they were glad to see their girls forming a circle of steady friends. The twins were excellent company, brainy and gay, but they had grown up as ugly ducklings, and their parents must have wondered if they would ever attract any male friends. I was not a very glossy prospect, fiscally, as a son-in-law, but I suppose I was a good deal better than nothing, being reasonably presentable and apparently honorable. Of course it was awkward to have twin girls to dispose of and only one hesitantly manifesting suitor.

The Davidson twins knew Buddy, of course, from casual meetings about the university, where he was very busy with his music and related studies in languages, but they had never met my younger brother Paul, and it occurred to me that I ought to do something about that. Paul was now a schoolboy of about thirteen or fourteen, looking promising. He was gay and bright, growing tall and athletic, particularly at tennis, with fair skin, blue eyes, and lightly curling dark blond hair, all beginning to attract attention from the girls. One day I packed him into our old car and drove out to the Davidsons' in Castlewood. When we arrived both of us suffered a failure of nerve, and I went in by myself. When Frances Davidson realized that Paul was waiting in the car she insisted on going out to talk to him. When she came back to the house she was fairly giggling with girlish pleasure. "Why Ben," she said, "he's cute as a button. Go out and bring him in." I did so, still with misgivings. He was given a cold drink of some kind and installed in Morris Davidson's big armchair. There he sat straight upright and delivered to us all an impromptu lecture on his current work in social studies, something to do with European history, all very circumstantial and accomplished, after which he chatted easily with the twins and their mother. They were charmed with him, and the occasion had turned into a great success.

Jane and I were pulled quickly closer that spring, in a painful and mystifying way, by a strange illness that attacked her—a major nervous crisis, which I learned was a recurrence of trouble she had had over several years, taking the form of a frightening general tension of mind and body barely short of hysteria. She could not eat or sleep or read or think, she could only suffer. She who had always been plump and cheerful was suddenly thin and sallow and weepy. She shook all over with chills and fearfulness, and she seemed to need to be held and comforted like a baby. I spent many hours with her, baffled but willing, doing what I could. Gradually, after several weeks, the tension began to pass and she slowly recovered her confidence and cheerfulness. In the process our relationship had begun to feel fatally domestic.

That summer the athletic department got me a job at the Adler-Royal Manufacturing Company, which was situated within walking distance, a mile or so from our old building on Thirty-fourth Street. Adler's main product was wooden radio cabinets, most of which seemed to be going to Sears Roebuck to house Silvertones. At our factory the cabinets were cut out from the raw wood, shaped, assembled, finished and shipped off to various points where their works would be installed. As a newcomer and presumably temporary, I stood at the bottom of the wage scale, and that was very low indeed. I was made a "trucker" in the "Rub Room," and my job was in many ways similar to my old one at Louisville Chair, though considerably simpler. Here again I was dealing with pieces of furniture at the end of fabrication, preparatory to shipping. At the chair factory nobody had ever heard of anything so fancy as a hand-rubbed finish, but here was a whole department that did nothing else. On the whole I was impressed with the quality of the product, and once again I got fascinated with the technical process, sensuously engaged with the handling of the wood. We dealt with mahogany-veneered cabinets in every size from small table models to big floor-model consoles with hinged tops. I functioned simply as a heavy-errand boy and general mover-about.

When the cabinets came from the drying room, each swinging in a cradle hung from an overhead conveyor track, and each glaring vulgarly in a coat of fresh lacquer, I lifted them off and pushed them into rows in a big open room to harden. Later I would push them into the next big room where the rubbers labored to civilize the high gloss of the lacquer. It was hard, dull, painstaking work, rubbing away all day with pads of rags and burlap dipped in pumice and various oily pastes until the finish had been tamed to the right point between glare and dullness. My basic job was to keep the cabinets moving about the floor, to the right persons in the right order. From the rubbers the cabinets went to the cleaners, women who wiped off the muck, then to the polishers, and from them to Louie, the foreman who doubled as inspector. He either passed the cabinet as satisfactory, returned it to the rubber for more work, or consigned it to a finish-patcher for a tricky minor repair. The patchers were skilled men who worked to mask any imperfections in the skin of the wood, using small heated spatulate knives that they applied to sticks of hard shellac of various shades. They would drip the stuff carefully into the wound, smooth it to match the surrounding surface, and then paint on a false grain to fill out the interrupted pattern of the real wood. The patch would be buffed and toned in so as to be undetectable; but sometimes a big patch would have to be sprayed with a fresh coat of lacquer and sent back for spot-rubbing. Utterly fascinating. When cabinets were all done I pushed them to the back corner of the room where the floor was pierced by a conveyor of clattering wooden slats, and hoisted each cabinet onto the padded cleats, periodically appearing, to travel to the floor below for shipment.

As in my other factory job, I found myself deeply interested not only in the processes but in the people around me, their tough gaiety and durability, their skill and instinct for craftsmanship, adding up to a kind of intuitive integrity, simple and unrationalized but very impressive. Why bother to do such dull hard things so well? The rubber's or even the patcher's work was not nearly so complex or interesting as the upholsterer's, or so satisfyingly visible in its results, yet these men managed to work with pride and style. It was their way of staying sane—that and the endless chat and banter that went on alongside the labor. My simple job was peripatetic by definition, and I was on the go all the time from one workman's bench to another. My situation was peculiar in other ways as well, being low and temporary; and there was also the problem of my "superior" education and social class—notwithstanding the fact that every man in the room was eating better at home than I was. None of this kept us from being friends, though our portion of the room's banter was carried on in rather different terms and tones. I liked these people and was pleased that they seemed to like me, and I tried to work as honorably at my low task as they worked at theirs. When I happened to see a personnel report that Louie was turning in at the end of the summer, I was proud to find myself described as "best trucker that ever was in rub room." Hardly imposing as a classification; but I had never been called the best of anything before.

Our foreman Louie felt that as a trucker I was wasting my talents and I ought to move toward higher things, beginning with the next stage of learning to be a rubber. But the hard repetitive dullness of the task repelled me, and I argued that in any case I was only at Adler's temporarily and there was no point in acting as if I were going to make a career of it. But when September came it was clear that the family was again dragging the bottom of our chronically low economic orbit, that we could not do without my wages and I could not hope to go back to college. God knows what we had been eating on for the past two years. So all through the fall and into the winter of 1940 I kept on with the job at the factory and the half-hour walk at either end of the day, no longer comforted by the thought that I would soon be going to classes and playing basketball again. It was a gloomy time. I wondered if I would ever be able to finish an education and find some hopeful shape for my life.

Then I heard from Jane Davidson that Bill Hall, the father of her friend Stacy Hall, was assembling a small sales crew at the dairy where he was sales manager and would put me on, and Buddy, too, if we wanted to have a crack at it. The logic of the scheme was that the members of the crew would solicit house to house for new customers for home delivery, in the process preparing themselves to take over delivery routes of their own, peeling off one by one as routes fell open. The sales crewmen were paid a small, barely decent weekly wage, but the real milkman's pay on a commission basis was said to be pretty good. Buddy and I liked the thought of working together, and we had no better prospects of any kind, so we decided to give the thing a try.

SEVEN

Works and Days

Fenley's Model Dairy was one of a half-dozen small dairies in Louisville, most of them creations of a single family who had begun as large dairy farmers and then decided to institutionalize themselves with a commercial plant in the city. The Fenley family still operated a big farm south of town, but that produced only a small part of the dairy's requirements, which were filled out by purchases from all comers. The company tacitly encouraged the fiction that it was a farm-to-you operation, the product moving from a model farm to a model city plant and thence to the home; but it was long since the case had been that simple or pure. The whole operation had grown more casual and a bit run-down over the years. In fact the bottling plant at Sixth and Hill and the huddle of little buildings around it had got downright shabby, a model only of a seedy workaday persistence, and one hoped one's customers would never see it. The company was now in the hands of R. B. Fenley and his sister Consuela, Mrs. Geiser, a tall fat flushed hectoring woman, very nasty. Mr. Fenley too was formidable, but in a more tolerable and civilized way; a big blocky middle-aged man with much of the countryman about him—quiet, concentrated, single-minded, with some tendency to the kind of bullying that comes in part from shyness and a submerged sensitiveness that he did not know how to deal with.

Bill Hall, the sales manager, when we met him, turned out to be a tall good-looking dandy with black hair and snapping black eyes. He dressed with an elegance out of all proportion to the modesty of his enterprise, his expensive brown scotch-grain brogues being especially noteworthy. He was a chatty, humorous, even-tempered man, very easy to like. Along with three other young men, my older brother Isaac (Buddy) and I joined Mr. Hall for a few days of training before being loosed on the streets. I have forgotten the others except for Eddie Farmer, a short blond bespectacled citified country boy of a type familiar to me, a folksy, droll, unscrupulous country smoothie. The six of us met in a tacky bare little former bedroom of a house next door to the dairy, a room where all the drivers did their book work at the end of the day, furnished only with a table and chairs and a big blackboard on which was posted a running record of the performance of all the routes, arranged in a comparative and competitive structure. After a day or two of rambling study of the chemistry of milk and its processing, we got down to our basic sales matter. Our problem was to persuade housewives to take their milk from our drivers rather than buying it at the store where they could save a penny a quart, or to take it from Fenley's rather than from one of a score of competing dairies. At that time home deliveries were being made every day, or rather night, between midnight and breakfast time, so we were to bear down on the steadiness and flexibility and general convenience of having a whole range of fresh dairy products brought to the doorstep to begin the day.

Mr. Fenley's dairy had been a "model" one in the sense that it had been the first to introduce a couple of authentic innovations: homogenized milk, and the paraffined paper "Pure-Pak" cartons on which we had a monopoly for the moment. Neither of these novelties had then swept the field, as they did later. People tended to judge the "richness" of the milk by the depth of the cream line on the bottle, and many people liked to be able to pour off the top of the milk for coffee or cereal. With homogenized milk there was no top cream to pour off and no way to judge quality by the look of the uniformly white milk. The Pure-Pak cartons were light and space-saving and disposable, eliminating the chore of washing and returning bottles, but they had disadvantages: occasionally one developed a leak that created a mess; being opaque they did not allow one to inspect cream line or color; the air space at the top of the carton tended to jostle and stir up the cream; a good many people objected to juxtaposing milk to paper, even with a paraffin coating—which sometimes unhappily flaked a bit and left a deposit of chips that looked too much like bits of glass. So we salesmen had to learn how to emphasize the advantages of our novelties and to talk down their shortcomings. At the same time Fenley's had had to keep among its options the old-fashioned staple item, cream-top milk in a glass quart bottle, and on that we had a truly admirable gimmick—on top of the usual cardboard plug cap, a hood cap of heavy waxed paper that came well down over the top of the bottle, where it was caught and crimped tightly under the lip by a loop of stainless steel wire that was spot-welded and chopped off with a short dangling end as a pull for opening the contraption. All in all we could feel that we really did have a good product to offer—of high quality, attractively packaged, and interestingly varied.

For several days in our shabby overheated upstairs room we discussed and practiced our strategy for countering the classic reluctants we would meet: the housewife who preferred to shop at the store and save her penny, the women who did not "want to run up bills," the women who felt an old loyalty to another dairy or another milkman—respectable positions to all of which we could offer attractive alternatives, if we could get inside the house and turn on our charm and powers of persuasion. For that part of the problem we had a simple and ingenious strategy: we would come bearing gifts. When our knock was answered by the woman of the house we would say, with a big smile: "Good morning! I'm from Fenley's Model Dairy and I've brought you a present"—holding up a gleaming quart bottle of our cream-top milk. When the woman reached for the bottle with a smile of her own, we would ask permission to step in and tell her briefly about the peculiar virtues of the milk. Having shown her eagerness to accept the gift, she found it awkward to refuse admittance. Once inside we asked to be shown to the kitchen where we tried to get the woman seated at her table in a relaxed and confidential mood, in which we sounded her delicately as to how much milk her family ordinarily used, where they got it, and so on, after which we knew what line to take and in fact whether we stood much chance of success. Then we would extol in general terms the richness of taste and texture and the high nutritive value of our milk, a consequence of the "controlled feeding program" on our supplying farms.

All of this was by way of preparation for our moment of drama: we would whip the cream *off the top of the milk* (this was the real reason why we needed to be in the kitchen). We were carrying with us, as nonchalantly as possible, a pint glass bowl, a low-geared rotary hand beater with a flat serrated blade, and an ingenious "cream lifter," a little aluminum cylinder about five inches long with a simple float valve. The housewife was usually dazzled by this notion, accustomed to thinking of whipped cream as luxurious and costly, and not realizing that the top of any bottle of standard milk can be whipped under the right conditions: the trick is to see that the milk is not stirred up at all, to take the very top, and to see that everything is cold—the milk, the lifter, the bowl, the beater. We opened our bottle, pausing to praise the seal-hood cap, dipped in our little lifter which filled magically from the bottom, tipped the cream into our glass bowl, and then with an unspoken abracadabra whanged away with our beater. In about a minute we would have a thoroughly usable bowl of stiff whipped cream, which we would contemplate with admiration before scraping it into the housewife's own bowl and putting it into her refrigerator. Then we would ask permission to rinse our equipment at her sink, after which we would turn around and start really boring in for an order for regular home delivery of Fenley's Model Dairy products—so various, so delectable.

Finally we had to brave the street, and I know Buddy and I were both a little terrified, being shy young men far removed from high-pressure types. The crew worked out of an old black Buick sedan, a Fenley castoff. We would pick up our tools, ice down a couple of cases of milk in the trunk, and with Bill Hall at the wheel set out for a neighborhood of his choice. At first, to build up our confidence, he chose neighborhoods where he thought we might find a ready welcome and some quick success. We quickly began to see into the economics of the case: the people who were easiest to sell were those who were least able to pay their bills; the good credit risks were the hardest to sell. I am afraid it was literally true that one could go into one of the city housing projects for Negroes and write one order after another. The black people found it hard to say no to a white man; they preferred to give the order and then find their own intricate ways of evading or exploiting the consequences. They had had to work out their own devices for surviving in a white economy. On the other hand you could spend a whole day going from house to house in the Highlands without a single success; one saw only servants or women who were rarely rude but tended to pride themselves on their imperviousness. We tended therefore to concentrate on middle-class neighborhoods, where we would get a fair number of new customers who could be trusted to stick and to pay their bills. I learned now for the first time of the existence in the city of a central credit-rating bureau where the bill-paying habits of citizens were a matter of record. (I shuddered to think what they would have to say about the Reids.) Each new customer we signed up was screened for a credit rating which was then given as a permanent instruction to the milkman on the route, authorizing bills ordinarily for a week, two weeks, or a month. People who were notorious nonpayers would be marked *cash only;* if the route man chose to give them credit he was held liable for the consequences.

Bill Hall would park the Buick and we would sit for a few minutes plotting our strategy for the neighborhood. We must have looked like gangsters in the big black car full of smoke. Being at once bored and edgy, we all smoked a good deal, and Eddie Farmer was addicted to a cheap pipe tobacco called Model that tended to turn my stomach in my queasy state. Using a city directory, Bill would assign each of us to a house and give us the name of the family supposedly living there; it eased one's way if one could address the housewife by name when she answered the door. We soon learned that the directory was only half reliable, and we formed the habit of asking the name of the woman next door at the end of each pitch. A presentation might last anywhere from five minutes to an hour, depending on one's reception and the housewife's loquaciousness, which was sometimes staggering. Many families used so little milk that the whole question was moot, and we tried to get out of such places in a hurry. The ideal prospect was the woman who used three or four quarts of milk a day and had to carry it home from the store. It was much harder, naturally, to deal with the woman who was a contented customer of another dairy, though it was heartening for the future to see how loyal she was to "my milkman." An interview might end with an outright acceptance or an outright rejection, but more commonly the end was inconclusive. The woman would promise to "think it over," or she might promise to "call in" her decision by telephone; if we thought she was a real prospect we would ask permission to have the route man call by and see if they could come to an agreement. The commonest ploy of all was to say that she would have to consult her husband, often referred to simply as "him": "I'll have to ask him." Then we would try a cajoling appeal to matronly pride: "Oh come on now, you make those decisions yourself, don't you?"

So it went on, day after day, and longer for me than for anybody else. One by one the other amateur salesmen ("Salesman Sam," we called each other, after a contemporary comic strip character) dropped away or were assigned to home delivery routes that fell open. Buddy was given a not very desirable route on the edge of the downtown business section, where there was much transiency among his customers and many apartment-house stairs to climb. I was led to suppose that as an educated gent with good manners I was being saved for a classy route in the Highlands (but hadn't Buddy had the same qualifications?). One day Mr. Fenley took me aside and asked me if I wanted to train for a post in the management of the company. I had begun to understand that self-made men of his type were likely to take a wistful, almost mystical view of the virtues and powers of "education"; they felt abashed in its presence. I had to explain to Mr. Fenley, as to the people at Adler's, that I would give him the best service I could but I had no ambition to climb in his hierarchy; I meant to go on with my education, and if I ever made a career I doubted that it would be in business. He was sorry but not surprised or offended: such freaks were to be expected among educated folk. Finally it got to the point where I was taking the Buick out by myself and working alone all day. I felt a little silly, though I rather enjoyed the privacy. After a couple of weeks of this, when it began to appear that no route in the Highlands was likely to fall open, I was assigned to the next vacancy, which turned out to be Route 22, and I got to know it very well over the next three years.

My route occupied a long rectangle roughly fifteen blocks by eight, bounded by Broadway on the north, Hill Street on the south, First Street on the west, and Shelby Street on the east—an elderly, somewhat shabby portion of the central city. The route had the advantage of lying with one corner within easy reach of the dairy at Sixth and Hill, so that there was no long trip to be made at the beginning and end of one's daily run. My population ranged from middle to lower middle to low class, with a small enclave of blacks at the northeast corner covering the same social range as the whites. The northwest corner, covering parts of First, Brook, Floyd, Jacob, Clay, and enclosing my old high school at Brook and Breckenridge, had once been an area of some elegance, with many tall red brick town houses, but it had all run downhill and the big houses were now cut up into flats or even into furnished rooms (one soon learned to beware of that itinerant crowd). But most of my people were modest sturdy folk living in single-family houses and working hard for a living.

The moment of truth had arrived now, when I had to start running the route and show I could handle all the parts of the task, and could survive its crazy time-scheme. My working day began about midnight, when I would have been going to bed under a saner regimen. Johnny, one of the veteran drivers who lived in our end of town, had offered me a regular ride, and he would toot once under our windows on Thirty-fourth Street and sit with his motor idling and his heater running while I, with three or four hours' sleep behind me, rolled out of bed, pulled on my clothes, and fumbled down the dark stairway. We would converse in grunts on the quarter-hour ride to the dairy, where I would back my little green-and-silver truck out of the dark garage and pull it into line behind the others waiting to load. Each driver ordered his day's supply at the end of the preceding day's work, on a long white sheet. In my turn I pulled my truck into the loading dock, stopping with the folding right-side door open and as close as possible to the bottom of the conveyor of rolling steel rods that ran out of the cold room.

I shouted out "Twenty-two," then stood on the running board to swing my load off the conveyor into the interior: the heavy cases holding twelve glass quarts, lighter wooden cases holding twelve Pure-Pak quarts, shallow cases holding half-pints of cream, the hinge-top wooden butter-box with butter, eggs, and cottage cheese. In addition to "homo" and "regular" (cream-top) milk, we carried chocolate milk, orangeade, tomato cocktail, and several kinds of buttermilk. The quantity of butter, eggs, and cream a driver carried was a pretty good indication of the class of patrons he served; my proportion of these costlier items was on the low side. One tried to stow one's load so that the most needed items were easiest to reach, and as one worked through a day's deliveries used cases would be pushed back and full ones pulled forward. It became a familiar and not unpleasant sort of rhythm. Our trucks were not refrigerated and in warm weather we carried big sacks of broken ice which we threw over the tops of the cases where they melted peacefully as the load itself melted. When the load was all aboard I pulled out and stopped at the curb to check my cases carefully against the order sheet; one was charged with everything on the sheet and every item had to be accounted for in some way every day.

Now I was ready for the day's undertaking. At this point most drivers stopped at an all-night restaurant somewhere for a hearty, grumpy break-fast before beginning deliveries. I tried that a few times, but I found that I had no real appetite at that hour and I decided to go straight to work and save the breakfast money. The Bible of the route was "the book," a sturdy leather loose-leaf spring binder in which each customer occupied a separate page. One could estimate a route's prosperity by the thickness of its book. Each customer's page was ruled off vertically by a list of the company's products and horizontally by the days of the month, so that each sheet held a month's record of everything delivered and accounts owed and paid. We "posted" the whole book at some time every day, to keep the record current. The book served also as a map of the route, and one rode with the book held by a spring clip to a slanted steel shelf projecting from the dashboard on the right, turning the pages as one moved from house to house, posting at once any variation, up or down, from the routine order, and clipping in notes that needed future attention.

I felt a distinct quality of phantasmagoria about those next several hours in the dark city, in which I ran straight through my whole route, more or less headlong. Because it was such a nuisance to keep opening and closing them I always rode with the folding doors open on both sides of the truck—except in the coldest weather when the milk would freeze inside the truck. Because I had to be able to read my book and see my load, I always rode with the dome light on. That meant that the whole interior of the truck would be reflected back from the dark windshield as the headlights bored ahead down a black street—the torso of my seated body, the open book on the shelf to my right, the tops of the cases ranging back in a plane behind me. The reflected tableau gave me the sensation of floating, as in a ghostly ship or perhaps a sleigh. In fact the constant accompanying jingle of the load, the cases against the steel floor, the bottles in their wire cradles in the cases, was much like the sound of trace chains on a horse's harness. The darkness and quietness of the city were spectral and strange. Especially at the beginning of a run, one felt already tired, yet not sleepy; nerves were tight and one's movements felt tense and badly coordinated, semispastic.

When I first began working at night I felt alone in the sleeping city, an abandoned world. Then I began to see that there was a whole night world with a small whole society: night-shift workers in factories, hotels, office buildings, hospitals, restaurants; cruising taxi drivers and policemen; wholesale truckers and other delivery men like myself; insomniacs, night women, drunks. But still one often moved about in the dark for hours without seeing another living creature—aside from the true citizens of the night, the cats and the rats. The numbers of rats in a large city are an incredible apparition. When I first saw them skittering back and forth across the street in my headlight beams I could hardly believe my eyes. One began to wonder if perhaps they were not the real proprietors of the place, letting us use their town in the daylight hours while they were sleeping off the night's debauch. In the old, rather shabby part of town where I delivered I saw rats everywhere, on streets, sidewalks, alleys, porches, stairways. When I first met one on a stairway I gave him fair quarter and stood aside to let him pass down. Night was cats' time too, and they prowled endlessly, after the rats and each other. I had a horror of running over a cat, and they were stupider about vehicles than dogs were. My eyes got very good at catching a flicker on the edge of vision that meant a cat about to make a dart into the street in front of me.

As I had anticipated my new job I had told myself that so much privacy would give me a lot of time to think about my writing and I would plan out stories and poems. But I soon found it didn't work that way; you really had to keep your mind on what you were doing, essentially simple as that was. One soon memorized the basic route, the sequence of customers and their standing orders, and felt that one could easily run the whole route without ever opening the leather book. But it was a foolish thing to do, for customers and their orders did not hold still but kept moving up or down or sideways, and unless you concentrated on the task you were soon making mistakes that cost you labor and ill will and ultimately cash. Out of personal pride and because the family needed money, I wanted to do a good job, and I found I took a keen quiet pleasure in doing it well, with care and some style. As Thoreau says, there is an aesthetics in all things. So I read my book, laid out each customer's probable order in the hand carrier on top of the butter box, and posted any variation at once on her page. That way I could let the mind and the eye wander a bit in the intervals of driving, and I did occasionally come up with an idea or a detail that I could use in writing.

The fact that the job involved healthful outdoor work was one of its satisfactions, and having resolved to treat it as a form of athletic training I literally ran the whole route, rather than walking my deliveries. Pulling up in front of a house I took my flashlight in my left hand and the customer's order in my right and set off at an easy lope, keeping the light in front of my feet and generally watching my step—especially after a few encounters with rats, and after tripping once on a curb and sprawling out on the sidewalk with two glass quarts in my hand; weeks after the cuts had healed a big square shard of glass worked its way out of the base of my thumb. I climbed a great many stairs, to second or third or fourth floors, and I always took those two or three at a time. One moved as quietly as possible so as not to disturb sleepers, and set down bottles and picked up empties without a clatter. Then the trot back to the truck, often to return with some item ordered by note; and so on through the remainder of the night. The sky would begin to go silver, then rose and gold, and soon there would be the visible, tentative sun. For me that was the sad, lonely time of night.

By six or so I was ordinarily through with deliveries and well ready for breakfast. Sometimes two or three drivers would arrange to meet at a common spot to eat and talk and work on their books. My favorite place was a German bakery and lunchroom on South Shelby Street, just off one corner of my route, where for a quarter one could get small fruit pies about six inches across, apple or cherry or peach, flaky and hot from the oven. One of those pies and a cup or two of coffee were my habitual breakfast. In the working-class neighborhood of my route it was safe to begin the second trip, devoted mainly to collecting bills, by eight o'clock, and so I dawdled a couple of hours over breakfast, smoking, yawning, chatting, posting my book, making out itemized bills for the day's collections.

As most of my people were wage-earning folk who got paid weekly or biweekly on Friday, and one needed to catch them before all the money got away, Saturday was my heavy collection day. But there were scattered collections on other days, and always errands to do. The collection call was the only time one saw most of one's customers, and one's only chance to create a personal and cordial relationship; so I always took along my hand carrier full of tasty items, hoping for extra sales, and always tried for a bit of friendly talk while making change and signing the receipt. Most women were either lonely or harassed, depending on their current domestic situation, and not sorry for a chance at a minute or two of unstrained conversation. If a customer showed signs of needing extra milk, one tried (if she was "good pay") to nudge up the standing order. Then one was always looking for new customers, and existing customers would sometimes lead you to new ones if they liked you. I did a good deal of cold soliciting at houses near my own customers, and it was a rare satisfaction when I could sign up several houses on a single block. One was always trying to thicken the texture of one's route, but that was not easy in the fierce state of competition. The best prospects of all were new people moving into a neighborhood, particularly those from out of town; those who were only moving within the city tended to bring their old loyalties along. I kept a sharp eye on empty houses and apartments, and bounced in with a big smile and a sample quart whenever I saw signs of new life; but like as not I would find a half-dozen other milkmen had been there before me. We were pretty good at our simple trade.

Except on Saturdays I was usually finished with my second trip before noon, and free to head back to the dairy, where I heaved my returns of empty cases and bottles and my unsold products into a conveyor window. It was a humiliating day when one had to return whole virgin cases of milk that had only been taken for a day-long ride about the city. Then I pulled on down the alley and gave the interior of the empty truck a good sluicing out with a hose to remove the day's dust, broken glass, and leaked milk. On a hot day things could get pretty ripe in there. After garaging the truck I still had an hour's work in the salesroom, posting collections in the route book, clipping in receipted bills, totaling collections on the adding machine and checking them against the actual money in my pocket, writing up "start" orders for new customers, if any, and finally filling out the long white order-sheet for the next day's round. Some days Bill Hall would be there for a bit of conversation and general bucking up about the state of things on one's route. We were good friends. When I had climbed the steps next door and turned in my money to the cashier and my route book to the bookkeeper, I was through with the day's work. It had been a long one—twelve hours or more.

Now I was tired and sleepy, especially if the previous night's sleep had been a short one, as was usually the case; but whatever civilized living and sleeping I was going to do had to be accomplished within the ten or twelve hours before Johnny's horn tooted under my window again. One of my motives in taking on the job at the dairy had been the notion that I could enroll in an afternoon or evening class or two at the university and so keep my education from lapsing altogether. I had already lost another whole semester while I was working at Adler's. Now, in the winter of 1940, thinking I had better begin rather tentatively and test possibilities, I enrolled in a single afternoon class, Ernest Hassold's course in literary criticism. That went all right and I got an A, so I felt my way was clear if I could stand the pace. In fact I was to spend the next three and a half years in part-time study before I finally got my degree in 1943 at the University of Louisville—four years late.

But the routine made a long hard day, particularly if I tried to crowd in an episode of a social or amorous sort. By the time I had made my way out to campus on class days, done a bit of necessary reading or writing, sat through the class itself, and traveled home by streetcar, it was time for supper and I felt both exhausted and abused. The obviously sensible thing was to go to bed right after supper, but I had trouble sleeping then, and I often persuaded myself I would be just as well off if I spent an hour or two with Jane or Virginia. The upshot of that was that I got by on three or four hours' sleep except on my day off, or on Sunday when I could quit at dawn after the first trip through the route, then I would turn in and sleep a solid ten or twelve hours that I drew upon all the rest of the week. On ordinary days I often fell asleep on the streetcar and rode past my stop, like a drunken man. Life at its lowest ebb was taking the long streetcar ride home from the Davidsons' at ten o'clock on a cold night, knowing that the horn would toot in two hours' time for another long day.

Much of the disorderliness and hardship of my schedule was relieved within a few months by a providential event. Awakened by a noise outside his door, a sleepy householder had taken a pistol from under his pillow and loosed off a shot; when he took a look he found he had shot the milkman. The wounded man survived, but only barely. Protests were made to the city fathers, who passed an ordinance prohibiting home delivery before seven o'clock in the morning. This made a radical improvement in our lives: we no longer had to stagger about in the dark and our workday became shorter and more efficient. In order to be loaded and ready to go at seven o'clock, we still had to roll out of bed in the small hours, but it was now more nearly possible to get a reasonable night's sleep. And in delivering by daylight we could make most of our collections as we went along; instead of the old double trip over the whole route, we could get by with a single slower trip and a few unavoidable calls back. Most drivers could now finish their work by early afternoon, and our lives had suddenly got far more civilized. We felt better physically and spiritually, less tired and gloomy and subterranean. At first we feared that we would lose many customers, but in fact nearly everyone accepted the new schedule peaceably and stayed loyal. The milkman who took the bullet had done us all a terrific favor.

Like all men who deal regularly with housewives in numbers, milkmen talked an elaborate folklore of seduction and conquest, stories of their successes with eager lonely women. Most of it was ritualistic, fantasy and tall tale, the kind of things with which men solace their drab lives. Things did occasionally happen. Eddie Farmer got besotted with a blowsy blonde on his route, wrecked two marriages, and lost his job when he ran himself into debt and started peculating. No doubt I was more naive than most men in sniffing out such opportunities, but I seemed to come across mighty few flirtatious women in my rounds. The main experience I had of this kind came as a shock and a mystery to me, and it very nearly went all the way. I was wary of taking on customers in rooming houses because such people were notorious for moving about without paying their bills; being unencumbered with possessions, they could pack and flit in an hour. But I had accepted an order from a young couple on the second floor of an old house on Gray Street, largely, I think, because the girl was so beautiful that it seemed worthwhile to run the credit risk just to look at her occasionally. I never saw the husband. The wife was very young, no more than twenty, of medium height with light blonde hair to her shoulders and eyes that were dark blue, almost violet. In face and body she was perfectly formed, perhaps the most naturally beautiful girl I had ever seen. One pictured her immediately in a Hollywood film, partly because of a certain coarseness of manner that felt real enough yet curiously superficial, not the essence of her nature but something overlaid, less professional than protective. It was the kind of hardness one often saw in girls from farms and small towns, like those I had known at the chair company and at Adler's, an earlier toughness and sensual wisdom than city girls developed.

She had told me to leave her milk inside the door of her room rather than exposed in the hallway. One summer morning as I climbed the stairs I saw her talking and laughing with another roomer, a squatty dark young woman, in the hallway, and I sensed that they were talking about me. I said good morning, and when I entered the room to set down her milk, she stepped in behind me and closed the door. Then she simply stood facing me, smiling, in her cotton robe and pink slippers, apparently inviting me to make something occur. I reached out and put my hands lightly on her shoulders, and when I did that the whole robe fell open and showed the whole of her, naked underneath. It was a classic male erotic fantasy, coming in full flesh out of nowhere, happening.

We must have stood there like that for ten minutes. Her body was so beautiful, so rich to me, that I wanted mainly to stare at it and to touch it only lightly. I ran my palms over her thrusting brown nipples, and held the back of my hand aganst the warm hollow at the bottom of her belly, against her amazing triangle of crisp blond hair. She stood quite still, her hands at her sides. "Why doesn't it feel this way when my old man does that?" she asked me, musingly. I said I didn't know, but I understood what she meant; it felt miraculous to me too. Later I remembered the lines from Canticles, "Thy belly is an heap of wheat, set about with lilies," and they made full sense to me for the first time.

The obvious next step was to the bed, which stood only a few feet away, and no doubt that was what she had somewhere in mind; but we never got there. I suppose the simple truth was that I was afraid—of her husband, of her prying friend out in the hall, of a hullaballoo that would get back to my boss and cost me my job, above all of my own timidity and inexperience. I had never been all the way to bed with a woman, and this seemed the wrong way to start. Anyway I liked the scene as it was so much that I did not want to mess about with it and change it into something else. Next time, maybe, I told myself. I kissed her, finally, in a chaste sort of way, and left with my empty bottles. She made no move to hold me back.

I drove off down the street feeling excited, confused, exalted. Something mysterious and rather beautiful had gone on in that shabby rented room, something pure, not dirty. What had she wanted from me, that simple, beautiful, knowing girl? Surely not mere sex, and surely not money. Admiration, perhaps, and whatever else it is that men and women want from each other—call it love. I knew I had stopped too soon, and not just in the sexual sense. I had failed her, offered her too little of what she needed. Next day when I delivered there was no one in the hall. I knocked lightly and entered her room. She was in bed, sound asleep, covered with a sheet. I sat on the edge of the bed and touched her shoulder. She opened her eyes and stared at me, gave me a slow, crooked smile, and turned over on her side with her back to me. I sat staring at her bare shoulder, where the skin looked grainy and dull. It was all over; I had been dismissed, and I left. Next time I called she had moved out, gone forever, leaving two weeks' bill unpaid. I paid it, sadly and with goodwill.

War had been creeping up on us for years, but about that I had been remarkably stupid and impercipient, with a schizoid will to suppress any real recognition of the fact that it was coming and it must involve people like me and my friends, in good health and of soldiering age. Politically I was dreamy and undeveloped. In Justus Bier and Gerhard Herz we had had among us walking examples of Hitler's intolerableness, and a younger fugitive, a talented pretty little German girl named Susi Steinitz, had become a close friend of mine at the university; yet I was able to hide from myself the general and personal implications of such presences. In a general sort of way I was an idealist and a pacifist, though I hardly bothered to give names to my vague condition of mind. I still dreamed of things like the League of Nations and disarmament conferences as common sense the wisdom of which the world must soon see. I remember sitting in the living room of my friend Tom Crume's house near the university as he tried to beat some political realities into my head. But I was so fuzzy-brained, and so preoccupied with mere survival for myself and the family, that I could hardly let such alien pragmatical matter through.

But now real war was on in Europe and the American draft had begun, and Buddy and I were caught in it at once. Buddy astonished me by saying that he had made up his mind to register as a conscientious objector. Even if one were not an adherent of one of "the historic peace churches" such as the Quakers, the Mennonites, and the Brethren, one could claim total exemption from military service on grounds of conscience based on "religious or philosophical" conviction, or one could accept service in a "noncombatant" role, ordinarily as a medical corpsman. Because we had never discussed the matter, I was surprised by his action and by his resolute way of taking it. He was such a quiet, counsel-keeping fellow that we hardly ever talked about anything aside from practical daily affairs such as how to keep bread on the table, or his voice lessons which he had kept up systematically since we went to work at the dairy. It was a shock to see that he had been thinking about the implications of the draft much longer and more seriously than I had. He vowed, moreover, that he would go all the way and demand complete exemption from military service. If he made his point and was given CO classification, he would be inducted into Civilian Public Service, which meant virtually unpaid labor of a simple, publicly useful sort comparable to that done by the old Civilian Conservation Corps during the depths of the Depression. (In fact many of the old CCC installations were reopened and used by CPS.)

More radical positions than Buddy's were possible and were adopted by a few young men: one could refuse even to register for the draft; or one could go through the process of registration and classification and then refuse induction into any service, even CPS. Either course meant a severe prison term. Buddy preferred to go through the established processes and deal with his fate as it developed. Every registrant who claimed conscientious objection had to prove his case to his own local draft board—or to higher authority on appeal. The local boards were usually composed of ordinary straight patriotic types, many of them Legionnaires, inexperienced in dealing with ethical scruples and crises of conscience, and inclined to be impatient or contemptuous—though if one belonged to one of the "peace" sects they were more or less constrained to grant the CO classification. Buddy's arguments were religious and even biblical, but they were not acceptably sectarian, and at root they were matters of the most deeply personal morality. He wanted to take a stand not against fascist militarism, manifestly wicked as that was, but against all militarism including our own—against the inclusive evil of war itself as a moral outrage committed by the whole race against God and man. Ultimately, somehow, he made his "philosophical" point and got his CO classification. I suspect it was managed less by persuasion than by stubbornness; both of us had got pretty good at a final digging in of the heels.

The draft situation made a crisis for us all, practically as well as philosophically. Dad was earning nothing. Paul was in high school, and Buddy and I were supporting the family between us. Mama was constantly unwell and in low spirits, and Buddy and I felt that one of us had to stay on hand to see that she took some kind of care of herself and saw a doctor occasionally; we had given up hope of getting her to a dentist. We knew we had a legitimate case for deferment on grounds of economic hardship, but we doubted that it would work for both of us, and we suspected that anyone who registered as a CO would be inducted swiftly, in a punitive spirit. That suspicion was confirmed by the quickness with which Buddy was whisked out of town after he was classified—sent off to a camp in the Blue Ridge Mountains where he would be working on forest trails for an "allowance" of fifteen dollars a month. He was the first CO to be drafted in Louisville, and the *Courier-Journal* printed a photograph of him looking handsome and cheerful in the midst of his rather embarrassed draft board. He had created a distinction they did not crave. At home the disappearance of his quiet, even, good-humored presence left us feeling vacant and lost.

My own situation remained complicated and I was troubled and confused. I felt that Buddy was right in his pacifist principles, and I admired the simplicity and nerve with which he had held on to them and stood up to scorn and incomprehension. I meant to follow his course, if I could make my nerve hold. At the same time I felt the powerful pull of the war excitement and the warm capillary attraction of the common urge drawing in most of my friends. Julian James was going into the Air Force, Bethel Ream into the Navy, Jess Cusick into the Army. If I took a pacifist stand, I told myself in the grand terms I had learned in talking about literature, I would be refusing the great comprehensive experience of my generation— negative and immoral as I felt that to be. Again it was easy to believe that this was one war in which the good guys and the bad guys were easy to distinguish, and right was on our side. But still I felt that was the short view, and morally unsound: I hated war worse than I hated Hitler. I feared it, too. When I really thought about it as an affair of actual flesh it scared me to death. But I was dreamy enough not to think in such real terms often. At the most fundamental level my feeling was simple: it was wrong to take a life, even an enemy's life in time of war. I simply could not see myself drawing any kind of trigger against any human being. A poem like Hardy's "The Man He Killed" shook me to the roots—it was so heart-breakingly, enragingly right. Then why not take the option of noncombatant service, probably in the medical corps, where one's function was to patch and preserve life? I thought a long time about that, and ended up feeling (as Buddy did) that that course was an evasion of the moral issue: in making oneself any part of the military machine one was helping the big trigger to be drawn.

Now I felt clearer in my head and my heart, but that was no help with the practical problem: who was going to feed the family and take care of Mama? With Buddy gone, my case for deferment as the family provider seemed incontrovertible. Yet I was convinced that if I declared myself outright as a CO the economic hardship would be ignored and I would be drafted on the spot. I felt trapped into a tricky strategy of playing for time. I would not declare my pacifism unless I was forced to do so by imminent induction, then I would fight my case. I did not let myself face the question of whether, if worst came to worst, I would go to prison rather than accept military service. My low scheme worked, in that it kept me out of the draft for two years and kept the family more or less solvent; but my flesh crept all that time at the thought of my own deviousness.

Shortly before Buddy was actually drafted, while he was still running his downtown milk route, we went through a disaster that did us no direct injury but shook us up badly. We had got hold of a second-hand Studebaker sedan that we drove back and forth to work, picking up another driver on the way. At about five o'clock of an early summer morning the three of us, with me at the wheel, were proceeding up Hill Street with only a few blocks to go to the dairy. We approached an intersection where the cross street came in from the right at an acute angle and vision was blocked by the buildings on the corner. I knew the crossing was dangerous, even at an hour when few cars were on the street, but I was driving fairly slowly and I had a green light on the traffic signal. We passed one of the little horse-drawn home delivery wagons that the Donaldson Baking Company had kept going in a half-antiquarian spirit; at the far left-hand corner of the intersection a wholesale bakery truck was parked and the driver was loading up his carrier at the back door. Suddenly, as we entered the intersection, there was a car in front of us, coming out of nowhere from the blind right side, and we plowed straight into the side of it; I hadn't even had time to touch the brake. The impact did not seem loud or violent, but it was enough to slew the other car around a quarter turn and into the back of the bakery truck, while we came to a stop in the middle of the crossing with our front end bashed in. For a moment one heard a sort of memory of breaking glass and a present hiss of venting steam; after that an awful bellowing scream from the back of the bakery truck. When we ran over there we found the young driver of the truck stretched out on the sidewalk with blood soaking the legs of his trousers, babbling and moaning, half dead with pain and shock. The spinning car had pinned him against the step at the back of his truck, crushing both his legs.

By now a crowd was gathering, many still in nightclothes, and we stood in their front, staring at our victim, feeling stunned and helpless and guilty. Somebody brought a pillow for the man's head. In a minute the police were there, directing traffic and asking questions, and soon an ambulance took away the moaning man. No one in either car had been injured. I talked to the driver of the horse-drawn wagon, and he agreed that the light at the corner had been in our favor. The driver of the car we had hit had been traveling with his wife and two young children and had been going through town in a half-daze after driving all night; he did not remember even seeing a traffic light. Nobody was "guilty"—only the design of modern life.

I dragged through the day with the load of that hurt man's suffering on my back, and in the late afternoon Buddy and I took a bus out to see him at the old-fashioned Catholic hospital, where a nun showed us to his room. He lay rolling his head, with his awful swollen livid legs propped up on pillows; but he was too heavily drugged to talk to us, or even to associate us with the mystery of his disaster. I felt like a figure in a Goya painting as we stood with the silent nun about the tortured body in the bare room with its pale distempered walls. My terror all day had been that he might lose a leg or even both legs—that they might even be gone when we got there. It never came to that, thank God, and the handsome blond young man would not even be obviously lame; but he would never walk like a young man again. For weeks after the accident I had to force myself into my truck every morning, and my leg muscles stayed in a spastic state, wanting to push the brake pedal through the floorboard. For me the stupefying thing about the episode had been the way it came out of nowhere, without cause and without control, making me the instrument of a terrible injury. I could feel neither guilty nor innocent, only corrupted.

In 1940, 1941, 1942 I pushed on with my part-time studies in afternoon and evening classes at the university, trying to get in as many credits as I could manage at any one time. Several times I had to take "Incompletes" because I could not finish writing assignments on time, but my teachers were patient with me, and I got things done eventually and my grades were good. I was still scorning everything not "modern," but Hassold forced me into a course in American language with David Maurer and one in the Romantics with Mary Burton, and I enjoyed them both and was grateful to him, after the fact. Everybody was trying to get me graduated. When I could not find a suitable course at a possible hour, Hassold or Webster or Bier gave me some sort of independent study to add to my credits. I was trying to keep up some original writing, in course or out, and I actually got a good deal of it done, stories and poems. Harvey Webster thought my stuff was publishable, or nearly so; and I was glad to believe him.

My milk route terminated at a point only a half a mile from campus, and when I had an afternoon class I would often park my truck on the edge of the campus, close the doors on my leftovers, and go on to class before checking in at the dairy—all with Mr. Fenley's permission, he still being a fan of education. I had long outgrown any embarrassment at wearing my uniform to class or at moving about in a general aura of sweat and cheese. I had also formed a habit of doing much of my writing, or my trying to write, in a bare round subterranean room that was really only a wide passageway under the front lobby of the Rotunda. A few people passed through but hardly anyone stopped, and I had the place mostly to myself in my peculiar hours of late afternoon and early evening. There was a Kafkaesque quality to the atmosphere of the place, with its tiled floors, yellow brick walls, stairways climbing two sides, the light at once dim and harsh, a dark corridor winding off to the right, that seemed to suit the buried phantasmagorical element in my own life. I had some strange visions there.

When I arrived I would first make the rounds of the sand jars on the ground floor to salvage any smokable cigarettes, then I would sit in my bare round room with a yellow legal pad on my knee and muse till something came or time was used up. One night the room and my mood there brought me a little German expressionist play, in which everything turned into literal corridors of the mind and heart, along which characters pursuing love moved and spoke a stiff ritualistic rhetoric. When I had finished it, the stage directions far outweighed the dialogue in the text. I called the little play "The Fourth Room." I liked it, and so did Webster, though neither of us quite knew what it meant. It occurred to me that it might stand a chance in the New Directions annual volume of "experimental" writing, and I sent if off to them. James Laughlin wrote back a kind note accepting the queer piece, it was printed, and I was actually paid—something on the order of ten dollars. I was a published writer. It made no difference, of course, except that I thought a little better of myself: I felt a distinguished if superannuated undergraduate. In all of my education from now on I felt elderly, out of phase.

I went on with the milk route, being called in periodically by my draft board, who grumbled but continued my deferment. Buddy wrote us cheerful letters from his work camp that surprised us by their chatty articulateness. Jim Read, our friend and history teacher at the university, had now married Sue Morton's older sister Henrietta, or "Henri," a lovely tall quiet blonde girl, and Jim too, as a Quaker, had registered as a CO and was expecting to be inducted at any time. His pacifism was not popular with the Morton family, whose only son Edward was a naval officer, and it induced nasty comments around the university, mostly sotto voce.

My stubborn unromantic love life had also gone on more or less as usual, divided between Virginia and Jane, with Jane pulling out ahead. I liked Virginia no less than before, but I knew I was not going to marry her, and I felt it was cruel of me to keep her dangling in hope. Jane had been graduated from the university, on schedule and with high honors, in June 1941. I told Virginia goodby with a wrench and many thanks, and she forgave me, bitterly. As I could not afford an engagement ring, Jane bought one herself, a zircon that made a reasonable facsimile. One day I drove my truck in to Fourth Street to meet Jane and her mother to pick out a plain gold wedding band. Mrs. Davidson seemed to want to make sure that I took at least one step that had a look of irreversibility. About that time I wrote a mannered, sentimentally bitter story that I called "In Place of Splendor," not realizing that the title was an unconscious recollection of the title of a published novel. My story rested on a self-pitying sense of deprivation, the drying and narrowing feeling of settling on one woman at last; resigning myself to monogamy, taking sad leave in the mind of all the girls I had been in love with, one by one, ending with Virginia. Very Hemingway. This time it was Jane who had to forgive me. On Harvey Webster's advice I sent the story to the agents Russell and Volkening, and they sold it to the *American Mercury* for a hundred dollars—big money by my standards.

Jane and I were married in the chapel of the Presbyterian Theological Seminary on Broadway on a stifling midsummer afternoon. My father conducted the ceremony and had a wonderful time with the whole thing. Jane's twin sister Ruth was maid of honor, and Hal Maynor came down from Lexington where he was doing graduate work in metallurgy to be my best man. Little Harry Cohen and Jess Cusick, both in heavy army uniforms, served as ushers along with Bob Lotspeich. Of the occasion I remember mainly the awful heat and the way I perspired. I swam in sweat from head to foot, and I prayed to get out of the chapel before I dissolved into a disgraceful puddle. As I had no car, Jane's aunt and uncle, Helen and Carl Franke, had offered us their grey Buick sedan for the wedding and the honeymoon, and we lurched away from the curb in that, after I fumbled the starting of the unfamiliar car.

The Davidsons held the reception at their house on Castlewood. Using the presence of Mom and Dad with their temperance principles as an excuse, they hoped to keep the affair nonalcoholic, mainly because Carl Franke and liquor were a fatal combination. Morris Davidson spent a fair part of his life trying and failing to keep the two apart. The temperance scheme did not bother me, for I believe that at that time I had never tasted liquor and had no intention of doing so. But the scheme could not hold; too many men demanded a drink, and Morris had to open his supplies. Before long there was a little group of serious drinkers, including Harvey Webster and Jess Cusick, sitting and talking peacefully in the dark back garden. They were still there when Jane and I finally got away late in the evening. Hal Maynor was with us as we drove off in the Buick, to some people's evident amusement. The arrangement seemed reasonable enough to me: Hal needed a ride back to Lexington and we could take a long loop around that way en route to our country Shangri-la in Harrodsburg. In my barebones impecunious habits of thought, I had not planned on having a honeymoon at all. It was Jim Read who insisted that Jane and I must of course have *some* kind of trip, and he who had suggested the Beaumont Inn, in Abraham Lincoln and Daniel Boone country. Naturally I had never heard of the place; I never went anywhere.

It was midnight when we reached the handsome old red-brick Georgian inn and were admitted by a sleepy elderly black porter. Following him upstairs, we felt tired and young and wicked. Our beautiful big airy bedroom held two enormous canopied four-posters, but we decided that one was enough, and I soon tasted the luxury of going absolutely to bed with a naked woman. Jane was weepy with tension and exhaustion, but we remained friends and even got a few hours' sleep. In the morning the waiters began stuffing us with the inn's wonderful food, especially the rich dark country ham that I could not resist. Over the next two days, which was as far as our money would run, we passed the time between a daze and a doze, eating, sleeping, reading a little, walking heavily about the grounds and the town. I hated to admit that I was bored with the unfamiliar leisure. When I told the old waiter that we had to leave because we were running out of money, he gave me a big grave smile. "We'll trust you all," he said. "You got a good face."

I was in the middle of my single week's annual vacation from the dairy. Jane had found us an apartment in Crescent Hill, and we went back to do some work on that. It was a decent, awkward, rather gloomy place, the ground floor of a two-story white frame turn-of-the-century house. Its attractions were its cheapness and its situation, in Kennedy Court, a quiet shady street off Frankfort Avenue, where a trolley bus ran downtown, and only a couple of blocks from the Hassolds, with all of whom Jane was in love—Ernest and Rosalie and their two teenage children, Christy and Stefan. We furnished our rooms with tolerable castoffs from our families and a few secondhand pieces we had bought, and hung the walls with cheap reproductions of favorite paintings from Justus Bier's art history classes. Within our first week Jane invited Jim and Henri Read to dinner, and I suppose that was the night I first faced up to the fact that I had married the world's worst cook.

We had hoped the apartment would grow on us, but as time passed it only seemed darker and more awkward to live in. After a couple of months Jane started looking about for another place, and one day when I was home alone Rosalie Hassold came by and read me a lecture on the need to find more genteel quarters. She was visibly offended to find me sitting about with bare feet, as was my country habit, and I was offended by her offence and wondered if Jane had egged her on to interfere. Shortly Jane did find a larger, nicer apartment on South Birchwood, only a few doors away from the Hassolds' house. It was half of the ground floor of a sizable frame and stucco house, pleasant bright square rooms with white wood-work and hardwood floors. The landlord was the rather nasty ne'er-do-well brother of a friend of the Davidsons, and he lived upstairs with his half-crazy neurotic wife and their three unhappy children, including a little boy with a clumping heavy lame leg. The rent was twice what we paid on Kennedy Court, but that still came to only thirty-five dollars a month, so we decided to risk it, hoping to see little of the family upstairs.

I still had my mother and father and their place to support, and we would all be living hand to mouth, but there was nothing new in that. We ran on the thinnest of margins and were chronically nearly penniless. I remember one morning when we had exactly fifteen cents in the house; I had to start for work before daylight and Jane had to go downtown a couple of hours later. The fifteen cents would buy two bus tokens. The only way we could figure to manage it was to go together to the bus stop, where I would hop on and buy the tokens, wrap one in paper, and drop it out the window to Jane panting along in pursuit. That is what what we did. Poverty is often undignified. We were to spend large parts of four years in the apartment on Birchwood, through many vicissitudes.

Typically now I was taking two courses in a term at the university and I enjoyed them all, but it was hard to find time for reading and writing after my job and my classes every day. I usually sat up till midnight, then poor Jane would have the struggle of getting me out of bed and off to work at five in the morning. If I actually got moving I was all right for the day, but I had a nasty habit of falling back onto the bed after dressing, and sinking into a second deep sleep out of which she had to drag me, literally. When it became clear that I would finish 1943 just one course short of graduation requirements, it was Justus Bier who pointed out that I could get those credits by passing a special examination in a given subject matter. So he set up a special examination in modern art for me, I passed it with an A, and I was graduated in June 1943 "with honors in English and Humanities." Owing to deficiencies in classics and in the library, the university had been turned down for a Phi Beta Kappa charter, but both Jane and I were elected to the Woodcock Society, our parochial equivalent, and we were proud of that. Still, I felt a strong lurking suspicion that my teachers had been overrating me all along.

When I left the university in 1943, eight years after I entered, I was not only married but a father. Jane had returned to campus in 1941–42 to take the "education" courses needed for a Kentucky teacher's certificate, and to make a beginning on an M.A. in English. She had taught briefly in a junior high school in New Albany, just across the river from us in Indiana, but they had let her go when she told them she was pregnant; then she was fired for the same reason from the book department of Stewart's, downtown in Louisville. After that she hated the world until our baby daughter was born. Using Jane's first name and my second, we named her Jane Lawrence. I hoped she would be called Lawrence, for I liked the old southern custom of using family names as given names, for boys or girls, but everybody started calling her Laurie at once, and so she has remained ever since. She was a classic fair-skinned blue-eyed blonde, a chubby, healthy, happy child from the outset, and very pretty, or perhaps I should say handsome, for during the first couple of years while her hair was short she looked like a little boy.

Poor Morris Davidson had hoped hard for a boy. He had lived all his mature life in a house full of females—mother-in-law, wife, twin daughters, a wonderful black maid and cook, Hattie, and a portly pit bull named Jennie—and he used to say that he sometimes looked out the window to see if he could spy a male squirrel. Morris had inherited the presidency of his printing business downtown from his father, the founder. He had brought the company through the Depression by the narrowest of margins, by terrifically hard work, and by taking on a huge burden of personal debt. Now, when the business was paying its way again after a dozen exhausting years, he was looking for an heir to keep it going in the third generation. He had invited me into the company when it became clear that I was serious about Jane, but I had turned him down, as gently as I could. Once more I had to explain that I felt no talent for business and no drawing to it, that I meant to be a writer or a teacher—or more likely both, as I saw few signs in myself of the copiousness that makes a living for a writer.

Morris accepted Laurie's sex with humorous resignation, and was soon doting. Indeed all the Davidsons were crazy about her, and Jane's mother and her grandmother, Mrs. Coleman (she had been Jennie Lind Dick), immediately showed a possessiveness that left me worried and sore. I blamed Jane for submitting to it. It seemed to me exactly the kind of ingestive domination that had kept Jane and Ruth from growing up and standing on their own. Of course it had its convenient side for us; when the baby was in the Davidsons' hands Jane and I were freer to move about, to go to a movie, or to see friends, which was the extent of our social life. But it irritated me to see that whereas Frances itched to get her hands on Laurie, she always acted as if it were a great favor and a great personal sacrifice if she kept the child for an afternoon. Laurie herself loved her grandparents and her great-grandmother, but with a humorousness and sanity remarkable in a small child; she had a mind of her own, and she was soon sorting things out in a thoroughly reasonable way, staying serene even amid the quarrelsomeness of daily life in the Davidson house. The three elders were strong-minded and intolerant, about as stubborn as people can be. They quarreled violently and more or less constantly, and I found them a shock, especially at mealtimes, which were often spectacular. My family had been gentler and quieter, even in its quarrels, especially in the last few years when illness and resignation had diminished Mama's early fire.

Mrs. Coleman at this time was an indomitable old lady of about seventy. She had divorced her husband, whose name had originally been Kohlmann, after a few years of marriage, and had supported herself and her only child by working as a bookkeeper in the office of the Louisville Cement Company. In fact she still held her job there, preparing payrolls, and the company was forced virtually to derrick her out finally a few years later. She never gave up anything willingly. She was very short and quite fat, and somewhat crippled with arthritis in her hands and feet. She

walked with a sort of quick flat-footed penguin shuffle that made a pecu-
liarly characteristic and irritating noise in the Davidson house. She still
rode the little Chestnut Street car to and from work, a sort of Toonerville
Trolley that made its loop at the foot of Castlewood a quarter of a mile from
the house. Late every afternoon one would see her stumping with heavy
briskness, in her long black clothes and no-nonsense hat and scornfully
mastering her ivory-handled cane, down the back walk to the house.

In the house she was never not busy. Except when there was company
and she came out to the living room to be officially social, she was in her
bedroom reading or writing or figuring or playing cards with herself. She
kept meticulous accounts of her modest finances and spent many hours in
the week on her figures. Every evening about nine o'clock she would shuffle out to the kitchen and spend an hour squeezing fresh oranges to provide juice for the whole family. Then she would shuffle back to her room
for another hour with her figures and her Bible before the long bathroom
ritual that preceded her retirement for the night. She had a powerful sweet
tooth from which I often profited, and she always kept ice cream in the
refrigerator, a cake in the sideboard in the dining room, and a box of candy
in her bedroom, chocolates or the delicious rich Modjeska caramels with
marshmallow centers that were a specialty of Bauer's downtown on Fourth
Street.

As the twins were growing up they had spent at least as much time with
Mrs. Coleman as with their parents, and they loved her in a warm, humorous, long-suffering style. Until they were nearly grown she would read to
them by the hour as they sprawled on her bed, and at least once a week the
three of them would go downtown for lunch and a movie. Frances was lazy
enough to value her mother's possessiveness, but Morris resented it as an
alienation of his own intimacy with his children. Mrs. Coleman and her
daughter and her son-in-law were all in their way passionate, opinionated,
inflexible, violent people. Mrs. Coleman had lived with the Davidsons
throughout their marriage, and Morris had got in the habit of identifying
her with all his frustrations in business and in marriage, such as his wife's
sexual coldness and her otherwise general passionate negativism. He
would come home tired from business and drink several strong bourbon
highballs while reading the *Courier-Journal* and the *Times,* which he despised for their liberalism. By dinnertime he would be either resolutely

merry or in a sullen rage, his day's resentments swollen and ready to discharge. At the last minute Mrs. Coleman would come down the hallway with her heavy shuffle, and he would lay down the knife with which he had been expertly carving to hold her chair while she maneuvered painfully into position. She was a picky, fastidious eater who cut all her food into tiny bits, a habit that sometimes sent him into a crazy fury. I have seen him cut a thick slice of rare roast beef and then fling it from the fork the length of the table full into her face. Yet the three elders were linked by humor as much as by hatred, and I have seen all three of them roaring with laughter until they all had to wipe away tears. Mrs. Coleman lived to be ninety-six, by which time Morris was of course an old man himself, and it touched and amused the rest of us to see that it was he and not Frances that loved and took care of her in her last years, carrying her trays, wrapping her swollen joints, helping her back and forth to the bathroom.

My situation in the draft had been moving toward a point of no return. I was called in for another physical examination, classified I-A, meaning ready for immediate induction, and told that there would be no more "hardship" deferments. The time had come when I must either declare my pacifism or go for a soldier, so I wrote a letter to my board saying that I must refuse military service on grounds of conscience. Not surprisingly, the members of the board were furious and they refused to give me the CO classification. But I had a right to appeal, to present my case before an appointed officer, and I petitioned for such a hearing. The hearing officer, a Louisville attorney, was neither unimaginative nor unsympathetic, but he was properly skeptical. He wanted to make sure that my convictions were real, that they fell within the legal sense of "religious or philosophical," and that they had some personal history—were not merely a timely ruse for avoiding any sort of public obligation. I could surely show a generally religious background and training. The fact that my older brother had been serving as a CO since the first year of the draft was a point in my favor, implying a pacifist tradition in the family. In the hearing I argued my position in the simple stubborn terms that were the only ones I knew: I was not only an American but a citizen of the race at large; the racial enemy was not Germany or Japan but the toleration of war as a human instrument; holding life sacred, and seeing the enemy soldier as a prisoner of the war system like ourselves, I could not conceive of trying to take his life, or of sharing in a structure that had that end in view. The hearing officer invited me to submit testimony to the fact that I had held these views for some time, and I got Jim Read to write a corroborative letter.

My petition succeeded and I was reclassified as IV-E, making me officially a CO. I had escaped military service or prison, but I knew my induction into Civilian Public Service would be swift. I felt resigned, ready, and in some ways even eager to go: it would be an interesting change in my life, and I had never liked the feeling of being immune to the big general obligation of my generation. The thought of leaving Jane and Laurie, and of going into a celibate world for an indefinite period, made me sad and panicky; but those conditions would simply have to be endured. The problem of money was acute, of course, as I would be making nothing but the government allowance of fifteen dollars a month. Mama and Dad would have to go back to living on nothing a year, and Jane would have to find a job. Then who would take care of the baby? I foresaw Jane and Laurie installed with the Davidsons, and I knew that then Jane's mother and her grandmother would take charge of both their souls. Frances, particularly, had made it clear that she despised my pacifism, taking it as a personal embarrassment and affront, and I knew she would make Jane suffer for having brought a coward into the family. I pleaded with Jane to try to hold onto the Birchwood apartment, and thereby to her independence, but I could not tell her how she was to accomplish the feat.

As things worked out, Jim Read was inducted shortly before I was, and the fact that he was installed as deputy director of the CPS camp in Gatlinburg, Tennessee, where I was assigned made the prospect seem a good deal less lonely. I packed all my equipment, including the writing materials with which I hoped to make a bit of helpful money, into a huge brown duffel bag and boarded the bus for Gatlinburg on a morning in the early autumn of 1944. I was sad and more than a little frightened, but I had traveled so little in my life, not having set foot outside Kentucky since the Texas interval in early childhood, that even the ordinary daylong bus trip was exciting: I had never traveled alone, never seen Tennessee, never seen a mountain. I tried to think like a writer, storing up impressions.

EIGHT

Pastoral

T hough some attempt had been made to tart it up a bit as Park Service headquarters for Great Smoky Mountains National Park, Gatlinburg was still a rather sleazy little valley town at the foot of the hills. The CPS camp was situated a few miles east of town, an old CCC camp that had been dusted off for our use. It was a group of rough and ready low frame buildings arranged around a clearing in the woods: a long bunk house, a mess hall and kitchen, a barnlike recreation hall that enclosed an undersized basketball court, the director's house including the camp office, and several scattered outbuildings such as a carpenter's shop and a vehicle shed. Plain and plentiful meals were served at picnic-style tables with attached benches, made of heavy unfinished planks worn smooth by use and scrubbing. In the bunk house the sixty or seventy narrow beds were closely ranked down the two long sides of the building. The effect always made me think of a Civil War military hospital. There was no such thing as privacy. Details of everybody's biology, psychology, and economy hung out in general view.

All of this made a completely new way of life for me, and at first I found it exhilarating as well as tense and tiring. Aside from the novelty of it all, the major excitement came from the men themselves, so many of them and so various. The CO position was one that had to be reached by independent thinking or at least by stubborn conviction, and it brought together groups marked by strong personality and on the average by high intelligence that was usually original and often downright cranky. The Gatlinburg group came from all over the country, half of them rural, half urban, and probably about evenly divided between the "religious" and "philosophical" options recognized by the law. In age the men ranged mostly from twenty to thirty, with a few well into their thirties. The married men, perhaps a quarter of the group, could be recognized by their older, more sober, more worried look. By the time I arrived, comparatively late in the war, there were quite a few men who had been in CPS for as long as four years and had passed through several such camps as Gatlinburg, and among them one saw a certain hard stoical competence and a good deal of bitterness and cynicism, sometimes a sullen reclusiveness that seemed close to pathological, real sickness.

The "peace church" objectors were Quakers (Friends), Brethren, Mennonites, and Jehovah's Witnesses. The few Mennonites and Brethren were stolid hard-working farm fellows who had acted out of straight sectarian discipline and who were rarely troubled by an idea. The JW's, as we called them, took the position that they were all ministers by definition and entitled to appropriate consideration. They tended to be rather low-grade, marginally citified types, not only non-intellectual but anti-intellectual, fundamentalists who feared ideas and behaved with an often nasty defensiveness that amounted to a kind of hysteria. They were the hardest of my new mates to like; in fact nobody liked a JW but another JW, and they trusted nobody but themselves.

The Quakers were another and pleasanter matter. Though there was a much wider range of type among them than among the other sects, as a class they struck me as the nicest and most interesting people I had ever come across—bright, humorous, thoughtful, kind, able. They came from all over the country, California, the Middlewest, the South, but mostly from the Philadelphia area that included New York City and New Jersey, and these last were an especially attractive group, more sophisticated than I had been accustomed to know, even at the university. Most of these young eastern Quakers were products of Ivy League colleges or of such excellent small Quaker colleges as Haverford and Swarthmore, and I soon learned to envy them their education, more traditional and richer than mine; they simply knew more of solid stuff than I did. There were solemn or dull ones among them, but most of them wore their Quakerism very lightly, and as a group they were notable for nerve and energy and gaiety. They spoke their Quaker idiom with a humorous ironical deprecation that was not in the least irreverent. They referred to each other as "Quakes," and made every issue, great or small, a "concern." One of them said of a good meal: "That speaks to my condition." Another translated the popular song "Juke Box Saturday Night" as "Juke Box Seventh Day Eve." They were enchanting young fellows and I found my best friends among them.

For the most part the Quakers fitted in easily, as the other sectarians did not, with the numerous "philosophical" objectors in camp. They were equally thoughtful and knowledgeable, and in their gentler way equally sophisticated, worldly-wise but withal spiritual. You could tell the Quakers by their serene moral earnestness, a charitableness so natural that it seemed genetic. The "philosophers" included some fairly headlong characters, Marxists and anarchists and general activists and loud habitual naysayers. But these more secular types, many of whom refused to profess any religion, also included men of deep sweetness of nature who seemed actually to incarnate Christian pacifism. They also included some absolutely first-rate brains, authentic and able intellectuals. I am speaking now of my general experience of CPS men, not only the group at Gatlinburg.

The camp had its own work to do in the immediate neighborhood, but it also served as a staging area from which men went out in groups of six or eight to operate small subsidiary work camps, called "spike camps," in the mountains within a radius of twenty-five or thirty miles. The work of the home camp was routine maintenance of a part of the beautiful forested park, clearing hiking trails, repairing shelters, roads, culverts, bridges, guard rails, and so on. All the men in base camp or spike camps were on permanent standby duty as firefighters in the event that fire broke out in the woods anywhere within reach, and we were given some rudimentary training in the techniques involved. (In some of the western camps volunteers were trained as "smoke jumpers" to be dropped by parachute on the scene of a fire.) I was relieved that no fires occurred during my tenure; the films we were shown of forest fires struck me as pretty terrifying.

For my first week in camp I was assigned to the "rock crew" in an old quarry near camp, a purgatorial operation involving breaking huge stones into smaller ones for repairing walls. We got up at seven on the clear, chilly mornings and set off for the quarry after breakfast carrying sandwiches for lunch. It was hard, dull, frustrating work, and impossible to see as anything but pointless and punitive. One was bound to feel like a prisoner sentenced to hard labor. There were indeed rude skills involved, but they produced little result, and most of us could not learn them anyway. The foreman of the rock crew was a middle-aged local man named Rankin, tall, pale, rawboned, bitter-tongued, a classic Scotch-Irish type. He seethed with contempt for our pacifism and saw us all as cowards and shirkers; he liked to tell us about his two sons in the Marines. Scorning us, and scorning himself for consenting to direct us, he gloated silently over our ineptitude. One of us would flail away with the heavy sledge at a huge knobby stone for half an hour, striking sparks and releasing a few powdery shards. Then as he would pause to pant and sweat, Rankin would lounge over, take the hammer, give it one nonchalant swing at a mysteriously selected point, and the stone would fly into a dozen shapely portions. "Plumb ruint that rock," he would say, looking at the heap meditatively; then he would spit and go back to his lounging. None of us could learn the trick, and he preferred to see us labor to produce nothing rather than teach us his country mystery. After a week of this stupefying comedy, with no profit in it except to one's brute muscles, I was delighted when the rock crew abruptly became the bridge crew. We were to repair, sometimes to reconstruct, rustic bridges over streams and gullies crossed by a winding graveled mountain road.

We worked out of a dump truck, with simple tools, long-handled shovels, axes, crosscut saws, light sledgehammers with long handles that had a bit of whip in them. Rankin was still our foreman, and he did most of the tricky ax work himself. His skill in notching and shaping the heavy timbers was a sight to see. We would pull up to a bridge and pile out to give it a general inspection, looking for punkiness in the underpinnings, the floorboards, or the guardrails. Usually we had to replace only a few members, but sometimes the unsoundness was so general that Rankin would decide to do the whole thing over from scratch. I became a specialist at nailing in the oak flooring boards, heavy rough-sawn planks about three inches thick and anywhere from four to ten inches wide. The spikes were longer than railroad spikes and much thinner, really just enormous common nails about eight inches long and about the thickness of a lead pencil, with flat heads. I took a sensual pleasure in the big handsome nails and the potent, graceful hammer. I seemed to be the only man who could master the craft of driving the nails through the tough oak without bending them. If you knelt on the floorboards and tried to drive the nail with careful short strokes, you were sure to strike untrue and bend the nail; but I discovered, suddenly, that if you knelt only to start the nail, then stood up and flailed away with a full cocky overhead swing, the nail would travel straight through into the timber stringer underneath, and the whole operation turned into a physical and aesthetic pleasure. The stroke made me re-member the one I had seen railway repair men use when I was a child in Crestwood, as two or three men swung hammers in tandem, spiking the long steel rails into the crossties. Once or twice I saw even Rankin watch-ing me perform my art with a glint of approval.

There was variety and point in the bridge work, time passed much more quickly than in the absurd quarry, and everybody's spirits lifted sharply, even Rankin's. I wrote to Jane several times a week, trying to make my letters full and circumstantial, documents that I might come back to later and possibly turn into some sort of publishable account of the CPS life. I was a good deal happier with the camp life than I had been at first, though still sick for home and family, and tortured by sexual desire. I remember that in one especially horny interval I asked her to send me some clippings of pubic hair; she obliged, sweetly, without even commenting on the per-verseness of my whim.

After about a month on the bridges, I met one weekend the young crew from one of the spike camps, returned briefly to the base camp. Having talked with these fellows and found them especially lively and engaging, and learning that they were looking for a recruit, I decided at once to sign on with them. Their spike camp was situated at Big Creek, some thirty miles into the mountains across the North Carolina border. We made the trip that night, the most uncomfort-able journey of my life, riding on backless wooden benches in the rear of a canvas-covered dump truck over rutted winding gravel roads that gave us a terrific pounding. Big Creek camp turned out to be nothing but a pretty little clearing in the forest with a single low frame building that housed a kitchen–dining room and a bunk room large enough for us to rattle around in.

As most of these men have remained my good friends I had better intro-duce them in some detail. Basically they were a Haverford group, with outriders of whom I had just become one. Hubert Rohrer, a young CPS man from the Middlewest, was straw boss of the camp and tended to keep to himself, not really sharing in the strong central warmth of the group. Hubert did all the cooking, such as it was, and the necessary marketing and errand running, and he figured that satisfied his obligation to us and to Selective Service. He was a rawboned unimaginative cook and a penny-pincher, but though we complained bitterly about things like fatback bacon and powdered eggs and milk, he maintained that the budget he was allowed would permit nothing better. Hubert's streak of Calvinist sadism made him think we all had a bit of suffering coming to us, which he was pleased to administer. I would not be surprised to hear that he turned back the money he saved on our food to the base camp.

The Haverford College group numbered four, three splendid fellows and one cull. Oddly enough they were all about the same size, well-made athletic young men a shade under middle height. They were nearly of an age as well, twenty-one or twenty-two, making me about four years their senior. They did not make me feel my antiquity, or my oddity in being married, but welcomed me into their established intimacy. All were "birthright Friends," not "convinced Friends," as they called converts. The youngest and least attractive of the group, Phil Vail, was the only one who had not finished at Haverford. Phil was a spoiled-brat type, with lingering adolescent traits that got on everybody's nerves, though generally we tried not to embarrass him by pointing them out. Even his voice was irritating—precise, dogmatic, and adenoidal, with a thread of whine running through everything. He was lazy and self-indulgent, and though he lacked the nerve to be an outright malingerer, he took care to preempt that part of any task that required the least strenuous or least continuous exertion. He was childishly pretentious and boastful, but again he managed the matter so as to obscure his vanity from himself, dropping his boasts into the texture of ordinary narrative, so that we learned that his family scorned to burn anything but apple wood, and always stayed at Grosvenor House on their (evidently frequent) trips to London, as parts of standard domestic tales. After a time we took to calling him "The Grosvenor Kid," or, in direct address, simply "Grosvenor." Phil was a snob, but too unconsciously so to be really promising at it.

Bill Ambler was the quietest and I suppose the simplest man of the group. He was a chunky, muscular, powerful fellow, very quick on his feet and a fine strong worker. In college he had been a star in football and baseball. Bill, or "Willem" as we often called him perhaps in token of his Dutch look, had pale skin, long straight light-blond hair, snapping blue eyes, and a slightly crooked, shyly friendly smile. His academic interest had been in mathematics, and in later years he went back to Haverford to work in the administration and eventually became director of admissions. Words did not come easily to him, and in fact he talked very little. One felt kindness and generosity in him, and perfect straightness and integrity, not a false note anywhere. I liked him enormously, but never felt an easy closeness to him. It was hard to penetrate the reserve that followed from his shyness and inarticulateness. But one of the nicest people I ever knew.

The most charismatic figure, the most obviously vivid personality in camp, was Jerry Myers. Jerry had gone to Haverford from the Providence suburb of Cranston, where his father was a high school athletic coach, and Jerry had been a standout in track, baseball, and wrestling. But he was even better as a pure student, and he had made a brilliant record in philosophy, the field in which he had already made a beginning toward a Ph.D. at Brown before the draft caught him. Jerry's mind was absolutely first-rate, quick, incisive, tenacious. He was a man of many moods and a master of all of them. In fact there was an element of theater, if not of outright fabrication, in everything he did. With his long black Indian hair, clear skin, and bold beaky nose, Jerry was a good-looking fellow, and evidently very attractive to females. His sexual drive was insistent, unscrupulous, and efficient, and he had been a successful womanizer since puberty. He often entertained and tortured the rest of us (all virgins except me, I suspect—and he made me feel inexperienced) with details of his serial conquests, none of which one felt inclined to doubt. He did not talk in a boastful spirit but simply to share the data of real experience that he knew would fascinate us as it amused and interested him.

I don't doubt that Jerry copulated well, for he did everything with zest and ease—working, playing, eating, drinking, smoking, chatting, arguing, studying, writing. He was marvelous company, though his pace was exhausting to others. When he had tired you out he would shift to a lower key, or simply go off and put on his glasses, light his pipe, and read philosophy for several hours with complete concentration. Among his incidental gifts were a good baritone singing voice (not quite so good as he thought) and the ability to play a very persuasive jazz piano by ear, with a pounding boogie rhythm. Ordinarily when we went to town we behaved unobtrusively, for the local bully boys thought us professing pacifists easy pickings, and there had been incidents in Gatlinburg and elsewhere in which CO's had been attacked and beaten. But one night in Newport, the nearest sizeable town to Big Creek, Jerry took over the old upright piano down front in the movie theater, swung out in his hypnotic footpounding style, and soon had the whole house singing, whistling, and stamping.

I liked Jerry very much, and I was to see a lot of him in CPS and more of him than of any of the others in later years when were both teaching in New England, part of the time at the same college, Smith; yet I never felt a simple trusting intimacy with him. With Jerry the problem was the reverse of Bill Ambler's shyness and reserve. He possessed, or was occupied by, an egotism that was curiously like Phil Vail's snobbery but much more complex and interesting—an innate thing, built into his character, almost unconscious and hardly a matter of will at all. It would not do to call it vanity, a question of manner and pretense and self-deception. Jerry's competence and confidence were natural absolutes that took possession of one and became overbearing without any intention of doing so. One felt diminished by him, and unwilling simply to trust a man with whom everyone's motives and feelings got taken up into his splendid gifts and his unwilled but automatic self-reference. He was not arrogant or unkind or ungenerous. If he ever showed or felt any of these tendencies, I suspect it was in his relationships with women. Perhaps there was an unscrupulousness about his formidable sexuality; but there, too, I think he tried to be more than a lucky and cynical exploiter. Jerry was the only man I have ever known to whom women actually offered themselves.

My closest friend in the Haverford group, and one of the dearest friends of my life, was the fourth member, Edward Brinton. Ed's family were eastern Quakers of many generations' standing, but he had spent his boyhood in California, where his father, Howard Brinton, was a philosopher and teacher of religion, and his mother, Anna, was dean of Mills College near San Francisco. The family had come back east in the thirties, when Howard and Anna Brinton became directors of Pendle Hill, a Quaker study center in Media, Pennsylvania. The family lived in Upmeads, a pleasant plain stone house on the grounds, and Ed and his three sisters attended the Quaker prep school, Westtown, before he went on to Haverford. He had been a good flexible student with a special interest in marine biology, and after the war he went on to take a doctorate in oceanography at Scripps, in La Jolla, California, where he has remained and made his career in teaching and research. Ed had a quick, muscular, lightly built body, and in college he had been a swimmer and soccer player and played excellent tennis. He was a good-looking boy, with a merry, high-colored face, eyes of very light blue, and crisply curling short brown hair. Later when I met his father I saw that the two resembled each other to an almost comically detailed extent; they even walked and stood alike.

Ed was solidly and brightly amiable, and it was impossible to dislike him. His was a beautifully poised and flexible emotional and intellectual nature, with a marvelous capable sanity about it. He did not have Jerry's brilliance of mind, none of us did, but he was very bright indeed, with a strong true common sense and charitableness, and a fine warm unsentimental sweetness in his relationships with people. I quickly came to feel for him something I would not have been ashamed to call love, and I was proud that he seemed to value me too.

My other close friend at Big Creek was the other Haverford outrider, John Forbes. In a very different and cranky way, John was as vivid and striking a character as Jerry Myers. He was a "convinced Friend," a convert, and a devoted Quaker. He came from a well-to-do Chicago family, makers of the Lincoln Logs of everybody's childhood, but had gone to the University of Rochester, before beginning graduate work in history at the University of Pennsylvania. Eventually he was to marry Ed Brinton's older sister Lydia, and make his whole teaching career at Blackburn, a small self-help college in Illinois. (It is noteworthy, though by no means untypical of select CPS groups, that of the seven men at Big Creek at least four, John Forbes, Ed Brinton, Jerry Myers, and I, became college teachers, and one, Bill Ambler, a college administrator. I do not know what became of Phil Vail or Hubert Rohrer, but I would not be surprised to hear that one or both of them had also ended up as academics.) John was very tall, at least six feet three, with sandy-red hair and thin fair heliophobe skin that fired up easily when he was vexed, which was often. He was strongly built and rather clumsy afoot, and in fact there was a slight spastic tendency about all of his actions, physical, emotional, or intellectual, something erratic and unpredictable, not altogether under control. He was a dear man, gay and risible, with an appreciative eye for absurdities in human nature. His nurturing had been the most conventionally elegant of our group, and his manners, his social instincts, were exquisite, though in execution they could be awkward like everything he did. He had the only kind of good manners that really matters, based on an intuitively accurate consideration of the needs of other people.

John was fundamentally a happy man, but he was also high-tempered and sensitive and easily wounded. He was forever doing or saying something headlong and a bit absurd, and that awkwardness of his made him vulnerable to teasing, which he did not take well for long. He was said to have come to Big Creek to escape a bitter-tongued marksman named Jim Mattox, who had elected himself gadfly to Forbes at the base camp. Now Jerry rather set himself to play the Mattox role, and indeed we all teased John a bit, though we learned to leave off when we saw he was about to feel wounded. We valued his natural good humor, and the general lonely camaraderie of the group, too much to set up a real discord. Seeking privacy for study and meditation, John had moved his bed and a table into a little anteroom off the kitchen, and he soon invited me to share it with him. I moved my bed in and we made a private stove out of a small steel drum we found about the place. We had fine evenings there, reading or writing or chatting quietly. He was a warm and nourishing nature, John, and I'd give a good deal to hear his booming laugh again.

Nearly everything well went at Big Creek, and the two months we spent there came as close to an extended idyll as anything I have ever experienced. The setting was simple and rugged and beautiful, a feast in itself to city boys with old wilderness dreams. We were so isolated that I sometimes felt that I kept the universe alone, like the man in Frost's poem. The late fall and the early winter stayed mostly fair, with crisp, cold mornings, sunny, invigorating days for working, long quiet evenings, and nights with a high, still, star-filled sky. You could feel health moving into your body. We worked and ate and talked and read and slept, and that was all there was to life. We were a congenial little society, forbearing and mutually entertaining, and we got on so well together that one thought of the gentle Quaker phrase, beloved community.

At Big Creek even our foreman was a pleasure, after the surly Rankin. John Crozier Hopkins, whom his friends called "Cro" but whom we always addressed respectfully as "Mr. Hopkins," was a mountain man of about sixty from the hamlet of Mount Sterling. He was a small, agile, talkative man with pink cheeks and shrewd blue eyes and a constant little wicked smile on his nearly toothless mouth. Mr. Hopkins respected our energy and was amused by our ineptitude, and I think he actually liked us as well as finding us curious exotics, good copy for yarning with his cronies. Certainly we liked him. He was a great country raconteur, especially on the subjects of hunting and fishing, and his stories usually carried a tinge of comparatively innocent salaciousness. I remember only one of his tales: of a friend of his who when he went off on hunting trips without his wife always took along an old hairbrush "to have something to lay his hand on at night." I appreciated that one.

Like the rest of life at Big Creek, our work was single, simple and interesting. We were to build a stone retaining wall to shore up a crumbled stretch of the embankment of a forest road where it ran along above the creek a few hundred yards from our camp. Essentially we were putting together a big heavy jigsaw puzzle on a vertical slant, out of pieces that lay in plenty, in all shapes and sizes, along the banks of the stream which amounted to a small shallow river at this point. Mr. Hopkins worked directly with us all the time, as our master mason, talkative and skillful. For structural soundness, and because our own muscles were our only lifting power, it behooved us to make the first courses of the more majestic stones and to descend to smaller stones as the wall gradually mounted. The first stones were immensely heavy and required two or three men to move them, working with crowbars and cut saplings. Some of them must have weighed half a ton. It did not take us long to learn how much easier it was to roll a stone or flop it end over end than to pick it up and carry it. We worried about hernias and strained backs, but we learned to take care and nobody ever suffered anything worse than a turned ankle or a smashed toe or finger.

Mr. Hopkins perched on top of the wall as it slowly rose, squinting and chattering, and shifted and tinkered the stones we brought him into place. Occasionally he would take a hammer and whack off an awkward knob, but usually he left the stone as it was, fitting around its peculiarities and taking pleasure in turning a knob into a key, a binding bit of structure. We got gradually cleverer at sizing up the needs of his situation and scouring

the bank and the stream bed for the right stone to fit into a cranky hollow.
Mr. Hopkins talked all the time, in his mountain man's racy hyperbolical
monologue, or questioning us about our homes or families or education,
about which he showed an impressed curiosity. We liked him so much that
it was a pleasure to please him; indeed the whole process gave a dense,
rich, simple satisfaction. The work was slow and hard, but it was rarely
boring. The thing we were making needed making, and you could see it
forming, and feel the accomplishing of it in your back and legs and hands.
I thought our wall was a splendid thing, and I have often wanted to go
back and find it again and see if it still looked so beautiful.

Only occasionally at Big Creek did we see anybody but each other and
Mr. Hopkins, who disappeared into the mysteries of Mount Sterling at the
end of each day. Once in a while the park ranger, Lawless, would come by
in his pickup truck to have a sneer at the CO's and strut about in his James
Oliver Curwood suit. We could see that Cro thought him as harmless and
absurd as we did. Before I came to the spike camp the men there had
somehow met in Newport an odd and interesting young couple, James and
Wilma Stokeley. I heard a good deal of talk about them, and I finally met
them when they came out to camp to spend a rainy Sunday afternoon with
us, bringing along a friend named Anne, a tall dark quiet girl in her early
twenties. She had a stunned, disoriented look, like a strayed Electra or
Cassandra, and she was so beautiful that we all stood about salivating.

I took it that the three of them pretty well comprised the aristocracy and
intelligentsia, the beauty and the chivalry, of Newport, Tennessee. Certainly it was strange to come upon them at Big Creek camp in the Smokies,
in a backwater of a backwater, and I suppose we were as exotic to them as
they were to us. We were a pretty odd apparition in ourselves, and we
must have seemed the most cultivated young cranks they had had offered
to them. I rather think the Stokeleys thought of making something of us in
the literary line, for both of them aspired to write, and in later years one
occasionally saw bits of higher journalism under one or both of their
names in organs such as the *Times* Sunday magazine. Wilma was the more
tightly organized and I thought the more able of the two, a sandy-haired,
slender, wire-drawn physical type, alert, watchful, quick-minded. James
was tall, dark, slender, loosely composed, with patrician good looks.

James was the scion of the Stokeley family of canners, and I got the impression that he was pretty much living on the family fortune, with no occupation but reading, writing, and talking, especially talking. He called himself "the uncanny son of a canner," and in fact there was a fey element in his makeup that was partly touching and partly frightening, smacking of real pathology in a worrying way. One liked him and felt troubled for him; he looked like a man headed for trouble. The great thing in James's life was the legend and example of Thomas Wolfe, and when he called himself the uncanny son of a canner he was making a Wolfeian phrase, spoken with a deprecating twist of the mouth but with an intention that was less than half humorous. For James really saw himself as Wolfe redivivus, and believed it was his destiny to be the Eugene Gant of the new generation in the Carolina mountains. I had never encountered that kind of identification with a dead man's spirit before, and the experience was disturbingly spectral.

Watching James working at the process of observing, thinking, and feeling like Thomas Wolfe, and talking in a loose, rolling, prodigal, agglomerative rhetoric, trying to *be* the dead man, I trembled for the act of impersonation, the evacuation of personality that was taking place. I did not think Wolfe was worth such a sacrifice of self, for one thing, and moreover the performance was not really accomplished enough to sustain itself. Had it been more fully achieved it would have been less worrying. James was abandoning his own personality in order to imitate another that was seductive but not particularly worthy, and ending up with a shaky incoherency, a fabrication of a fabrication. It was a curious little demonstration of Plato's warning about the dangerousness of art, a created thing at three removes from the truth. I could see Wilma watching James with a kind of habituated apprehensiveness. One trembled for both of them but especially for him because one liked him so much: he was so handsome and passionate, so generous and eager, so vulnerable.

The Stokeleys' friend Anne hardly spoke during the afternoon, but sat watching the general rattling and irreverence like a baffled and titillated vestal. She was so quiet that it was hard to guess how much brain she possessed, but she was so dark and beautiful that the question hardly signified. She appeared to accept the principle that her role in life was to be ceremonial and ornamental, and she sat with her slender ankles crossed and her long hands in her lap, watching and watched. I could already tell that her beauty was taking hold of John, and of Jerry as well in a different way, half simple lust, half spiteful and mischievous instinct to frustrate John. Both of them pursued Anne after that day, John in a clumsy, worshipful, unhopeful way, Jerry asserting his *droit du seigneur* over both John and Anne, meaning to take her to bed and move on. But in her quiet apparently pliant style, she was too tough for either of them. Jerry, who was accustomed to seeing women tumble before his charm, fell back baffled by the simple invulnerability of a southern Calvinist nice girl who knew very well what her viginity was meant for. And she was quite shrewd enough to realize that neither Jerry nor John nor any of us gay overeducated impecunious Yankee CO's could possibly fit into her plain and pragmatical dream of the future.

The fact was that we had little opportunity for romance or for social life of any kind. We built our wall by day and studied in the evening and went to bed early, satisfactorily tired. We broke the routine of our work only once in the two months at Big Creek, and that occasion produced the only mildly dramatic episode in which I was involved. Frank Lawless hauled us higher up into the hills for a couple of days' work cutting and carrying firewood for the fire guard who manned an isolated tower looking out over miles of forested mountains. It was a wild, ruggedly beautiful spot, covered with wind-stunted oaks and conifers, with a long grand rolling terrain visible in every direction, the mountain tops impaled by what looked like huge bones or candles, the grey-white standing trunks of the majestic chestnuts that had perished in the great blight of twenty years before, wiping out the species, leaving not a single mature tree alive in the whole country. We cut our wood with crosscut saws in a little clearing under the knoll on which the tower stood, and that was pleasant enough; but then we had to carry the two-foot, seventy-pound logs fifty yards up a steep, rocky, rain-rutted path to a shed at the base of the tower, and that was killing work. When one had toiled up the path, lined with thickets of wild rhododendron whose stiff tubular cast-off leaves made a slippery brown carpet underfoot, one had to stand and pant for several minutes at the top and look out over the wild landscape.

On the second day, as we sat eating our lunch with our backs against a sunny spot in the tower wall, listening idly to the intermittent squawk of the radio with which the fire guards conversed over miles of mountain forest, it suddenly dawned on me that my name was figuring in their talk.

After a minute the guard came out onto his balcony over our heads and called down to me. A message had come through from the base camp in Gatlinburg: I was ordered to move to another spike camp fifty miles away; a truck was being sent to meet me and carry me there. I was shocked and angry, and after I had thought the matter over for a minute I knew I would refuse to go. Why should the director pluck me, with no reference to my wishes, out of a situation for which I had volunteered, where I was happy and doing a useful job well, when he had fifty other men at hand at the base camp? It struck me as arrogant and silly paramilitary behavior, and I made up my mind to resist it. "Tell them I won't go," I called up to the fire guard. "Tell them to send one of those deadheads at Gatlinburg." The guard stared down at me, spat, and went back inside the big glass-walled room, where I heard him talking angrily with Lawless. What right had a fucking CO to refuse a direct order? I kept silent. After a bit I heard the guard again at his radio: "This son of a bitch says he won't go." He reappeared on the balcony: "They say the truck has already started out to meet you." Sorry, I still wouldn't go.

So it was left. We returned to Big Creek that night, and I heard no more of the matter until I got a sharp reprimand from the director when we met a couple of weeks later. The other men had sympathized with me, though not all of them thought I was right to defy an order. Still, they all felt, it was my affair and I was right to act on my own principles, if that was what they were. We all heard the movement of the magic word conscience. More than anything else I had been offended by the director's assumption that a man made himself a chattel when he became a CO, and must submit to any authority. Eventually I made a story out of the episode and it was published in *New Directions*. I changed the scene of the confrontation to the room at the top of the tower, drew out the action quite a bit, and added tasteful gothic details such as a captive rattlesnake with which the guard threatened me before revealing that he had "drawed" its fangs. I called the story simply "The Tower." It did not please me greatly in itself, but it was a satisfaction to be making even this much in the literary line out of my CPS experience.

Happy as we were at Big Creek, with the place, the work, the companionship, we all feared it was not an idyll that could go on forever, or even that it should be countenanced for long. We felt the unhealthy hermetic

and self-indulgent element in our situation. We all loved the healthy physical strenuousness of the life, but we had to face the fact that only our
muscles were being well used; our brains and real talents, if any, were
hardly being tested. Moreover we foresaw the day when our close and
warm little group must be recalled to the base camp and lose its identity in
the mass there or be scattered into other spike camps. Casting about for a
way to stay together and at the same time to do something more intellectual or at least more humanely useful, we began to look more closely into
options being offered in what was called "alternative service"—alternative,
that is, both to military duty and to the countrified conservancy practiced
in the camps under the National Park Service.

The possibility that appealed to us most was that of serving in CPS units
set up to replace or supplement civilian employees in hospitals in the East,
especially mental hospitals. Apparently the most immediately feasible
place was Eastern State Hospital in Williamsburg, Virginia, the oldest
mental hospital in the nation. At Eastern State there had been a blow-up of
some sort between the CPS men and the director of the hospital, and some
men were being transferred out. We did not like the sound of that, but we
knew our kind well enough to know that we could be hard to get along
with, and that a disagreement did not necessarily mean that the director
was a monster. Most of our Big Creek group sent in applications for Eastern State and we were quickly accepted. Hubert Rohrer and John Forbes
decided against the move, but five of us—Ed, Jerry, Bill, Phil, and I—
would be going. Williamsburg had certain obvious attractions in itself,
such as the presence of William and Mary College, the general historical
interest of the town, and the restoration that was being carried out there
with Rockefeller money. I was very sorry to be separated from John, indeed
we all were, but he had got into one of his cranky independent moods and
would not be persuaded.

I had about a week's furlough time saved up, and I decided to spend it on a
trip home before making the move to Williamsburg. In Louisville all the
things I feared had occurred. Jane had found a job in a branch library, but
she had had to sublet the Birchwood apartment and move in with Laurie at
her parents' house, where the formidable Frances had taken them over
physically and spiritually. Frances resented everything about my pacifism,
its freedom from war's risks, the fact that I was earning nothing, the idea

that a CO should be thought entitled to leave time, to be spent sponging on his patriotic connections. Morris shared some of those feelings, but he had enough generosity and humane sympathy not to show them. Jane and I did get free of the family for a couple of confused and exhilarating days in a made-over carriage house in St. James Court, lent to us by Ethel DuPont, a cranky brilliant friend of Jane's parents' generation, a comparatively poor relation of the big-bang Delaware DuPonts. Unluckily Eppie had forgotten to tell her tenant that she had invited us to stay in her own absence, and we lay naked and quaking in the young woman's bed while she fended off her amorous escort of the evening outside the alley door, unaware that we were within.

Laurie was my delight during that week—fat and funny and boyishly handsome with her short blonde hair. She was about a year and a half old now and had been walking for many months. She used her body busily and efficiently, but so far she had refused to talk, though one felt she was ready to talk the moment she saw any point in it. Meanwhile she was getting her way in the world with a system of imperious gestures and soprano grunts. The three of us went down to Thirty-fourth Street twice to see Mama. Dad had got hold of another of his strange short-term jobs and was out of town somewhere. Mama as always broke my heart with her haggard beauty, her habituated vulnerability, and the old wit still occasionally flashing. She and Jane had always liked each other, and Mama was gently mad about Laurie, treating her first grandchild as a miracle vouchsafed late in a life that was not supposed to produce any miracles. She and the baby played and grunted together on the bed under the front window where Mama spent most of her time now. Her dispersed minor ailments had come to a point in "heart trouble," only vaguely explained. Her cheeks flushed prettily with the pleasure of seeing us, and I could see a slight puffiness in the tissues of her face and hands.

NINE

Wards and Warders

1 made the long trip to Williams-
burg, about six hundred miles, by day coach on the Chesapeake and Ohio,
traveling over country I had never seen before, much of it very beautiful,
especially the Kanawha River region of West Virginia. The time was late
February of 1945. Walking across Williamsburg to the hospital I found the
scene flat and gloomy, though there was certainly a pleasant sense of proportioned space about the restored areas along Duke of Gloucester Street,
and beauty of tone in the warm dark brick of the old college buildings
designed (as I learned later) by Christopher Wren. I was looking for the
other campus, that of the hospital, which, though it lay only a couple of
hundred yards from the restoration area, was tucked in behind a bit of
slope, out of sight and unmentioned in the guidebooks furnished to tour-
ists. It had a melancholy beauty of its own, with walks and drives lined
with old elms crossing the grass and linking the buildings, the oldest being
massive three- and four-story blocks of cut granite and sandstone with
pillared porches enclosed by heavy steel screens with locked gates. Before
entering the grounds I walked down the street that formed the western
perimeter and looked up at the backs of the grey buildings, noting with a
sinking heart the stench and the miscellaneous hubbub from within, the
iron rust on the walls below the barred windows, at which an occasional
motionless figure hung as if crucified. Suddenly a whole roll of sodden
toilet paper sailed out of a second-floor window and landed at my feet.

I found my friends behaving like old hands, busy and apparently happy,
and eager to introduce me to the new life. They looked natty and professional in the hip-length white cotton jackets, which, together with a cluster
of keys on a long chain from the belt, formed each man's insignia of office
as an attendant—pronounced "tennant" by most of the patients. The CPS
unit was mainly housed on the top floor of Sequoia, a comparatively mod-

ern building that otherwise served as a general admissions headquarters for the whole hospital. On the ground floor was the staff dining room where we took all our meals, in cafeteria style. The second and third floors were given over to relatively new patients who were undergoing observation and diagnosis and who might, at least for the time being, be judged hopefully as candidates for early release.

On the fourth floor we were high and bright and airy. On one side we looked out into the tree-studded central grounds, but on the other side we overlooked the most depressing sight in the whole hospital, a low frame barrack called Nine-Camp, with an untidy fenced yard at one end. In warm weather when our windows stood open a wavering but unending cacophony washed up to us from Nine-Camp, from inside the building and from the yard where a few men patrolled the path they had worn along the fence or snuffled about in the long grass like pigs and sheep in a barnyard. These were the patients who had been judged hopeless and harmless, so low in brain power or so totally disoriented that they could only be tended as animals. Many had physical deformities as well. Most of these men had passed their whole adult life in these quarters.

Our rooms, some single and some double, were strung along both sides of a long bare central hallway, all the rooms and the hall lined alike with walls of glazed yellow brick and floors of asphalt tile. The effect was plain and bright and comparatively spacious but monotonous and remorselessly institutional. At the center of the corridor the floor stood open for the full width of the building, for a general gathering place with a few tables and sofas, a ping-pong table, and a bulletin board bearing notices from CPS and Selective Service and announcements of events at the college and in the town. Off this little lobby stood a room for showers and another of toilets. A few of the married men in the unit had gone so far as to import their wives, who had found jobs in the hospital or in town; these young couples were housed more spaciously if not elegantly in older buildings on the grounds. My room at the extreme end of the corridor struck me automatically as a cell. At first I had the room to myself, but soon I had a roommate, Phil McLellan, who was rather quickly succeeded by Ross Groshong, a grave, handsome, dark-haired fellow who became a good friend.

In degrees, depending on taste, energy, and available cash, most of the men had tried to make their rooms more comfortable and gracious, with effects in one or two cases that approached the sybaritic. For aesthetics and to save space, nearly everyone got rid of his heavy iron hospital bedstead and put springs and mattress directly on the floor, couch-wise. Remarkable things could be done with rugs, curtains and bedspreads, prints and hangings, lamps and bookshelves. Everybody had books and most men had phonographs, some of them elaborate and excellent. Except in late night hours the hall was hardly ever empty of music, and there were occasional confrontations between music lovers and night-shift men trying to get some sleep and finding no charms even in Mozart.

In my first day I met most of the men of the unit, beginning with Calhoun Geiger, called "Cal," a friendly, burly, rosy-cheeked, blond young man who served as our director while working on the wards like everyone else, and whose younger brother Vernon was also on our list. I was given a quick general tour to show me where things were and how they worked. The male attendants had nothing to do with the female patients, except that one of us might be called in, rarely, to help control a woman who had got out of hand; and we saw little of Front Building, where the quieter, untroublesome men were housed, and which with its peaceful, pastoral air reminded me a good deal of some of Vincent Van Gogh's madhouse paintings. Most of us who were ward attendants were assigned, on one shift or another, to Montague Building, whose three floors held the three wards of the more or less chronically "disturbed" men, an umbrella term that covered everything from harmless restlessness to outbursts of extreme hostility and physical violence. Ward Four on the ground floor, entered by a broad stone porch under massive round pillars, was made up mostly of older men who suffered from some form or phase of senility, along with a few younger men who had physical problems that made them too vulnerable for the more violent wards upstairs. The porches onto the second and third floors, Wards Five and Six, were closed in by heavy steel screens, as were the stairways between the floors, and the steel gate at each level could only be opened by an attendant with a key.

One's first impressions of the place were confusing, frightening, depressing. The stench and the din projected a hundred feet from the walls, and one had to nerve oneself to penetrate that climate even before entering the building itself. The walls and floors of the building were indurated with more than a hundred years of tobacco juice and spilled food, of sweat and urine and feces, to the point where soap and wax could only compact the effect. Ward Four, where many of the patients were incontinent, smelled even worse than the other two, though it was less hectic to the eye and ear. The distinction between Five and Six, the true "disturbed" wards, was not easy to see; Six was perhaps a little less crowded and explosive. What made the attendants' situation tolerable, and less perilous than it seemed at first glance, was the fact that the disturbed patients almost never acted in concert; it was rare for even two of them to have the same dangerous idea at one time. Apartness, the isolation of the troubled psyche, was of the essence of their disease. By the same token, though almost all of these men were steadily or intermittently disturbed, it was fairly rare for the impulse to take an aggressive form; and when aggression occurred it was as likely to be directed at an imagined person as at one who was real and present. Moreover it was far more likely to take the form of words than the form of blows.

Looking down the long hallway on Ward Five or Ward Six at any random time, one's first impression was chaotic: bodies in veering, pointless, spasmodic motion, a hubbub of voices shouting, cursing, singing, weeping. It took a while to learn that all this was customary and in its weird way orderly, and that it was more varied and modulated within itself than one supposed. At a given time half of these bodies were still, though they might be tense; it was the restless ones that caught the eye and defined the tone. All of them were coping in some way, with whatever degree of consciousness or understanding, with the dreadful emptiness and endlessness of time, with a hospitalization that was really imprisonment. Most of them were getting no treatment whatever aside from custody; they were fed, clothed, housed, all minimally. If they had visible physical ailments they were treated, but not one, so far as I could see, was ever given anything resembling psychiatric attention. A good quarter of them, I concluded in time, could have functioned at least harmlessly in the ordinary world if anyone had been willing to take a little responsibility for them. In effect they had been put away out of sight forever because they were a bit of a nuisance or an embarrassment. I had seen madder people walking the streets of Louisville.

As things turned out I worked for about a month on Five and Six, and

within a few days the chaos had begun to seem muted and even systematic, without ceasing to be chaos. For the time being I was on the day shift,
sharing the duties of the ward with one or two other men, often Ed or Jerry
or Bill, who were very good at our craft, cleverer and braver than I. Our
job was almost entirely housekeeping or otherwise custodial. We came on
duty at breakfast time, when Willie Higgins (always called by both names),
a patient-trusty who organized all the meals, would be finishing up his
slapdash serving. Willie Higgins was a headlong old pirate with an inflamed face under wild white hair and a loud, foul, bitter tongue, who
ordered other patients about like the hogs he believed them to be. Except
for a few physically ill or acutely disturbed men who had to be fed off
private trays, all the patients ate in a bare room with picnic-style tables off
the central hall, which had to be virtually excavated after every meal, for
the food, both plentiful and totally unappetizing, got smeared everywhere
in pools and clots. For the rest of the morning and the long afternoon we
worked at the patients and the premises, talking with the men as much as
we could, cajoling and trying to reason and persuade, to give them bits of
rational companionship. We tried to keep clean clothes on those who
would wear clothes (the majority), to persuade them to go to the toilet (in
the toilet rather than on floors or walls), to see that they got occasional
baths and haircuts and shaves. We were expected to become instant bar-
bers, and most of us became reasonably proficient at the trade in time. On
the rare occasions when a patient had a visitor we scrubbed him up and
dressed him in his personal clothing, if he had any, kept labeled in the
central store room. Most of the hospital clothing was crude cotton stuff
made in the state prisons.

　　We spent a great deal of time trying to keep the dirt and stench of the
place under some kind of control. It was a local habit for tidier patients to
make use of big number 10 tin cans, of about two-quart capacity, as spit-
toons or urinals or both. Men who could afford or beg cigarettes or "mak-
ings" smoked, and most of the others chewed hospital-issue "Apple" tobacco, gnawed off hard brown cakes. Patients were allowed to carry
wooden safety matches but nothing to strike them on; we attendants were
expected to provide that: "Tennant! Got a striker?" More orderly patients
kept their cans by them by day and in their rooms by night, and emptied
and washed them out with some regularity; but the cans were forever

getting kicked over, or occasionally thrown at somebody, and that meant a fearsome job of swabbing up. A few patients were so disoriented or coprophilial that they would defecate on the floor of their rooms or in the hallway, or in their clothes if they were wearing any, and then paddle in the stuff and smear it on floors and walls and furniture or their own bodies. So we spent a great deal of time changing beds and clothing and scrubbing rooms and hallways. When we got a free chunk of time we scrubbed the long-suffering but still handsome hardwood floor of the long central corridor and then waxed it when it was dry, herding patients ahead of our work, or pressing a few of them into service. In waxing one man would pace up and down the length of the floor flicking bits of paraffin from a big cake with a nail-studded paddle, then a half-dozen men would march up and down, up and down, pushing massively weighted polishing brushes. For a few hours the place looked gratifyingly glossy and the smell, though it never seemed to diminish, grew at least more complex.

We were forever being summoned to open the big gate on the porch by a shout of "Tennant! Turn me out," or "Tennant! Turn me in." Of course one felt like a jailer, though the necessity of it all was obvious enough. Few of the patients on Five and Six were allowed outside the ward without an attendant, so we often got involved in escorting a patient or a small group to places like the canteen or the laundry or Brown Building, the infirmary. It dawned on me after a bit that the cannier men manufactured these errands for the mere pleasure of an outing, or for a chance to cross paths with womanhood in the form of groups of pathetic dowdies like our own in everything but sex. (I remember a cluster of that kind in the canteen one day that included two women in shapeless cotton dresses whose menstrual blood had run unregarded down their bare legs into their shoes. I have seldom felt so desolate.) A good half of the patients in Montague Building, the deep sunk and far gone, never left the ward from one year's end to the next, and they would stay there until they were carried out at last in the long wicker baskets, like mummy cases, in which dead bodies were shipped home. A few men were confined to the ward because they were known to be "runners," men who would "elope," in the hospital phrase, whenever they saw a chance, strike out down the road for home and be brought back in a couple of hours by a posse of attendants and state policemen.

Charlie Greer was such a runner, and consequently he was given very little freedom. He was considered one of the few genuinely dangerous men on the ward, and he was so and looked it. Within the prevailing indirection and anonymity of the place he was a striking figure: quiet, seclusive, decently dressed in his own clothes, a rather good-looking young man of about thirty. His intermittent intensity of purpose and his constantly menacing physical strength could be terrifying; certainly he frightened me. He was tall and immensely powerful, thick in neck and shoulders, with very long heavily muscled arms. Using a shy, confidential smile, he liked to seduce a person into shaking hands, then crush the bones of the hand together agonizingly. The trick was not so much sadistic as egotistic and monitory; he wanted to show us all that he was sly and powerful and to keep us on notice that he could do terrible things whenever he felt ready to act. It was wise to stay afraid of Charlie, yet it was impossible not to like him to a degree, and to pity him: he was intelligent, lonely, confused, utterly entrapped.

Charlie and the other younger men on the ward naturally appealed to us in a special way: it was hard to accept the conclusion that these were already wasted lives, that nothing could come of them. The most haunting single figure in the seething crowd was a lithe, handsome, blond Virginia aristocrat who had been a track star of Olympic quality in college. He was the closest thing we had to the classical schizophrenic, with all the symptoms in pure clinical form. He went through catatonic intervals in which he would pose for hours frozen in some tortured angular attitude like one of the mad figures in Pope's underworld, his muscles hard as stone. You felt that if you moved his arm, it would break off like a dry stick. Most of the time he sat unmoving on a backless wooden bench against the corridor wall, with one bare foot drawn up on the seat and his chin on his knee. Some days he would stand for hours in an angle of the hall, not caring whether he faced in or out; or he would pace the hall slowly with total abstracted gravity. I made a point of speaking to him every time I saw him, but I never got an answer, and in fact I never heard him speak a word. When you spoke to him you could see a little flicker deep in his eyes registering the fact that something insignificant had brushed his consciousness, but his gaze stared straight through you into the other world where he meant to stay.

Gordon Crockett was another who looked young, though I suppose he could have been anywhere from twenty-five to forty. Except when he was in one of his depressed phases he was always on the scene and always active, chattering, singing, dancing, grimacing, gesticulating, serially or with several modes in concert. He looked like some corrupt nobleman's freakish byblow. His back was short and rounded, almost humped, and his close-cropped bullet head sat tight on his shoulders, with a sallow hairy face and beautiful big dark eyes like overripe cherries. His arms and legs were long and wiry and his long thin hands fluttered constantly; he looked like a cross among a monkey, a spider, and a butterfly. Gordon had grown up through some shabby southern big-city demimonde, where he had learned his routine of song and dance and patter, and where he had come to grief at last. It was a queer, fragmentary, and fabricated personality, revolting, fascinating, and pathetic, with a thread of uncorrupted purity and sweetness running straight through the middle of the mess that kept him pitiful and winning. Gordon was almost the only one of the disturbed patients who showed a steady overt sexuality. A career as a male prostitute was apparently an aspect of his troubled past. He masturbated frequently and he had been caught several times "going down on" other patients in the lavatory. "I'm a cocksucker," he would say to you, with a sly, shadowed, wondering, from-under look, in a voice that seemed to mingle pride, contrition, and mystification.

Gordon had a companion, half chum and half keeper, who was universally known as "Boogie-Bear," sometimes called by either half, "Boogie" or "Bear." He was said to have been committed for "raping" his wife, meaning that he had used her sexually so brutally that she had finally had to take him to law. Boogie played the mountebank to Crockett's monkey, and liked to exhibit him in his song and dance routine with a derisory commentary delivered in the flat gravelly stentorian bass that was the commonest and loudest of the ward's many noises. It was his voice that had greeted me when I first approached Montague Building nerving myself to enter. Slouching on the porch with his fingers hooked through the screen, he bellowed at me in inquisition, command, and humorous contempt. He was a shrewd, blatant, nasty old man, but not dangerous—full of insult but a bit of a coward, and plenty smart enough to keep out of harm's way. He was the nastiest type of wool-hat poor white, his red neck obscured by hair and dirt, a classic cracker. Faulkner or Erskine Caldwell would have known him in a flash, but it was Mark Twain I thought of: Pap Finn with an overlay of the horrible old humbug who calls himself "the King" or "the Dauphin." Like both of them he liked to orate, and his quantity was prodigious; his blatant bass monologue boomed and rasped all day like recorded speech mechanically amplified. It was not pointless speech but full of mule-skinner wit and dirt and Thersitean excoriation. Boogie looked like Mark Twain's awful rogues, too, low and burly and slouching, black from head to foot in his shapeless dark clothes and hat, and with his red eyes and twisted wet mouth moving in a thatch of black hair and stubble beard. In his loathsome way he was an endless entertainment, clever, sly, outrageous.

A third of these histrionic characters was John Mansfield, a man of about sixty, tall and thin, with a long, sallow, hang-dog, jack-o-lantern face. In any other company he would have seemed spectacular, but alongside Crockett and Boogie-Bear he came through as comparatively quiet. In the sane world he had been a professional entertainer of low order, a carnival barker or something of that sort. He was master of an engaging line of patter, a joking spiel varied by a snatch of song, a complicated drumming act with his hands, a little soft-shoe buck and wing—a man of the old school. There was a good deal of the old-fashioned con man about John, an insinuating intimacy that could be winning when it did not descend to the transparently sycophantic. He liked to call all of us attendants "Cap'n": "Cap'n Ben Reid," "Cap'n Jerry Myers." We took to addressing him as "Cap'n John." When Jane came to visit me at the hospital I took her around to call on some of our more presentable characters, and she was charmed by John Mansfield; his manner with her was courtly and quietly gay, exquisite really. He was one of the people who did not belong in that place.

Apart from our routine care and feeding and shepherding about, the only actual treatment I can remember being given to our disturbed patients were a few administrations of electrical shock. The most spectacular instance involved the most spectacular of our patients, our classical raving maniac named Tom, who was kept locked up (in hospital lingo "secluded") in a personal pigsty on Ward Six, a bare room fitted only with a rubber-covered mattress. Sheets were wasted on Tom. Most of the time it was impossible to shave him or cut his hair, and he would wear no clothes. He squatted glowering in a corner, or ranted about his room, shouting and gesticulating, his whole body vibrating with rage. His body and the walls and floor of his room were smeared with his feces. Every few days several attendants would overpower him and give him a bath while another swabbed out his room. No one person could deal with him, for he would attack savagely, biting and kicking and scratching. So I was astonished one day to be summoned to Brown Building to help give Tom a shock treatment; it was my first experience with the process, and I could not picture Tom as submitting to any treatment whatever, unless he were sedated.

In any case the four of us who were called found Tom lying quietly on a treatment table in a bare clinical room. We watched as the electrodes were fitted to his head and the doctor in charge explained our function: to stand, two on either side of the body, to restrain it and prevent whiplash injury to limbs and spine in the severe convulsion that would follow the electrical shock. One man was handed a folded cloth to place between the teeth to prevent Tom from biting his tongue. But there was no way to prepare for the awful strength and intensity of the convulsion that occurred when the switch was thrown. It was exactly like a grand mal epileptic fit, quadrupled: the mouth flew open and emitted a loud sucking indrawn scream, the whole body arched in a stiff bow like a great flat leaf spring, then every part of the body vibrated powerfully within the confinement of the awful rigor of the muscles. Within half a minute the paroxysm had tapered off and the body lay flat and quiet and the man unconscious. It was hard to believe that a body, much less a brain, could suffer such fantastic tension and stress without breaking and tearing. Yet within a couple of hours Tom was up and walking about, looking tired and slightly dazed, but quiet, clean, and clothed—another person. You could carry on a civilized conversation with him; he talked not only rationally but intelligently, and he seemed as sane as anybody else. There was only one word for it: miracle. I watched him closely over the next few weeks. Within the first week he had begun to slip. Inside a month he had reverted to his old maniacal persona and become a caged wild man again, raving and naked and shit-smeared. The miracle had not held; and a man cannot live in electrical convulsion.

It was shortly after this episode that I was asked to move to Ward Four on the ground floor of Montague Building, where I was to spend the re-

mainder of my fourteen months at Eastern State. It would not be accurate
to call Four a senile ward; though old age and bodily decrepitude were the
commonest denominators, by no means all the patients showed all the
senile symptoms. And it was even more obvious here than on Five and Six
that many of these men had simply been parked to live out their days
because persons near them had found them a trial. There was a middle-
aged syphilitic, half blind and wobbly on his feet, but by no means mad.
One young fellow, hardly more than a boy, suffered from both epilepsy and
diabetes; he was stupid but certainly not insane. The first sight that met
my eye on the ward, actually taking the sun on the porch outside the door,
was two men in wheelchairs, one young, one middle-aged, neither mad.

The young fellow was thin, dark, birdlike, with big lustrous dark eyes.
He was kept generally in a wheelchair because he was gripped by a complicated spastic condition that made his movements unpredictable and
often uncontrollable and dangerous to himself. While he could walk at
times, and stubbornly kept trying to do so, he would usually start to fall
forward after a few steps, then break into a jerky run to keep from falling,
and perhaps fetch up against a wall with a sickening crack that could break
bones. He liked to play a game in which an attendant would set him on his
feet and moving forward like a clockwork toy, then follow close behind
him to catch him if he jackknifed. On the rare occasions when he made it
the length of the hall he would turn at the end with a grin of triumphant
sweetness. In his wheelchair the spastic problem was dangerous mainly
because of his passion for cigarettes, which he would smoke constantly if
permitted. Then his wheelchair companion would have to straighten him
up if he folded onto his lit cigarette or clutched it spasmodically against
some part of his body or clothing. The older man's devoted nursing was of
course a service to us all, and in fact he was valuable in all our work, for he
kept a shrewd general eye on the other patients and often knew before we
did when somebody needed attention. He was alert and intelligent and
surely as sane as any of us. In a year's close observation I never saw anything wrong with him aside from his poor useless sticks of legs. He was a
thoroughly presentable little man, neat and humorous and conversable,
perfectly clear in the head. What kind of fate put such a man among a crew
of mental derelicts?

But these were the odd only partly accountable types around the edges of Ward Four. The norm was accountable enough: old or ageing men, veteran schizophrenics and arteriosclerotics, pretty hopelessly confused in mind and generally frail in body. None was officially bedridden but nearly all were tottery. They spent most of their time lying down or sitting on chairs or benches. Several were blind or deaf or both, and others were nearly so. Most were intermittently incontinent ("untidy") and some were chronically so; they went to the toilet whenever and wherever the flesh moved them—in bed, in a chair, on the floor, in their clothes. Excretion defined the atmosphere; the air seemed solid with stink.

All of this meant a different balance of problems from that on Ward Five or Ward Six. Hardly any of these patients were physically dangerous, or able or concentrated enough to be a threat to "elope." But care and feeding and housekeeping problems were multiplied. Many men were on medication for physical ills, and one had to learn to administer such things as insulin shots for diabetes and injections of liver extract (with a barbaric four-inch needle in the buttocks) for anemia. Many had to be tended like infants: dressed several times a day, bathed, fed by hand, taken to the toilet (usually too late or too soon), put to bed, their linen changed several times in a night. It was endless, exhausting, exasperating work, and it would have seemed unbearable if so many of the men had not been so appealing and so helpless that one's heart turned soft and stayed that way. Harried and tired, one still knew one was a necessary benign proprietor.

John Rae was one of the most impressive men on the ward, and almost the only one who occasionally took a fairly efficient swing at one of the attendants; though he must have been pushing eighty, he was still strong and reasonably well coordinated. Tall, white-haired, with a fiery red face and beetling white eyebrows, he looked much like George Bernard Shaw, but even more robust and rubicund and angry. John had spent most of his life as a Virginia farmer, but he had been born a lowland Scot and he retained much of that accent. To talk with him in a rational interval was to realize that this had been a formidable and probably an admirable person; in his deep, smouldering blue eyes one saw character and intelligence. His manners were graceful and his voice was enchanting, deep and soft, its burr intricately modulated. John Rae did not know where he was but he knew he did not want to be there. He was one of the few who recognized his room as his own place, albeit a temporary one, and made an effort to keep it neat. Basically all he wanted from us was his freedom; he could not understand why we should have him in charge. He wanted to get out and go home, though he had no idea where it was or how to get there. Every few days he would gather his energy to a point and come glowering out of his room, dressed for travel, and command us to let him go. But most of the time he sat glooming and staring at the other patients in disgusted amazement, or pacing the hall in deep silent baffled suffering, a kind of walking crucifixion.

That kind of baffled pacing was a natural part of the general symptomatology on Ward Four, where one often saw a whole file of tottering specters heading nowhere with diffuse passion. An old Belgian peasant named Barricault patrolled the hall constantly at a brisk erratic pace that was almost a trot, his big puffy flat-bottomed feet always bare and the rest of him usually so. With his long arms, his short, thin, bowed legs, his big round bald head, and his broad face with its beak of a nose and wide gash of a mouth, he looked like an ambulatory gargoyle, set free to stray without a brain. Some of us tried to talk with him in French, but arteriosclerosis proved no more rational in French than in English.

Henry Rigsby came near to turning the patrolling attitude into an art or a profession. Having only recently quitted the great world, he was healthier and more vigorous than most of our old men. He looked like an old countryman who had dropped sociably by in the course of a long walk down a dusty road; and in fact that was precisely how he interpreted his situation. He was not quite sure where he was, where he had come from, or where he was going, but he was sure that he was only pausing briefly to rest and chat and he would shortly be on his way—as soon as he had picked up everything he could lay his hands on. His eyes popped with astonished greed at the quantity of plunder that lay about unguarded; he was a seasoned old rogue who saw that he had stumbled into a pilferer's paradise. After he had exchanged a bit of rustic-courtly chat with us, he began to glide about, picking up shirts, pants, socks, pillows, crockery. He secreted them inside his coat till that overflowed, then he nipped into a bedroom and came out with a big pillowcase into which he stuffed his surplus. Then he sat down with superb nonchalance and chatted again, carefully paying no attention to his bulging bosom or the bundle under his arm. After we had given him supper he thanked us gallantly, then strolled over to the door and said he reckoned he had better be getting on down the road. We persuaded him to stay the night, but he refused to take a bed; instead he stretched out on the floor by the door with his bundle under his head, ready to leave at first light. The whole charade was repeated each day for about a week. Finally he gave in and accepted a room, which he turned into a pack rat's den that had to be excavated periodically.

But my favorites among the patients of Ward Four, the ones that most entertained me and shook my heart, were three old men of less peripatetic habit. One was George Mitchell, a tiny, stooped gnome-body from Richmond. He had apparently been in Eastern State for many years, and grown old there, for he talked often of the day long ago when he had first been brought to "Dr. Brown's Building" for mysterious motives that he was still protesting. George was tidy and clean to the point of fastidiousness; he was always fully and neatly dressed in the hospital issue, and he scoured out his personal number 10 can in the lavatory a dozen times a day. Most of the time he sat in his chair carrying on an endless plaintive monologue, not loud, complaining in the most winning and reasonable tones of the injustice and hardness of his life. Actually he was most conversable, and he had an acute humorous sense of his own absurdity. If you sat down to talk to him, the crooked smile under his watery blue eyes and bald crown seemed to contain all the sweet sadness, deprecation, forgiveness in the world. An extraordinarily pure and gentle nature.

E. F. Heath came from Petersburg, as he loudly and repeatedly announced, evidently attaching much significance to his provenance. "E. F. Heath!" he would shout. "Ol' E. F.! Just an old Petersburg boy." As we gradually pieced together his rambling rants, we made out that he had been a trunk maker in a factory in Petersburg, and most of the time he believed that he was still there at work. Being totally blind and partly deaf, he interpreted the voices and movements around him as the stir of the factory floor, and as conspiratorial, aimed at himself. Feeble and tottery as he was, he was still very irascible and combative, and he would square off and cock his weak old fists and shout his pugnacious vaunt: "Ol' E. F.! The best man in the shop! Yeah! I can lick any man in the shop!" The jaw in the long, sallow, bloodhound face was set with horrid grimness. Alongside this professional cantankerousness was another totally different nature. If you addressed him formally and politely, calling him, as I always did, "Mr.

Heath," and speaking quietly and reasonably so that he understood that one was not among those plotting his downfall, then the old man showed a sweet and graceful social instinct, conversing and carrying himself with a natural courtliness of manner that could only be called beautiful. Jane was enchanted with him, and he with her, when she visited the ward. But Mr. Heath loved to chew tobacco, and in his situation that was about the only pure pleasure left to him. The consequences to his environment—floors, walls, the clothes of passing persons—were disastrous, however; when he had a mouthful of juice he simply let fly and splattered whatever he happened to be pointing at with a brown tide. I liked to give him tobacco, partly for the pleasure of watching the wave of pure euphoria wash over his face as his jaws began to work. If I had time I stood by with a number 10 can, trying to anticipate the direction of his discharge; but usually I had to leave him to fire his scattershot and return in half an hour with a bucket and a mop.

I suppose my supreme favorite was an old countryman named Henry Richeson, whom we sometimes called "Buck" because he himself was forever calling on a mysterious creature of that name: "Come on, old Buck," he would shout, or "Come up out of there now, Buck." We thought Buck might have been a brother or a son; but I finally concluded from the tone and the contexts that Buck was probably a mule, to his master half amusing and half exasperating. It was unwise of us ever to apply the name to Henry, for it only added to his hopeless disorientation. He was a handsome old fellow, with a hard stringy high-shouldered body, a cap of short snow-white hair, and rheumy blue eyes that once must have been bright as well as light but were now nearly blind. He walked with a brisk, choppy gait, very funny to watch with its decisive directionlessness, going nowhere with such an air of purpose. It was impossible to keep him fully clothed, for he would discard his garments one by one and end up stark naked or wearing an impressionistic remnant such as a shirt or a single sock, and ricketting about with his rustic dignity quite uncompromised. The effect was irresistibly comic because he was hung like a horse, with the largest, smoothest penis and testicles I have ever seen on a man.

Henry's temper, one could tell, was naturally sweet and social, and his voice was deep and musical. Sometimes, sitting quietly, or talking away to nobody about nothing, he would break out in a low, rolling giggle that was simply enchanting and seemed to contain all the amusement in the world. It was rare for any of the patients on Ward Four to receive a visitor; our old gents had been simply filed away by their thankful families, and nobody really wanted to see them ever again. But one day we were told that persons were coming to see Mr. Henry Richeson, and we scrubbed him up and shaved him, trimmed his cap of white hair, and dressed him in a complete outfit of his own clothing, trying to time the operation so as to assure that he might be at least half clothed when his visitors appeared. When they arrived they proved to be a half-dozen tall, grave, decent country people, a son, nieces and nephews, all middle-aged themselves. We sat them in a circle in the cleanest corner of the central crosshall, hoping that breezes from the front door might thin the urine-laden air. Henry sat sedately among them, his huge old work-worn hands fluttering over his bony knees, looking straight ahead of him at nobody, talking out his own mysterious reveries, emitting his marvelous irrelevant chuckles, and exclaiming "Eh, Lord!" every so often. As the visitors left they told me that Henry had not known any of them. They were glad they had come but they would not be returning.

Toward the end of my long tour of night duty on Ward Four, Henry Richeson suffered a terrible visitation of boils, like one of the plagues of Egypt, in which his scrawny old body erupted in great red carbuncles, a dozen at a time. I itched to get my hands on the things and squeeze them out of his flesh, but the doctor warned me to let them alone. At about three A.M. of one hot still night, when I was sitting at the desk in the ward office writing up a report, Henry's figure appeared in the open doorway, wearing one sock. He wandered about the office, scrabbling aimlessly at the bare walls and muttering and moaning faintly. I went on writing. Finally he came over to where I was sitting, turned his back to me, and bent over until his head nearly touched the floor, his great bag of testicles hanging down like an udder. He pulled his thin buttocks apart to disclose his hairy anus and a large red boil, an agony even to contemplate. "Looky here, boy," he said plaintively; "what kind of a place is that there?" I could only walk him back to his bed and tuck him in.

The hospital used a variety of euphemisms to sweeten the sound of ordinary crises. Nobody was ever "violent" or "raving," he was "disturbed." Nobody "ran away" or "escaped," he "eloped." The patients themselves used simpler idioms. When a man suffered an epileptic seizure they said he "fell out" (in the Tidewater accent closer to "oot"). I remember coming onto Ward Five one night and being met at the gate by Gordon Crockett with the news: "Charlie Greer run today." "Run?" I queried, mystified. "Run away," said Gordon impatiently. "Took off. For home." When a patient died the record always said he had "ceased to breathe" at such and such an hour—a poetical way, I supposed, to avoid committing oneself and perhaps to disclaim responsibility. Except for poor hopeless Gayle White who choked to death mercifully on a bit of food, deaths among the old men of Ward Four seemed always to occur at night, and so it fell to me to oversee several passings. I remember particularly one thin old fellow who died on the ward of pneumonia. I worked with him most of the night, trying to administer medicines and to get fluids down him, and taking rectal temperatures that finally read 106 degrees. His breath came faster and faster, shallower and shallower, more and more rasping. Finally there came an exhalation that was not followed by an inhalation. Mr. Watson had ceased to breathe. I looked at my watch and walked to the office to record the time. Then I returned to the room to shave the white face and wash the white body for shipment to a family who would feel, I imagined, little but relief. On a whim I inserted the thermometer again: 103 degrees—heading down toward room temperature.

Life in the CPS unit went on peacefully and on the whole pleasantly. I liked my mates at Eastern State, though we were all so busy that we had little free time together. Jane came twice for visits of a few days, traveling by train from Louisville, where she had now found a job teaching in a private girls' school, the Kentucky Home School. Sleeping accommodations were hard to arrange. She could not stay in our general bachelor quarters in Sequoia, and we could not afford a hotel. A young CPS couple lent us their room on the hospital grounds one night; a Quaker professor of political science at William and Mary lent us his house in town for a couple of days. One night we slept, or tried to sleep, in an apple orchard adjoining the hospital grounds: a very queer experience on the lumpy turf, with insects humming about us and cows snuffling in the damp grass. We trailed back carrying our blankets with birds singing in the dawn, feeling exhausted and peaceful. By day, in free hours, I took Jane to tour the tolerable parts of Montague Building, and she found it fascinating and frightening. She was charmed and touched by John Mansfield and E. F. Heath in particular, and sat down with each of them for a talk. She was very good at that kind of random, humane chat, and they adored her. Later we both tried to write some poetry about the strange men on the wards, but neither of us could bring it off. It was very hard to strike the right note; things kept turning too melodramatic, or pathetic, or rhetorical.

My best friends continued to be the Big Creek group, Ed Brinton and Jerry Myers and Bill Ambler, but I also found plenty of interesting new friends. I liked Hubie Taylor, burly and balding, a Philadelphia Main Line type and a young Quaker lawyer-to-be, witty, energetic, highly intelligent. One night as I approached Montague Building to go on duty, I looked up to the caged front porch of Ward Five to see Hubie dancing about in vigorous fisticuffs with a huge young man named Poitras who had tried to force his way through when Hubie unlocked the gate. Pacifists are not immune to anger. I also liked a very different kind of man, Larry Gorham, a blond, bespectacled New Englander with a humorous squint, odd and nervous and acute, a little fey. Another attractive fellow was a southerner named George Edwards, known as Buddy. He was a handsome, brown-skinned young man with a powerful body and a strong, well-trained voice. George gave us all a moment of glory when he sang the bass solo parts in a performance of the *Messiah* in the beautiful old Bruton Parish church in Williamsburg. Three fellows who tended to move as a group, Jack Gessell, Asa Watkins, and Carl Werner, were also good friends of mine, though I grew bored after a time with their *raffiné* style of living. Asa was a good painter of a melancholy symbolical cast, and all three of them were knowledgeable about music and devoted to it. The thing that finally got on my nerves was their obsession with decorating their rooms, which gradually took on a sort of Turkish voluptuousness, Ingresque, too thick and rich.

My closest new friends were two men who joined the unit midway in my stay, Roy Finch and Ross Groshong. Both of them had come on from the CPS camp at Coleville, in the high arid country along the California-Nevada border. The fact that they had known my brother Buddy, who had moved west to Coleville a year or so earlier, made an immediate bond, but I quickly admired and liked both men, two quite different types, in their own right, and they have remained my good friends ever since. Ross came from an Iowa farm and was a graduate of Antioch College, with an interest in labor economics and in communal living experiments. After the war he worked for several years as an organizer and a time-study expert in the hectic effort to unionize the textile companies in North Carolina, before going into industry himself. Ross was a handsome fellow with short, curly dark hair, tallish, with a classic cattleman's build, thick muscular shoulders, narrow hips, and long legs. At the hospital he worked on the farm rather than on the wards, and tramped off every morning in jeans and field boots. Ross and I had a good deal in common temperamentally, being persons of repressed intensity, rather dour and silent. When I had an opening for a roommate he moved into my bare room at the end of the hall.

Ross was a striking person, but Roy Finch was extraordinary, even in the remarkably fast company of our CPS unit, which brought together a couple of dozen young men of high character and ability. He was an impressive-looking fellow, about six feet two in height, slender but strong in build, very quick and purposeful in his way of moving; one almost never saw him really relaxed. He had long coal-black hair, clear brown skin in a long narrow face with a long jutting nose and fine dark eyes. Roy was my first experience of the New York Ivy Leaguer, and I found him imposing, even daunting, though he was not naturally an overbearing sort. At Yale he had been a philosophy student of summa quality, and after the war he took a doctorate at Columbia and went on to a distinguished career as a teacher in colleges about New York. He has been the kind of scrupulous, curious, ingestive scholar who writes little in proportion to his powers, and his production has been limited to several dense volumes on Wittgenstein.

Roy was the first man of my own generation to remind me of Ernest Hassold. He had Hassold's kind of copiousness in learning, not only quantity but range and variety, his kind of grace and power of mind, penetration joined with energy, and the same sort of analytical and combining instincts, so that he was constantly linking knowledge and making patterns; a bold, imaginative, compounding intelligence. I could not keep up with Roy's play of ideas, and I always felt stupid and tongue-tied in his company. But he must have been used to such unequal relationships; he admitted me to friendship.

Roy was new in another way to me, being the first accomplished and active politically radical pacifist I had known. He had already got into trouble a couple of times by defying Selective Service edicts that he thought intolerable. His political position was anti-communist, and I suppose it was more or less officially socialist, though at first it had looked to me like a kind of philosophical anarchism. After the war Roy became a national officer of the War Resisters League, and with David Dellinger, who had been his friend at Yale, he was a founding editor of the radical and pacifist magazine *Liberation*.

But Ed Brinton was still my favorite companion, funny, acute, energetic, generous in spirit, a thoroughly sound and pleasurable young man. We were often together on the wards, and we usually ate together, went to movies in town, played tennis on the college courts, took bike rides out along the hilly country roads. One warm day when we were both on night duty we rode out a few miles to the sluggish James River with the notion of sleeping on the sand banks. But we were so tortured by sand fleas that we had to give up and drag exhausted back to our rooms. Ed had a notion that an occasional bout of wildness was good for the soul, and it was on his suggestion that I got drunk for the first time in my life. We pooled our money and bought a couple of bottles of the oversweet table wine that was the only thing to be had locally, and chugged them down all too fast. At that time I had hardly tasted alcohol, certainly never in quantity, and the stuff hit me quick and hard. I had never felt quite so completely gay. We roved about the dark walks of the college, singing our loudest and calling to the girls to come out; when the campus cops appeared in the distance we fled shouting with laughter. Then we reeled about the hospital grounds, serenading our married mates, most of whom looked shocked and unamused. The climax of the evening came when I struck a match and set fire to all the bureaucratic notices on the bulletin board in our top-floor hall. Then we doused it with water and fell into bed. Twelve hours later I woke feeling fresh and euphoric after the best night's rest of my life. But the next time did not work so well. Nothing seemed quite so funny as before, and instead of sleeping soundly I woke in the act of heaving my whole stomach contents onto the bedroom floor. The stench was awful, and Ross leapt up with a curse and carried his bedding out onto the porch to finish off the night. That was the last of our sprees.

Recent news from my family in Louisville had been scanty and as usual confused and gloomy. Dad had found another of his desultory little jobs, working on a weekly newspaper in

LaGrange, about twenty-five miles from Louisville. He was boarding in LaGrange and coming home on weekends. After finishing at Shawnee High School my younger brother Paul had tried to get into one of the army programs for training doctors, but he had failed in that and had to settle for a Navy V-12 program at the University of Louisville, where he would be trained as a dentist and would live in one of the temporary barracks that had been thrown up on campus. Hence Mama was alone in our old shabby little apartment on Thirty-fourth Street. Jane kept in touch with her by telephone and tried to see her as often as she could, usually taking Laurie along. Jane wrote that Mama was spending much of her time in bed, with our spooky old neighborhood medical man, Dr. Clark, in frequent attendance. He was devoted to Mama, in spite of the fact that his bills rarely got paid. Jane thought Mama seemed just worn out, listless and low-spirited, though she livened up remarkably when Jane and the baby came and showed some of her old natural gaiety and brightness. One night when Mama had not answered his phone call Paul went to the apartment and found Mama dead in bed. Her tired heart had given up.

Next day Cal Geiger handed me Dad's telegram with a solemn face. I had a few days' leave time accumulated, but no money for the long train trip, so the fellows in the unit got up a purse for me, to be repaid or not as I was able. I left Williamsburg in a day coach filled with men from the Navy and Seabee units that seemed to surround the town, feeling conspicuous and uneasy as the only able-bodied young man not in some kind of uniform. The journey took nearly twenty-four hours and I was rarely able to snatch any sleep in such circumstances; but for some reason I fell sound asleep near the end of the trip. I awoke all alone in a silent stationary car. When I looked out the window I saw we were resting in a wilderness of rails and fragments of trains down along the Ohio River. I had slept peacefully through the arrival in the station, the general disembarcation, the breaking up of the train, and the shunting of the car out to the yards. Like one in a disturbed comic dream, I jumped to the ground with my duffel bag and made my way through a quarter-mile of tracks to a point where I could catch a streetcar out to the Davidsons' house.

The dazed condition of my arrival seemed to last through the next couple of days, while Dad and Paul and I, supported by Jane, waited for Buddy to cross the country from California. It was torture to sit with Dad for hours at a time in the shabby little room where Mama had died alone, both of us depressed and silent. Mama's life would not bear talking of. My grief was wordless and sullen with anger at the pitiful waste that life had been for my brilliant and beautiful dark little mother. I hated Dad for failing ever to provide the grace and stability her nature needed, and I was enraged at the heartless hurry of time that had taken her away before her sons could show that they could make a better job of life for themselves and for her. I had dreamed for years of working a resurrection of the mother I had known as a child.

Being out of our hands, the funeral was well conducted. Dad had bought a lot in the pretty green country graveyard outside Crestwood, where there was a handsome fake Gothic chapel of grey stone, and I was pleased with his choice of the town where we had been happiest as a family. I had expected to loathe the formal service, but in fact I felt nourished and comforted by the slow ceremoniousness that took notice of the fact that something worthy and beautiful was being mourned. I loved the dignity of the leave-taking, and when I stood in the sun by Mama's grave with my brothers and father, healing tears poured down my face in sheets. I had never wept so well.

TEN

New Directions

The war wore on. I seem to have had little sense of the fighting as a progressive affair that our side was slowly winning. I felt as if the war must drag on more or less infinitely, leaving me suspended in my lonely, pointless, impoverished state. Things were about to change, however, even for me. For one thing I had got drawn into the margins of a strange phantasmagoric scheme concerted by Roy Finch and a friend of his named Lewis Hill, whom Roy had got to know in Coleville as an intellectual and radical activist like himself. Hill had now been invalided out of CPS with a chronic bad back, a symptom of the bone disease that would kill him in a few years, and he was now living in an apartment in Washington. The two men had kept in close touch, and both of them longed to do something that would make of pacifist protest more than the passive, negative, inconspicuous affair that gave no embarrassment to militarists and public officials. They dreamed of a gesture public enough and dramatic enough to show that pacifism was alive and tough and international, a bona fide alternative to the habit of war.

For good reason, Roy and Lew were keeping very quiet about their scheme in its early stages, and it is not clear to me why Roy chose to confide in me in Williamsburg, for my pacifism was the simple, stubborn, stoical type that bored him. Perhaps, under his influence, I sounded bolder than I felt. In any case, he sounded me out on the plan. Their principle was to create a direct and visible contact between war-hating American citizens and comparable ordinary folk in Japan—to suggest that the confrontation of the two immense war machines did not express the monolithic will of the two peoples, who were in fact ready to meet in love not hate, were they not separated by military interdict. Their device was to be a peace ship: a sailing vessel manned by peace-loving Americans would set out from San Francisco equipped to make the voyage across the Pacific; when the vessel

222

was well out to sea its errand would be announced with as much publicity as possible; in Japan the crew would be welcomed ceremonially by peace-loving Japanese, particularly Christians, previously alerted by means that remained mysterious.

My jaw dropped at the boldness and illegality, not to mention the practical improbability of the scheme. I had no intention of setting foot on that ship, but I agreed to give Roy what small help I could in early stages; if he wanted it, I wanted him to have it. He and I used a couple of days' leave and took a bus to Washington to see Lew Hill and discuss ways and means. It was my first sight of the city, and I insisted on spending half my time in the National Gallery. Hill impressed and rather frightened me, with his Strangelovian deadly serious fixation on his plot. He was pale, almost white, from head to foot, with straight blond hair and a cold colorless face with a rigid jaw, all of his movements stiffened by his bad back. The quickness and economy of his mind were obvious from his first words, and he knew me at once for what I was in his context, a bumpkin dilettante. He did not take kindly to my skeptical cracks, brushing them aside and plowing on toward the center of his purpose. The meeting was meant as a general strategy session, and we were soon joined by a couple of other CPS men known to both Hill and Finch, and by a mysterious young man in army uniform whose role in the proceedings I could not fathom. My own function was almost nugatory; I was really there only out of loyalty to Roy, and sat about feeling what I was, marginal and outclassed, as plans were laid.

The main things needed, obviously, were money and people: money to buy or charter and fit out the sailing vessel; qualified and committed people to sail the ship or travel on her; other influential people willing to lend their names as sponsors of the enterprise, vouching for its seriousness and purity of purpose. Most of the conspirators' time that day was spent in making up a list of such persons: secular pacifists who might be counted on for nerve, influence, or cash. Those with all three qualifications formed a very short portion of the list. The scheme was obviously complex and risky, in fact foolhardy. Its foolhardiness was half its rationale: to show the world to what extreme lengths certain ordinary citizens were willing to go to make their voices heard for peace. The voyage was to be both reality and symbol. I had often felt I had stepped through the looking glass in my life,

but never onto such a high and windy plane. My head whirled, and I was
scared. In fact I found my main comfort in the hopelessness of the scheme,
surely too complex to be brought off with the means and time available. I
could not have felt less heroic; I trusted we would be defeated before we
fell into the hands of the law.

The oddest thing all this time was that my personal pacifist impulses
were turning in an opposite, more conservative direction. I had just about
decided to abandon my absolutist stand, and to accept noncombatant military service as a medical corpsman. That option had always been available,
and I had been tempted by it from the beginning of the war. Mama's death
had brought my restlessness and disgust with the pattern of our lives to a
point, and I felt sullenly angry at what I had seen of Jane's unhappy and
unhealthy dependence on her parents, which I was helpless to change
when I was earning nothing in CPS. Much as I loathed the idea of war, I
still felt that if there were any shreds of right in this war they were on our
side. I did not like setting myself above the danger and responsibility and
even the guilt of the war, and I had never got past my romantic feeling of
deprivation at missing the great general experience of my generation. It
still seemed to me unthinkable to man a weapon against any enemy, but I
found it harder and harder to draw a line between ministering to madmen
in Virginia and ministering to wounded men in Europe or Asia. Had it
been feasible to tend the wounded of both sides, enemies as well as friends,
my problem would have been pretty well resolved. I pictured myself as a
general healing spirit, a wound-dresser like Walt Whitman.

When I had made my decision to accept noncombatant service I spoke
of it first to my friends from Big Creek, knowing they cared about me, and
feeling that they were entitled to a chance to try to talk me out of it. In
abandoning CPS I was giving in, as I well knew, to arguments and feelings
that had tempted my friends and that they had resisted after a hard struggle. I felt like what I was: a traitor to my friends and to a fundamental
principle of true pacifism, the refusal to take any part in the machine of
militarism. They waited on me in a body, Ed Brinton and Jerry Myers and
Bill Ambler, friends for whom I felt love. As always, they were both humorous and serious, hurt to think of losing me and my loyalty, and troubled
for the health of my soul, and I was moved close to tears to feel their
affection and the depth of their concern. They were constrained, of course,

by having to confront our deepest principle of all, every man's obligation to work out his own moral destiny. It was what had put us all, singly, into CPS in the first place. My own constraints were powerful, but I knew that morally they were shallower than those that kept my friends faithful to their adamancy. I was being directed by boredom, restlessness, curiosity, poverty, shame, and an egotistical need to test my own nerve.

A complicating and invigorating new factor was the appearance in Williamsburg of brother Buddy and his close friend Kingman Grover, who had got fed up with the high-dry boondocks of Coleville and applied for transfer to Eastern State. Soon they were wearing white coats and carrying keys like the rest of us. The two were best friends, and Kingman soon became a permanent friend of my own. It tickled me to hear Kingman call Buddy "Socko": nobody could have been less Socko than Buddy, who was his old quiet engaging self. I questioned Kingman about the nickname, and he said it was a play upon a Jewish form of Buddy's given name of Isaac: "Itzak." Kingman was a few years older than Buddy and me, and much farther advanced professionally. After graduation from Amherst he had gone on to a graduate degree at Syracuse and done some teaching there before being drafted early. Kingman was a quiet dark shortish man, elegantly and unpretentiously civilized and humorous. After the war he went on to a career as a teacher of humanities at Cooper Union in Manhattan, and he and his whole delightful New Jersey family became and remained friends of us all.

My friends were persuasive, more by their humane presence than by their arguments, which they were reluctant to press in any case, feeling that I had the right to make a wrong decision. But my mind was made up, and in that condition I was always stubborn. I told Cal Geiger what I was about to do, wrote to my draft board to say l was ready to volunteer for service in a noncombatant function, and wrote Jane that I was coming home. In a few days I was back in Louisville, unaware that I was beginning one of the queerest intervals in my life.

I had expected to be whisked off to boot camp at once, and when I checked in at my draft board downtown I was told to hold myself ready for an early call. My situation was tense and uncomfortable. With nowhere else to live I could only pile in with Jane and Laurie on top of the Davidsons, who made me little more welcome than if I had come back upon their hands as a purer pacifist. I had no money, yet it seemed to make no sense to go back to work at the dairy, or to try for any other job, when I expected to be called up any day. In a penitential spirit I made myself as useful as possible about the house and yard. I tried to read and write but found I could not keep my mind on any subject for more than half an hour. The days became weeks, and I felt more and more restless and disoriented. I wrote long homesick letters to my friends in Williamsburg. When I inquired again at the draft board they refused to name a likely day: I should wait and count my blessings. But I felt I simply had to find some sort of function and some means to achieve a bit of privacy and independence for my little family.

Ed Brinton had suggested once that at some point Jane and I might want to spend some time at Pendle Hill, the Quaker religious and educational center in Media, Pennsylvania, near Philadelphia, where his parents were the directors. It struck me that the time had come. I wrote to Howard and Anna Brinton, explaining the limbo in which I found myself, specifying our pennilessness, and asking permission for the three of us to come for an indefinite stay. They replied that they would take us in and give us bed and board in exchange for whatever work Jane and I could do. The draft board gave me permission to await my call at Pendle Hill. Somehow we scraped together enough cash for our train tickets. Characteristically, the Davidsons let us go with great reluctance; it seemed to them merely one more of my harebrained schemes.

Pendle Hill turned out to be a little green suburban estate, pretty if rather untidy, with half a dozen rambling structures scattered over several acres. It was named for the spot in England where the early Quaker father George Fox had had his Bunyanesque visions of a better moral world, a life of "beloved community." The institution had never known quite how to describe itself. It had no formal academic standing, and really aspired to none, though some pretty sophisticated intellectual work did get done there in individualistic ways. It was usually referred to as "a Quaker study center." In the spring and fall a modest program of more or less formal courses was offered, discussion groups led by shifting staff members and attended by residents and commuters. Outside groups such as a "labor institute" sometimes occupied the place for short concentrated programs of their own. Quaker studies and Quaker worship went on fairly constantly, whatever the population. There was a small publishing program that issued chiefly pamphlets and small books on religious and sociological subjects. Pendle Hill also served steadily as a training and staging area for individuals and small groups who were preparing for work in one or another part of the world under AFSC, the American Friends Service Committee, which had for many years coordinated the traditional Quaker "concerns" for international humane endeavor. My irreverent young Quaker friends sometimes referred to this body as the "Circus Committee."

All of these semiformal programs were going on in the same times and spaces, working together with an energetic untidiness. Only a few couples had private living quarters. Most meals, plain and plentiful, were taken in common in an airy countrified dining room, where everybody pitched in on the chores of preparation, serving, and cleaning up under the eye of a resident dietician. An excellent small library got heavy use, especially by graduate students from several universities busy on research projects or theses. Pendle Hill was given its tone partly by this ramified busyness, partly by its hospitality to a small shifting population of lame ducks like me and my small family. I remember a silent, furtive young man, a psychic casualty of army service, who spent all his time mooning about the grounds, occasionally pushing a hand lawn mower. A year or so after we had left, Pendle Hill brought over from Japan, for rest and treatment and hopeful reconstitution, a group of young women who had been maimed when the first atomic bombs were dropped: "the Hiroshima Maidens."

Howard and Anna Brinton had given up their formal academic careers in California to come east and take charge of Pendle Hill. In the Quaker style they were universally addressed, even by each other, by their full names unaccompanied by "Mr." or "Mrs.," as Howard Brinton and Anna Brinton, and they ordinarily used the Quaker "thee"—never "thou." Both were highly qualified scholars, he with a doctorate in religion and philosophy, she with a doctorate in oriental studies. I first saw Howard Brinton when he visited his son in Williamsburg, and I almost laughed aloud at his precise resemblance to my dear friend Ed; it was as if somebody had taken Ed and suddenly clapped thirty-five years on his shoulders. They even walked alike. Howard Brinton had a compact, active body and bright blue eyes and fair skin under a plume of snow-white hair. Anna Brinton was comparatively tall, with a slight portliness that was rather becoming; she wore her grey hair in long braids wound round her head, which shook with a constant small tremor; her shrewd, humorous face was of a broad, rather Slavic conformation. Jane and I admired and liked the two of them, though I think we were both a little daunted by Anna, or A.B. as she was often called. The local habit was to guard Howard Brinton like a tribal treasure, to keep him as free as possible from practical concerns and save his time to read and write and think. In most terms he did teach a course in one or another kind of religious subject matter, and he usually presided informally at the "meeting for worship," which was often totally silent. Anna Brinton thus became the real executive officer of Pendle Hill. She was a woman of such formidable intelligence and energy and such impatience with dithering that she found it hard to conform to the Quaker principle of democratic consensus in making decisions.

Because we were Ed's friends, and because there was really nowhere else on the grounds where we could be housed together, the Brintons generously took us into Upmeads, their own house, and gave us a big bare lightstruck room on the top floor, with a crib for Laurie and our own bathroom. Upmeads was a fair-sized house of wood and grey stone in an adaptation of Pennsylvania Dutch style, its handsomest feature being a big library and living room in a wing to itself, two stories high, with an open beamed ceiling, a big stone fireplace in one end, a big trestle table running nearly the whole length of the room, a scattering of shabby, comfortable chairs, walls lined with shelves filled with the Brintons' large personal library, and oriental treasures of a subdued cast filling window niches and hanging from the facings of the shelves. The room was a peaceful battleground of motives gracefully reconciled: Quaker austerity, personal unpretentiousness, love for things that are handsome and exotic but not gaudy, an active intellectual and spiritual life. It stays in my mind as one of the most beautiful rooms I have ever seen, so elegant and withal so simple and so much a place for use.

There was no blinking the fact that we were refugees at Pendle Hill, but we wished to be more than objects of charity and we tried to make ourselves as useful as possible. Jane helped out in the kitchen, the library, and the publication office, as needed; at first I performed chores about the grounds and buildings, but soon Anna Brinton turned me into a chauffeur and general errand man. In the community station wagon, an elderly Ford with a wooden body and a limping engine, I drove A.B. about on tribal missions, shopped and marketed, carried people to and from trains and buses.

At first Laurie was a serious problem, as we had feared she might be—having never been away from home before, and being accustomed to the hovering solicitude of her grandmother and great-grandmother (Iddly and Bigty as she called them later). Laurie was attracted by the busyness and variety and the new faces at Pendle Hill, but she was frightened too, and she clung to Jane's hand or skirt. There were a half-dozen small children in the community, and in order to free their parents to live and work, a nursery school was set up in charge of Joan, the youngest of the three Brinton daughters, a pleasant brown-haired Westtown student of fifteen or so. Laurie spent her first morning weeping and vomiting, and Jane had to be called to the rescue; but things soon began to go better, especially after Laurie got interested in George, a little boy who used to wander about the grounds under a big black umbrella and wearing a long slicker and high rubber boots. Laurie was now two and a half years old, but though she had walked early, she still showed no disposition to speak. Quite suddenly now, inspired no doubt by her chatty new young friends, she began to babble language in a torrent. We would be awakened in the morning by Laurie bouncing excitedly in her crib and shouting: "Bell ringy, Mommie! Time wake up, Mommie, now!" It was enchanting, even at seven o'clock.

I had of course written Roy Finch to describe my queer limbo situation, marking time at Pendle Hill while my military induction was mysteriously delayed. After a bit he wrote back suggesting that I meet him and Lew Hill in New York for a conference on the peace ship scheme, and I accordingly took the train up from Philadelphia. We met at the Finches' tall red brick town house on East Seventy-fourth Street, where Roy was the only one in residence, and I was fascinated to explore the high narrow house, the first of its kind I had ever seen. Roy and Lew had been calling on persons who might lend money or influence to the scheme, and I went with them to see one of their more exotic prospects, a certain wealthy New York woman married to a priest of a Zen cult. It was a Yeatsian situation in which she received us in trailing robes and talked to us in a hushed voice in a draped murky room so dim that we could hardly see each other. I had the feeling that she and I were about equally baffled by the complex and dangerous proposition of a folk peace mission to Japan. She promised to discuss the idea with her husband, but we felt fairly sure that in the long run she would not commit herself or her husband or her money. It was hard to believe that a decision or an action ever took place in that house.

Later that afternoon the two conspirators and I their ineffectual satellite sat on a bench in the sun in Central Park, our conversation as desultory and mournful as that of the pigeons about our feet. We had seen a newspaper and it proclaimed V-E Day, the end of the war in Europe. Were they going to pull the war out from under us, before we could make our *beau geste?* Secretly I hoped so. But Roy and Lew were very depressed, caught in anticlimax—not too depressed, however, to appreciate the comedy involved in pacifists' lamenting the coming of peace. Later, having remembered that the war with Japan was still going strong, they cheered up a little.

A week or so later Roy telephoned from Williamsburg to ask me to put our proposition to two men who were working, separately, in upstate New York at the time: Scott Nearing, a writer, teacher, and pioneer environmentalist, and Milton Mayer, a stiff-necked free-lance journalist of pacifist leanings and some fame. I wonder now, as I could see Anna Brinton wondered then, where I got the money for those trips. Certainly I had none of my own; I think Roy must have sent me some cash. Anna Brinton looked at me with a wary and mistrustful eye: why was I accepting Quaker charity while tootling about by train and plane on mysterious and perhaps seditious errands? She could not bring herself to speak her suspicions, and I refused to volunteer anything. We remained friends. She was a generous woman.

With Scott Nearing I had a good confidential talk, and he got the point of our queer proposal so quickly and shrewdly that I went away impressed with his intense solidity and with a new respect for the dignity of the scheme itself. My meeting with Mayer came to nothing; in fact it was not really a meeting. I found him on the point of departure from a summer stint at a junior college in the green countryside near Ithaca, surrounded by a score of capering young people who had evidently turned him into a cult figure. The tribe was about to accompany him on a bus to the airport, and I crowded onto the bus with them and rode along for a dozen miles while Mayer and his friends laughed and cracked jokes in a kind of private patois they had apparently worked out over the summer. It reminded me of a bus full of school kids singing "Old MacDonald Had a Farm." It was all hilarious and frustrating; quite impossible to find any privacy in which to talk sense to Mayer, who had struck me as bold enough to be useful.

Not long after I returned to Pendle Hill the bombs fell on Hiroshima and Nagasaki, and the comedy turned ever grimmer. The community in effect queued up to offer national apologies and sympathy to the little Japanese gardener, who assured them all in his politest broken English that he did not hold them responsible for the fortunes of war. It seemed obvious even to my obtuse political perceptions that the war could hardly go on much longer. Yet I still assumed, unrealistically I suppose, that the system had kept its eye on me and would still call me up for service somewhere. I decided that we should go on home to Louisville and ask my draft board to get on with the job and take me out of my suspended state. But when I presented myself they only mumbled, and a few days later they wrote me that I was free, discharged of any obligation. The war was just about over and I had contrived to miss it after all.

My basic needs were the same as ever: a place to live, a job to feed my family, a chance to get on with my education. I expected vaguely to put my education to direct use some day, but for the moment the sensible thing seemed to be to go on with my old job that gave us a tolerable income and allowed me some time for classes and study. So before long we had picked up our old life exactly as before it was interrupted by CPS: I was running a milk route for Fenley's Model Dairy, I was enrolled in two graduate courses at the university, and we were back in our old apartment on South Birchwood. Our plan was to keep on in this way till Jane and I had finished M.A. degrees, then to look about for academic jobs of some kind. During the war Jane had got ahead of me in her graduate work, and she was highly regarded by her teachers, for good reason, for she was a genuinely brilliant if impressionistic student. My own slower mind was having a good time with solid courses in Shakespeare and northern Renaissance art, taught by Dick Kain and Justus Bier, respectively. My milk route was not my old one in midtown but a classier territory in the Highlands, where one saw maids rather than housewives, and where most bills were paid by monthly checks. My clientele was comparatively small and not easy to enlarge, and it actually paid me less than my old route; on the other hand I had little direct collecting to do and so had more free time for classes and reading and writing.

Money was short, but otherwise life seemed pleasant and reasonable, and it was a deep satisfaction to be back together as a private and independent family. Moreover Jane now found a part-time job that gave her a good deal of pleasure in itself and helped us to make ends meet. This was in the "Talking Books" program of the American Printing House for the Blind, situated a simple bus ride from home down Frankfort Avenue. Jane was blessed with an attractive reading voice, and she enjoyed the reading aloud for the discs that circulated as an oral library for blind persons all over the country. There was small room for trash on their concentrated list, and much of her reading was in classic novels, English and American. Helping to make the job feasible for Jane was the fact that our gay new sister-in-law was now living with us.

Paul had been sent to continue his training in dentistry at St. Louis University, and he had fallen in love with Kathie Lambrechts, the daughter of a dentist in practice in the city. The only bar to their marriage was the fact that the Lambrechts family were devout Catholics, and Paul had surmounted that by turning Catholic himself. We were all a bit sore at what seemed to us Paul's tame acquiescence to an arrogant requirement, but I think religious forms meant little to him compared to the girl herself, and when we met her we were quickly charmed in turn. Kathie was pretty, dark-haired, full of life, a great singer and dancer and mistress of joking repartee. In our rather subdued tonality she seemed at first a bit raucous, but she brought us an invigorating access of energy, capacity, common sense, and high good humor. The war had ended with Paul's training unfinished, and he had come back home to complete his degree at the University of Louisville, where he could live and study more cheaply. He and Kathie were hard up, of course, and we offered to take them in with us in exchange for some fairly steady babysitting. That worked out very well, for Laurie and Kathie quickly became the happiest of chums. Laurie thought Kathie's comic routines hilarious; one heard them giggling together all over the neighborhood, and their progress homeward was audible a hundred yards away.

In fact Kathie brightened us all up, in conditions that must have been trying for a new bride. Paul was working hard in his clinics, and he often brought laboratory work home with him. One would find pink prosthetic devices lying about on the table or the mantelpiece or boiling pungently on the kitchen stove. Though we all kept happy enough, living was tight. Our rooms were fairly large, but Jane and I occupied the only real bedroom, and Laurie's crib had to go into a corner of the dining room. For the newlyweds we could only set up a mattress and spring on blocks under the front window of the living room, where it sat all day and was visible from the street. Mrs. Heil, our semihysterical landlady upstairs, complained bitterly that she could not approach the front door of the house without being affronted by glimpses of bare bodies in the window. The humorous or amorous sports of the young couple were sometimes noisy, though I felt they kept within the bounds of taste. Late one afternoon Paul and Kathie had retired to our bedroom and were romping and giggling on the big double bed; Jane was off at her job at the printing house, and I was sitting in the living room, barefoot as usual, working at a paper on *Troilus and Cressida*. Suddenly there came a peremptory knock on the French doors that opened onto the front hallway. When I opened the door with my paper in my hand, there stood, with a thunderously censorious face, Mr. Lightfoot, our Hudibrastic young neighbor from across the hall. He denounced me for carrying on with another woman while my wife was away and subjecting his young children to the noise of my lechery. I enjoyed pointing out my visible innocence, though I could not deny the noise, which continued as we stood talking.

Life rocked along in these pleasant untidy ways until the spring of 1946, when I stepped off the street car at Sixth and Hill early one morning to find an astonishing sight. Several trucks were pulled up blocking the loading dock at Fenley's, most of my fellow drivers were milling about in front of the dairy, and several strange men were strolling up and down the sidewalk carrying placards. I crossed the street warily and was met by a little cluster of my friends: "We're on strike." Having had no warning of the situation, I felt stunned. Apparently the decision to strike had been taken at a union meeting, involving drivers of all the city dairies, only the night before. I had long ago quit attending union meetings, having found them intolerably empty and boring. The union plan was to strike Fenley's and to use the wage benefits gained there as a pattern for all the dairies. Our men had accepted the scheme, but with uneasy doubts as to the loyalty of the other drivers about the city; we all feared that our customers would be gobbled up by the other dairies and that a long strike would leave us with no routes to run. Reluctant and a little dazed, I joined the picket line. I had no faith in the enterprise, but I felt constrained by loyalty to my mates—who seemed rather surprised to see me take the common part.

It was the most miserable sustained experience I had ever been through. Walking a picket line, as I did for the next six weeks, is life at its lowest ebb. The boredom is stupefying: hour after hour, back and forth, nothing to do, nothing to say. Soon you are hating not only your bosses but your companions, yourself, life itself. In the disorientation of total boredom you begin to do extravagant things. I stole the keys of a scab truck and threw them away in the weeds of a vacant lot. I got drunk on a quart of Old Forester that we passed around, then threw the empty bottle like a grenade in a long looping arc from the back window of a car, over the roof of the car and across the street and under the wheels of another passing scab truck. We talked seriously of dangerous and brutal schemes for disabling the trucks that were still running and even the few men who had refused to join the strike.

In the long run the strike threw all our lives off course, and it finally destroyed Mr. Fenley and his business. When a group of pickets tried to block his car in an early stage of the strike, he drove into the crowd in a panicky rage, and one of the men, a driver for another dairy, was tossed and badly hurt. Mr. Fenley was taken to court, and though he got off with a fine, he was deeply shaken by the incident and by the general shock the strike was dealing to his paternalistic notions of himself in his business. He began to turn religious and to lose interest in the struggle, and after trying for a time to operate the dairy on an exclusively wholesale basis, he finally sold out altogether. By that time I myself had turned in a new direction, then in another more conclusive.

As the strike dragged on in a stalemate, and as the damage it was doing to our lovingly tended individual routes began to seem more and more excruciating, I began talking with a driver friend of mine, Joe Taylor, about a way out of the mess. Joe was a thin, stooped country fellow with lank blond hair, a sallow rat face, and an entertaining line of bumpkin talk. He and I always got on well, and we usually called each other "Sam" after our old favorite comic strip character Salesman Sam. As we were mourning together on the picket line one day, Joe said: "I believe if I had me a truck full of milk I could go out on my old route and sign up every one of my old customers for myself." I agreed. We began to consider the idea seriously. Why not take a stab at it—set up as independent distributors? All we needed was a decent vehicle and a dairy willing to supply us. I had noticed a used Ford panel truck for sale at a gas station on Frankfort Avenue, seven or eight years old but apparently tight and neat and painted a discreet dark green. I described it to Joe and he allowed it sounded all right if only we had some money. The price was six hundred dollars. Joe was broke and so was I. I mentioned the notion to Jane that night, hopelessly. To my amazement she said that she had six hundred dollars—quietly squirreled away a dollar or two at a time. She was willing to spend it on the truck, and so, of course, was Joe. We put our proposition up to the head of a small dairy, Walnut Grove, whose products we had both admired for quality and appearance. He would supply us, at a rate that sounded to us very fair. We bought the Ford truck and parked it in front of my apartment, to Mrs. Heil's renewed outrage. Joe, who owned a serviceable 1936 Chevrolet sedan, set to work trying to sign up his old Fenley customers in South Louisville. Enough of them agreed to give us the nucleus of a route, and we were ready to start deliveries.

But the new venture was to last only a few weeks in the summer of 1946 for me, for Jane had taken another initiative that succeeded surprisingly and prevented me from spending the rest of my life as a more or less contented milkman. She had consulted with our neighbors the Hassolds about our general prospects, and Ernest had urged that we try to make a beginning at something that would make better use of our training and our brains, which he rated higher than I did. He suggested that we register our credentials, such as they were, with an agency in Chicago that tried to match prospective teachers with openings in college and university faculties. I agreed to this, but not hopefully. The idea seemed much too exalted; I could not believe that any college would look at us twice. But the bureau began sending us notices of jobs available, we applied for those that sounded vaguely feasible, and to my amazement we got several nibbles. What I had not considered was the working of the new GI Bill: a wave of returning servicemen was entering the colleges and they had to have teachers. Jane and I were invited to Galesburg, Illinois, for interviews at Knox College, which I knew of as a decent liberal arts college whose football team charmingly lost all its games. As I expected, nothing came of the long bus trip. We applied for openings at Iowa State College in Ames, and shockingly, after an exchange of letters, we were both offered jobs without even an interview. It seemed miraculous and we accepted quickly before they could realize how unwary they had been. We would be instructors in English at salaries of just under two thousand dollars a year. With two of them we figured we could get by all right, especially as we would be getting meals and living quarters at a low figure. We would not be at the main campus in Ames but forty miles away at Camp Dodge near Des Moines, a former National Guard installation which was being converted to accommodate several hundred GI freshmen and the necessary faculty.

I told Joe Taylor the milk route was all his now, and we agreed to trade the Ford truck for his Chevy sedan with the mysterious bullet hole in a back window; so we owned a car for the first time. In the last summer, to our delight, Ed Brinton arrived for a visit and I persuaded him to stay on and go to Iowa with us. He helped us pack the car with clothing, books, and phonograph records. We would be leaving our apartment and its furniture in the hands of Paul and Kathie. In the middle of September Jane and Laurie and Ed and I insinuated ourselves into our cocoon of possessions and set out for the long trip to Iowa. Crossing the Mississippi for the first time I paid silent obeisance to Mark Twain. Driving across Iowa I was ravished to see whole fields full of pigs and piglets—always among my favorite animals. At the front gate of Camp Dodge we were met by a bulky, scoutmasterly young man in tan cottons who introduced himself as Wendell Bragonier, assistant director of "The Annex." He climbed onto the running board and showed us the way to our new quarters. As he proudly displayed our two small rawboned white rooms, we got our first taste of Iowa smarm. His innocence was reassuring, however: he seemed even less sophisticated than we felt. Maybe we could con these people into mistaking us for college teachers after all.

Postscript

1had vowed not to continue my
memoir beyond *First Acts,* but persons who had seen my manuscript professed a curiosity about our lives after 1946, so I will lay out the bare bones
of the untold story as shortly as I can.

Jane and I spent one year at "The Annex" of Iowa State at Camp Dodge
and a second year at the main campus in Ames. Then we were told that
they liked us but could not keep both of us: nepotism. I got the news in
New York where I had begun work in summers toward an M.A. at Columbia. I wrote letters helter-skelter and was surprised to be invited for an
interview at Smith College—largely I think on the strength of the fact that
I had published a few things. It turned out that Smith had only two-thirds
of a job; but Mount Holyoke College, ten miles away, offered me the other
third. Nothing was open for Jane but a readership at Smith; but the Shaws,
parents of Buddy's wife Eleanor, offered us a pleasant old house practically
rent-free in Williamsburg, a few miles from Northampton. So, persuaded
by the quality of the two colleges and trusting that we could avoid starvation, we accepted the odd appointment. Laurie entered the Smith College
Day School and commuted with us daily in Joe Taylor's old Chevrolet.

At the end of our first year Smith said they wanted me full-time. I had
really liked Mount Holyoke better, preferring their hard-working plain-
Jane style, but I felt I had to take advantage of Smith's full appointment.
Mount Holyoke not only released me, sweetly, but now gave Jane a full-
time instructorship; so we felt happy and prosperous: five thousand a year,
wow! But midway in our third year, a few days after Mary Ellen Chase (in
charge of rookies) had been telling me what a great man I was, the Smith
chairman Howard Patch fired me in the course of an apparently casual
conversation on the steps of the library. It was done with such vague gen-
tility that it took me several days to understand what he had meant to say.

237

Then Jane learned that her lease had run out at Mount Holyoke. It was all very symmetrical. It had taken us country people five years to focus on the basic academic biology: it was not enough to do a good job; you really had to produce the union card—a Ph.D. Jane and I both had M.A.'s by now, but that produced nothing but cocked snoots.

After a great deal of scattershot letter writing I was offered an instructorship at Sweet Briar College in the rural middle of Virginia; nothing for Jane, but maybe we could make do. By no design that I could see, we seemed to be caught in a pattern of teaching in women's colleges. I have never regretted the fact, or found it anything but benign happenstance. We all loved Sweet Briar, and we spent six happy years there. In our second year, 1952, we brought forth our second child, another burly blond, Colin. (It happened that *three* children were born on the same day in the small Sweet Briar faculty; everybody talked humorously of orgies at Christmas and confused parentage.) Laurie mothered the little man in a wholly delightful and helpful style, as did our wonderful black servant-friends, particularly Mary Morris.

It dawned on me tardily, as I began to think of myself as perhaps the oldest living instructor of English, that with the University of Virginia fifty miles away in Charlottesville I could actually get moving on a Ph.D., and I began driving over there a couple of times a week for classes. It also occurred to me that as my competitive profession honored and rewarded publication, I could turn my course papers, if I were clever and energetic, into publishable essays. So I began working systematically with a double motive; in fact I had begun to do so half-consciously already with my Columbia master's thesis on Gertrude Stein. So it transpired that my first two books, on Stein and W. B. Yeats, were really verbatim copies of my theses, and nearly all of my first published critical essays were virtual carbon copies of course papers at the University of Virginia. Why not do them well enough so that both teachers and editors could value them? My process was candid and clear; nothing secret about it.

My papers appeared in the good literary quarterlies in the East: *Kenyon, Yale, Hudson, Massachusetts, Virginia Quarterly, Sewanee.* My subjects were things that rose up and caught me in areas in which I was studying or teaching: from freshman English and introduction to literature to modern literature especially the Irish writers, the eighteenth century, American literature, literary criticism, even Shakespeare. When people ask me, what is your field?, I have never known how to answer. I have always taught in any area in which I was needed, interested, and felt some degree of competence. I never became a specialist or even in the traditional sense a scholar, an expert, perhaps not even a literary critic. I was always an impressionist, an appreciator, a chronic student.

I finished my doctorate at Charlottesville in the spring of 1957, at thirty-nine—mighty old. Sweet Briar at once offered me promotion, tenure, and a few more dollars. But I had been getting feeling-out phone calls for some time from old friends at Mount Holyoke College—Alan McGee, Jo Bottkol, Sydney McLean—who had been watching our progress for several years, and they called now to offer me an assistant professorship, *tenure* (unprecedented), and more money. Full of guilt and regret for Sweet Briar and our friends there, we decided to return to Mount Holyoke. It had been our favorite academic place; and we were influenced by nasty confusions in the Virginia schools following desegregation, affecting Laurie's future—but mostly by a vague comprehensive feeling that the time had come to shake up our lives, to make a move rather than fall back into old comforts.

In South Hadley things went well. Jane held a part-time instructorship at the University of Massachusetts, ten miles north. Laurie entered the Northampton School for Girls, Colin the college's child study center. Taking advantage of Mount Holyoke's irresistibly low mortgage loan rate, we built a house on a wooded lot a mile from campus. My Stein and Yeats books came out, essays were appearing, I was happy teaching good matter to good students. Soon I was promoted in rank and made chairman of the department—largely, I think, because the long-squabbling elders could not agree on anyone of their number. I was made full professor, and that staggered me, as did the realization that in 1963–64, after seventeen years of teaching, I would achieve my first sabbatical leave.

In summers studying papers in New York and California, I had begun work on a new kind of thing, a biography of the lawyer, collector, and patron of modernism in the arts John Quinn, who had puzzled and interested me as an undergraduate at the University of Louisville. I was given a Fulbright research grant to England, attaching me loosely to University College London, to work on my notes and to try to track down and interview the surviving people, few but famous, who had known Quinn in the flesh (he had died in 1924). Laurie had entered Radcliffe at sixteen, fallen in love with an admirable young Harvard student named Michael McAnulty, married him at eighteen and left college, and was living with him in Cambridge. Never having been outside the United States before, the rest of us spent a happy year in Walton-on-Thames, thirty minutes by train from Waterloo Station, getting to know London and using Colin's school holidays to make acquaintance with Scotland, Dublin and the Yeats country, Venice, Florence, Rome, Rapallo, Paris and provincial France. It was all hectic but informative, brand-new to us; and I had managed to talk with Mrs. Yeats, T. S. Eliot, Ezra Pound, and a few others.

After about a year back in South Hadley I felt ready to pull my Quinn material together, and I applied to the American Council of Learned Societies for a grant to free me for a year's writing. Again I was lucky. In London I had presented the Quinn project in outline to Jon Stallworthy of Oxford University Press, and they had accepted it for publication by their American branch. I was tickled when my finished manuscript numbered exactly one thousand pages. In 1968 Whitney Blake and his New York staff made a handsome job of the big book, which I called *The Man from New York: John Quinn and His Friends,* and I had my first public success. The book was well reviewed and reprinted, and I was astonished to hear soon that we had a Pulitzer Prize; I had not thought of such things and had not even known that the book had been nominated.

One summer afternoon I received a surprise visit from a young southern academic, George Core, grave, charming, concentrated, intelligent, who appeared in South Hadley simply as a fan of my critical writing. He was to prove himself my most warmly loyal professional friend. George manifested next as editor of the University of Georgia Press, and in 1969 he brought out a physically beautiful little book, *The Long Boy and Others,* reprinting my essays on Johnson and Boswell, Richardson, Fielding, Smollett, and Sterne. In 1971 the Kennikat Press reprinted, as *Tragic Occasions: Essays on Several Forms,* my papers on *Macbeth, Hamlet,* Keats's odes, *Moby Dick, Billy Budd,* and "The House of Yeats." Obviously I moved around a lot in my objects of attention; and I am sometimes embarrassed to see how much publishing mileage I have got out of my modest quantity of writing.

While going on with her part-time teaching at the university, Jane had been doing some notable writing of her own. Working from her old undergraduate base in "humanities" and from a fascination with the poetry of Rilke, she had written a series of fine essays in each of which she set out from Rilke's treatment of a particular subject—Leda and the Swan, Eurydice, Saint Sebastian, Judith and Holofernes—and compared it with the treatment by other poets and artists. Her papers all appeared in good journals, and they were the first visible movement of a very large work still in progress of which I will speak later.

I continued disenchanted with my own critical style and resolved to try another biography. I had thought of John Crowe Ransom and George William Russell (AE) as subjects, but I got forestalled on both by swifter men; so I turned with some reluctance to an unresolved case from the Quinn story: Sir Roger Casement, the Ulsterman who had become famous in Edwardian times as a British consul investigating atrocities on the Congo and the Amazon, had turned nationalist Irish patriot, conspired with the Germans early in the Great War, and been hanged for high treason by the British in 1916. Not exactly my artsy cup of tea; but when I began to dig into the facts and the mysteries of Casement's character and fate, I was sufficiently caught. With another sabbatical impending in 1971–72, I applied to the National Endowment for the Humanities and was given a senior fellowship to work on the Casement archives in London and Dublin.

We left Colin, with mild misgivings, as a freshman at St. John's College in Annapolis. He had had disciplinary problems, more ominous than we recognized, all through his high school years—in several schools. In London I worked in the Public Record Office and Jane in the British Museum and the National Gallery. In the late fall we moved on to Dublin, found a flat on a top floor in Yeats's Merrion Square, and worked in the National Library and the National Gallery. I collected masses of notes, and came to realize what a smoulderingly touchy subject Casement still was—in Ireland, England, and even America.

Then in midwinter came the shattering news from friends in Annapolis that Colin had gone wildly off the rails and had been hospitalized after confrontations with college officials and police. Laurie had gone up from Chapel Hill, where she and Michael were based, to try to deal with it all. Jane flew home at once and I stayed on, guiltily, working in Dublin and then back in London, hoping Colin's crisis would pass. But Laurie sum-

moned me home in April: things were bad. Jane and I extracted Colin from
the horrible little private hospital in Delaware designed like a carousel. I
shall never forget my first view of him, tall, gaunt, and long-haired, doped
and disoriented, shambling at the end of a straggling file of patients. He put
his arms around my neck and said wonderingly, "Papa?" We headed north
with no real place to live, our house in South Hadley being rented for the
year. A specialist in Holyoke diagnosed the boy as seriously, perhaps
chronically, ill—a classic manic-depressive. We spent some weeks in a
cabin on a lake in New Hampshire, then weeks in our rain-soaked place in
the Berkshires. "Medicated" and showing only his depressive side, Colin
slept most of the time, and I went to work writing up the Casement story.
It was a grim summer.

Because Whitney Blake had moved from Oxford to Yale, I had offered
the Casement idea to Yale and they had accepted it. But by the time I had
finished my manuscript in 1974, Whitney had left Yale and I had a new
editor, Ellen Graham. I liked her fine, but I was irritated when it took Yale
two years to make a book. They had nominated *The Lives of Roger Casement*
for a National Book Award, however, and it was one of the five finalists. I
was ordered to prepare an acceptance speech, and did so; but the award
went to another man. I was never able to persuade the people at Yale, or
anyone else, that Casement's strange, often melodramatic story was pretty
sensational stuff and needed to be exploited as such. I dreamed of a Master-
piece Theatre series.

While we were abroad David Truman had named me Andrew W. Mellon
Professor in the Humanities, to occupy a chair with which Mount Holyoke
had just been endowed. I was pleased to sit in the chair for the next ten
years, during which I went on teaching full-time and doing bits of writing.
George Core had moved on to the University of the South to be editor of
the *Sewanee Review,* where he has made a solid and imaginative success. He
put me on his editorial advisory board, and he went on printing virtually
everything I wrote of essay length. I had written most of my memoir, first
called *Dry Goods,* then *First Acts,* in two summers at Worthington. I hoped
for a book, but I was equally interested in making a contribution to some
sort of family history.

Jane and Colin and I went on reasonably happily in South Hadley and
Worthington, warmed by the neighborhood, in their retirement, of my

brother Buddy and his wife Eleanor nearby in Granby, and our old friends Kingman Grover and his sister Vanessa just around the corner from us. Periodically we were crushed by a manic or depressive spell from Colin, who had to be hospitalized again and again. Most of the time he was delightful company; but when he was bad he was horrid. He finally put together a University of Massachusetts degree in their University Without Walls. About ten years ago he suddenly began pouring out good poems, very good poems, and lots of them. In the spring of 1983, three weeks after winning a top prize in an international poetry competition, he committed suicide by swallowing his whole stock of prescription drugs. We are far from past that event. Colin had the best brain in the family, apart from its fatal twist, and the only true talent. Jane and I made a volume of his poems, which was published by Colin Smythe in England in 1986 under the title *Open Secret*.

In June 1983 I retired from Mount Holyoke after twenty-six years on the faculty. I grieve to say I haven't made very productive use of my freedom. Jane, on the other hand, has begun bringing in the sheaves of her years of loving work comparing treatments of single subjects across the spectrum of the arts. Hers is a reference work, a compilation, an index, potentially huge in scope, to be called *A Guide to Subjects in the Arts Since 1300*. Who did what-when-where with Adonis, for example? She is nearing the end of her work on subjects from classical literature and myth, to be published by Oxford University Press in two big volumes; and she has notes in hand for other possible volumes on, for example, classical history, the Bible, Great Books. I watch her with admiration and dropping jaw as she puts in hundred-hour weeks. Can she last? She shows no sign of quailing.